D1565824

Abortion Ecologies in
Southern African Fiction

Critical Interventions in the Medical and Health Humanities

Series Editors
Stuart Murray, Corinne Saunders, Sowon Park and Angela Woods

Critical Interventions in the Medical and Health Humanities promotes a broad range of scholarly work across the Medical and Health Humanities, including both larger-scale intellectual projects and argument-led provocations, to present new field-defining, interdisciplinary research into health and human experience.

Titles in the series

Forthcoming titles

Abortion Ecologies in Southern African Fiction

Transforming Reproductive Agency

Caitlin E. Stobie

BLOOMSBURY ACADEMIC
LONDON • NEW YORK • OXFORD • NEW DELHI • SYDNEY

BLOOMSBURY ACADEMIC
Bloomsbury Publishing Plc
50 Bedford Square, London, WC1B 3DP, UK
1385 Broadway, New York, NY 10018, USA
29 Earlsfort Terrace, Dublin 2, Ireland

BLOOMSBURY, BLOOMSBURY ACADEMIC and the Diana logo are
trademarks of Bloomsbury Publishing Plc

First published in Great Britain 2023

Copyright © Caitlin E. Stobie, 2023

Caitlin E. Stobie has asserted her right under the Copyright, Designs and Patents Act, 1988,
to be identified as Author of this work.

For legal purposes the Credits on p. x constitute an
extension of this copyright page.

Series design by Rebecca Heselton
Cover image © anna quaglia / Alamy Stock Photo

All rights reserved. No part of this publication may be reproduced
or transmitted in any form or by any means, electronic or mechanical,
including photocopying, recording, or any information storage or retrieval
system, without prior permission in writing from the publishers.

Bloomsbury Publishing Plc does not have any control over, or responsibility for,
any third-party websites referred to or in this book. All internet addresses given
in this book were correct at the time of going to press. The author and publisher
regret any inconvenience caused if addresses have changed or sites have ceased
to exist, but can accept no responsibility for any such changes.

A catalogue record for this book is available from the British Library.

A catalog record for this book is available from the Library of Congress.

ISBN: HB: 978-1-3502-5018-5
        ePDF: 978-1-3502-5019-2
       eBook: 978-1-3502-5020-8

Series: Critical Interventions in the Medical and Health Humanities

Typeset by Integra Software Services Pvt. Ltd.

To find out more about our authors and books visit www.bloomsbury.com
and sign up for our newsletters.

Contents

Acknowledgements

This book has developed thanks to the generosity of many colleagues, friends and institutions. From my years at the University Still Known as Rhodes, I am grateful to several mentors and peers for inspirational classes, conversations and work on southern African fiction including Minesh Dass, Yolisa Kenqu, Kharys Laue, Mike Marais, Sue Marais, Karen McCarthy, Lynda Gichanda Spencer and Beth Wyrill. At the University of Oxford, it was a privilege to work with the Fakes, Fabrications and Falsehoods in Global Health team led by Patricia Kingori, whose imaginative approach to medical ethics pushed my thinking to exciting theoretical domains.

It was a pleasure to discuss reproductive agency and literary aesthetics with great minds at the University of Leeds. My heartfelt thanks to Graham Huggan for his enthusiastic suggestions, attentive counter-arguments and confidence in this book from its earliest moments – back when it was a very different beast – and to Brendan Nicholls and Jane Taylor for sharing their insights on abortion in southern Africa with me. I am particularly grateful for the generous mentorship of Stuart Murray, whose guidance has been crucial in developing my critical thinking, as well as to Clare Barker and Amelia DeFalco for embodying a feminist ethics of care through their research leadership. It was a pleasure to think through posthumanist possibilities in postcolonial fiction with Maya Caspari, Frances Hemsley, Anna Stenning, Ryan Sweet, Emma Trott, Liam Wilby and others in the Medical Humanities research group. The Leeds Animal Studies Network (LASN) and the Environmental Humanities research group also kept me engaged with some very exciting work when writing this book. Many humans could be mentioned here, but particular thanks are due to Sunny Harrison, Becky Macklin, Sophia Nicholov, Dominic O'Key, Lourdes Orozco, Jonathan Saha and Tom Tyler.

Further afield, Christabelle Sethna is a researcher with shared interests in both abortion and nonhuman agency: I am grateful to her for her hospitality, and particularly for inviting me to speak at the University of Ottawa's HumAnimaLab. Thank you to Benjamin Klein for the invitation to speak at the University of Cambridge's Postcolonial and Related Literatures Seminar. Additionally, I appreciated the opportunities to present at two seminar series in Leeds hosted by Finding Africa and LASN. When writing this book I was lucky to correspond with Rachelle Chadwick, Greta Gaard, Rebecca Hodes, Susanne Klausen, Catriona Macleod, Ana Stevenson and Sebastiano Triulzi, who deserve thanks for warmly sharing knowledge and advice. I am grateful for the continued kindness of more scholars from different seasons of my life including Michelle Kelly, Bob McKay, Julie Parle, Derek Ryan and Laura Wright.

This book could not have been written without support from the University of Leeds through a Wellcome Trust ISSF postdoctoral research fellowship, which granted me time to complete the manuscript, as well as a previous Postdoctoral Fellowship from the Leeds Arts Humanities Research Institute. I am also grateful for travel grants from: Minorities and Philosophy at Leeds; The European Society for Literature, Science and the Arts; Leeds's Faculty of Arts, Humanities and Cultures; the Northern Network for Medical Humanities Research; Leeds's Centre for Canadian Studies; and the EU Marie Skłodowska-Curie Research and Innovation Staff Exchange. The generosity of these organizations allowed me to attend conferences and gain valuable feedback on my work. The Clara Thomas Archives and Special Collections at York University, Canada and the Amazwi South African Museum of Literature in Makhanda, South Africa granted me access to their archives: I acknowledge their help in significantly bolstering the scope and impact of my research. Special thanks are due to Open Society Foundations for funding my trip to Amazwi and 'Abortion & Reproductive Justice: The Unfinished Revolution III' in 2018. It was a privilege to present alongside internationally renowned academics and activists at my alma mater.

Thank you to Ben Doyle at Bloomsbury Academic for responding to this project with such efficiency and enthusiasm from our very first correspondence. Thanks also to Laura Cope for her assistance with the editorial process, particularly her help with text and image permissions. I am grateful to the Critical Interventions in the Medical and Health Humanities series editors and editorial board for their encouraging feedback on my approach, and to the reviewers whose detailed and attentive comments bolstered both my conceptual framework and the structure of my argument.

I am ever-thankful to Vic Clarke, Diana and Richard de Ritter, Clare Fisher, Amber Lascelles and Arththi Sathananthar for sharing food, laughter and wisdom with me over the course of this project. You made my time in Yorkshire feel much, much warmer. Faith Pienaar, I'm inspired by how you model growth, trust and vulnerability through both your public writing and our personal conversations. To Peter Adkins, who read and commented on all these chapters with both considerateness and precision: thank you for thinking with me, and for the much-needed rambling in the Dales. Thanks to my family, near and far, for everything: Bruce and Cheryl; Blake, Alison, Fintan, Juno and Otis; Melissa, John, Kieran and Cara; and Cora. Finally, special thanks are due to Ryan Turnbull for years of unconditional love and unwavering support.

Credits

The author and publisher gratefully acknowledge the permission granted to reproduce the copyright material in this book.

Figure 1. Ecological model of abortion stigma by the International Network for the Reduction of Abortion Discrimination and Stigma (inroads) © inroads, 2018. Reprinted with permission.

Wilma Stockenström, excerpts from *Expedition to the Baobab Tree*. Copyright © Wilma Stockenström 1983, English translation © J. M. Coetzee 1983. Reproduced by permission of Human & Rousseau.

Tsitsi Dangarembga, excerpt from *Nervous Conditions*. Copyright © 1988 by Tsitsi Dangarembga. Reprinted with the permission of Faber and Faber Ltd and The Permissions Company, LLC on behalf of Graywolf Press, Minneapolis, Minnesota, graywolfpress.org.

Zoë Wicomb, excerpts from *You Can't Get Lost in Cape Town*. Copyright © 1987 by Zoë Wicomb. Reprinted with the permission of The Permissions Company, Inc., on behalf of The Feminist Press, www.feministpress.org.

Excerpts from BUTTERFLY BURNING by Yvonne Vera. Copyright © 1998 by Yvonne Vera. Reprinted by permission of Farrar, Straus and Giroux. All Rights Reserved.

Some sections of Chapter 4 are adapted from Stobie, Caitlin E. (2021), '"Creative Ferment": Abortion and Reproductive Agency in Bessie Head's Personal Choices Trilogy', *BMJ Medical Humanities*: 1–10. Originally published by BMJ Publishing Group Ltd. Thanks to the journal editors for permission to reprint these materials.

The third-party copyrighted material displayed in the pages of this book is done so on the basis of 'fair dealing for the purposes of criticism and review' or 'fair use for the purposes of teaching, criticism, scholarship or research' only in accordance with international copyright laws, and is not intended to infringe upon the ownership rights of the original owners. Every effort has been made to trace copyright holders and to obtain their permission for the use of copyright material. The publisher apologizes for any errors or omissions in the above list and would be grateful if notified of any corrections that should be incorporated in future reprints or editions of this book.

Introduction

Abortion, discourse and ecological metaphor

I

Safe abortion/pain-free/same-day/call now

In contemporary South Africa, these words may be found plastered on any public objects ranging from lamp posts to litter bins. Promotional flyers by traditional healers make similar claims alongside promises to bring back lost lovers, enhance penis length and more. The supposedly painless abortion is often named first: most convincingly, perhaps, in a list of fictive achievements. Growing up in post-apartheid South Africa, I did not know what to make of the posters that appeared routinely in city centres and shopping malls. State school sex education classes in the 2000s were more concerned with circumventing HIV/AIDS through alphabetized slogans (Abstain, Be Faithful, Condomize) than discussing what happens if and when contraception fails. Sometimes adults spoke in hushed disgust of 'those adverts' when they materialized in historically white suburbs. Generally, this was the most my peers and I read about the topic. We did not know there could be safer forms of abortion beyond the metaphorical backstreets. And, to many, the termination of pregnancy was not something that we should be informed about.

South Africa's clandestine advertisements belie the fact that the country has one of the most liberal abortion laws in the world. Passed in 1996, two years after the sweeping victory of the African National Congress (ANC), the Choice on Termination of Pregnancy (CTOP) Act states that all women have the right to access safe and legal terminations of pregnancy for free at government hospitals or clinics during the first three months of pregnancy. Abortion is also available under certain conditions with a doctor's consent from thirteen to twenty weeks of gestation, and there is limited access for extreme circumstances after twenty weeks. The trimester system was ostensibly developed as a form of compromise to appease liberal pro-choice activists and conservative anti-abortionists: it is tolerant of abortion, but only for the first twelve weeks of pregnancy (when a developing zygote, which is referred to as an embryo up until the eleventh week of gestation, is generally considered to hold less agency than a foetus). Yet a 2005 study in the *International Journal of Obstetrics & Gynecology* revealed that more than half of a sample group of forty-six women who underwent illegal abortions in South Africa did so because they were unaware of the current law (Jewkes et al. 2005: 1236). It is very likely that these women would have been exposed to fake information about illicit abortifacients or operations instead of free government services. This is not to say that state-funded clinics are necessarily supportive of those seeking abortions, either; a survey of pre-abortion counselling services at public hospitals in the Eastern Cape province revealed that healthcare providers often attempt to coerce abortion seekers into keeping their pregnancies by framing the operation as immoral, shameful, traumatic or even life-threatening (Mavuso 2021: 4).

Of course, abortion stigma is not exclusive to southern Africa, or even Africa in general. In her archival research on historical geographies of abortion in Lancashire during the late nineteenth and early twentieth century, Francesca P. L. Moore discovered that euphemisms such as 'Herbalism' or 'Women's History' were used by archivists who sensed that any direct references to terminations of pregnancy might result in information being withheld from public records (2010: 265). More recently, Texas has introduced the so-called Heartbeat Act of 2021 that controversially bans abortion after six weeks of pregnancy. At this stage, many women are unlikely to even be aware that they are pregnant, while others still might not have had the time to fully contemplate or finance their available options. Campaigners for the act argue that embryonic cardiac activity may be detected by transvaginal ultrasound from six weeks; crucially, and despite the lawmakers' semantic choices, reproductive health professionals argue that this cellular activity is too underdeveloped to be classified as a heartbeat, let alone an indicator of sentience. These historical and ongoing challenges to accessing safe, legal terminations of pregnancy demonstrate how questions of language and narrative have always been at the centre of the so-called abortion debate – a debate where, more often than not, facts about foetal development are shrouded in fiction. Such cases may also lead one to assume that artists around the world have faced decades of censorship when writing about reproductive agency. Yet, during my studies in the university town where J. M. Coetzee's *Disgrace* ([1999] 2000) is partially set, something surprising emerged: the topic of abortion was inescapable. In an English lecture, one professor contemplated the ethical implications of Coetzee's narrative about a woman who is raped and refuses to abort the resultant foetus. A seminar on Zoë Wicomb's *You Can't Get Lost in Cape Town* (1987) degenerated into a heated class discussion on terminations of pregnancy. The word abortion even appeared on a secondary reading list about Olive Schreiner, one of the country's most famous cultural exports.[1] I was particularly surprised to discover that abortion narratives from apartheid South Africa and surrounding regions were not shrouded in veiled references such as the terms that Moore describes above. Rather, southern African fiction was theorizing reproductive agency in both frank and feminist terms during the height of extreme political upheaval.

Analysing South African, Zimbabwean and Botswanan fictional materials, this book traces creative formations of abortion from the late 1970s to the 1990s. It focuses on texts by Wilma Stockenström, Zoë Wicomb, Yvonne Vera and Bessie Head. The women in this study render creativity as a literal and symbolic force in their narration of social injustices; biological formations in their artistic forms are utilized to question the very nature of agency and materiality in southern Africa. I understand agency as the embodiment of personal and political desires rather than a teleological will for action or drive for power. My methodology interprets materialist feminism as a philosophy directing us towards the notion that all agencies matter, instead of positing that there is a scale of worth or comparative value between different subjectivities. New materialism emerged in the 1990s, positing a theoretical turn to considering the significance of matter and often operating in conjunction with philosophical posthumanism: that is, the anti-anthropocentric critique of human relationships with nonhuman organisms and materials. Yet new materialism's reliance on Anglo-European philosophies means that the field's supposed novelty is often asserted without considering perspectives originating beyond North America and Europe. Engaging critically with terms from postcolonial theorists and the new materialists – who are interested in recognizing agentive capacities beyond the binaries of human/nonhuman, organic/inorganic – I consider both traditional worldviews and the influence of colonial ideology upon southern African regions. Importantly, and contrary to many contemporary associations with terminations of pregnancy, the fiction in this study asserts that abortion is not the denial of a future. These formations of agency not only precede new materialist conceptions of the zygote and gestating environment, but also exceed such theory through creative experimentation with transgressive, and locally situated, alternatives.

This project is preoccupied with the concept of representation as formation in various senses. First, and perhaps most obvious, is the importance of informing the public and causing them to question what is normalized (or stigmatized) by received wisdom during times of censorship. Formation also evokes the momentous history of feminist rallies: political resistance movements assembling and marching to transform restrictive policies. It further calls to mind writers' creative approaches to tackling such subject matter through literary forms. Significantly, all senses apply in times of political upheaval against patriarchal control, when censorship threatens to silence authors writing against normative views. It hardly needs explaining that transitions from racist regimes to postcolonial independence in southern Africa would stage this politics of representation in a number of ways. Southern African fiction treats abortion as a political and ethical issue, involving discussions of collective as well as individual agency in a social and historical context in which both of these are severely curtailed. The texts in this study are also consumed by the concept of transformation, particularly when challenging traditional associations of sexual reproduction and biological growth with personal development. Their thematization of literal creativity (through environments and ecologies) transforms received wisdom positing that physical growth and procreation necessarily yield positive results. There is another sense of creation embedded here too: abortion is a source of potential creativity for the woman who writes autobiographically about, or in the wake of, the procedure.

This study refers to the fictions at its core as postcolonial rather than decolonial. Although my historical scope broadly aligns with moments of decolonization in southern Africa, not all of the texts were written or set during these periods. While postcolonial and decolonial theories share the objective of decolonization, Walter D. Mignolo notes that many studies in the former field are indebted to works emerging during the poststructural and postmodern turns such as Edward Said's 1978 text *Orientalism* (Mignolo 2011: 55), whereas decolonial thought is intertwined with trajectories of 'dewesternization', which are often driven by searches for 'new meaning' (Mignolo 2011: xxiv). Throughout this book, I am critical of the valorization of novelty – not only for its connections with literal matters such as abortion or natality, but also its linkages with 'new' materialisms and nationalism. A second and related point is that the authors engage with both Eurocentric literature and traditional beliefs; the environments, metaphors and metonyms that they centralize are distinctly southern African, but are often rendered with reference to Anglo-European literary traditions. Thirdly, while my textual analyses do adapt the work of several postcolonial theorists, most of these critics are male and do not address gender and sexuality in their writings. To a certain extent, and in cases where such frameworks fail to consider gendered oppression, I am using southern African fiction *as* feminist theory. This methodology is inspired by recent interventions in critical race studies such as Zakiyyah Iman Jackson's theorization of Black feminist posthumanism through literature (2020: 35). It remains unclear how the new humanity that decolonization movements promote may move beyond homogenized definitions of man (Mignolo 2011: 52). This is particularly apparent when they fail to account for gendered issues of embodiment and materiality that disrupt teleological models of progression, including the liberationist narrative of development from colonial state to decolonized nation. I am more interested in aesthetic coinages that are critical of humanism and legal personhood such as Bessie Head's 'New African', a metaphorical figure who melds her affirmative and political stances on agency with an ethics of refusal (as I discuss at length in my final chapter). Thus I interpret the prefix in postcolonialism as marking a hiatus rather than a complete and clear break, thereby avoiding tropes such as the 'birth of a nation' that is free from colonial influences. Similarly, Head and the other authors in this study experiment with a continuum between the humanism of postcolonial politics and posthumanist theorizations that unsettle anthropocentrism. The texts create playful subversions of uneven social structures to attain reproductive agency. Furthermore, they provoke notions from both schools of thought in order to counterbalance associations of agency with humanist personhood, on the one hand, and apolitical abstractions about embodiment on the other.

Agency is a term which recurs in postcolonial scholars' works to describe political power and freedom, but it is not without its problematic elements. A recent collaborative article by Elleke Boehmer et al., for example, utilizes Steve Biko's *I Write What I Like* ([1978] 1987) to interrogate adolescents' writing practices in contemporary South Africa while simultaneously acknowledging how Biko's narrative theorization of agency, and the broader Black Consciousness Movement (BCM), was sexist (Boehmer et al. 2021: 5). While agency remains a useful construct for centralizing southern Africa's history of racialized oppression, therefore, one must be careful not to replicate patriarchal discourse when using this term. In her monograph *Postcolonial Agency: Critique and Constructivism*, Simone Bignall argues that 'historical discontinuities mark shifts in public modes of *agency*', a term she uses to 'describe the relation through practice, of desire (will), power (authority) and subjectivity (use of reason)' (2010: 11; original emphasis). While I am inspired by Bignall's contestation of linear chronologies, and particularly her association of agency with desire, there are several points at which our analyses diverge. As the humanist undertones of her statement suggest, postcolonial analyses often consider agency equally alongside the reasoned capacities of a subjective agent. My use of agency is distanced from the concept of subjectivity or issues of access, although the historical analysis in this introduction shows that the latter are often congruous with violations of reproductive agency. It also strives to move beyond the human realm of political power, an association of the term that postcolonial analyses such as Naminata Diabate's *Naked Agency: Genital Cursing and Biopolitics in Africa* are only recently starting to complicate (2020: 6). Rather, I connect agency with materiality, or biological perspectives on interconnected embodiments, arguing that it figures for both ethico-political and physical desires. Formulating a continuum of material desires, I tackle a problem of agentive representation that exists for many postcolonial interventions interested in materiality – and particularly for postcolonial ecocriticism, as noted by Cara Cilano and Elizabeth DeLoughrey (2007: 72–5). They show how ecocriticism risks misrepresenting the agency of indigenous peoples and their representations of nature, particularly in settler colonial contexts including South Africa, and they follow Graham Huggan in arguing that postcolonial perspectives on ecocriticism are thus not 'new' so much as 'renewed' (Cilano and DeLoughrey 2007: 72). On a related note, I am interested in disrupting teleological narratives of development by using a continuum model of agency. In his essay 'Necropolitics' Achille Mbembe argues, through Paul Gilroy, that death is representative of agency (2003: 39). I am interested in pursuing the temporal entrapments underlying this statement, since my understanding is that agency encompasses desire as defined by both biological sciences and materialist theories of becoming. This continuum of material and metaphorical desires is used to chart differences between local and imported worldviews on abortion in the primary texts.

On her personal website, historian of sexuality Lesley Hall curates an extensive list of literary abortions (2019: 1); it is decidedly more a collation of data than literary analyses, but still crucial for anyone interested in the topic. As with several popular surveys of literary terminations of pregnancy (Wilt 1990; Weingarten 2011; Bigman 2016), however, Hall's study focuses on Anglo-American literature from the twentieth century: the majority of catalogued authors are white and/or women. The exclusion of race from such discussions may not be the result of oversight, but rather deliberate omission stemming from the desire not to speak for women of colour. Yet in her landmark 1986 essay 'Apostrophe, Animation, and Abortion', Barbara Johnson reads abortion as an event that triggers anxieties surrounding one's identity in terms of gender and race, as well as one's artistic identity. 'For a black woman,' she notes, 'the loss of a baby can always be perceived as a complicity with genocide. [...] Yet each of these poems exists, finally, *because* a child does not' (Johnson 1986: 36; original emphasis). She focuses on the technique of apostrophe, or narrative address by a first-person speaker, to argue that many poetic abortions animate the foetal addressee (Johnson 1986: 29–30). According to this reading, abortion as a literary theme does not symbolize the binary opposition of life and death, but rather marks a site of generative potential for rewriting masculinist literary traditions and notions of personhood or subjectivity. Johnson's study is truly inspirational in several senses. Firstly, the essay is still utilized in contemporary fields such as queer theory and the medical humanities. In their debut monograph *Animacies: Biopolitics, Racial Mattering, and Queer Affect*, Mel Y. Chen responds to Johnson's claim that 'the poem can no more distinguish between "I" and "you" than it can come up with a proper definition of life' (1986: 33), noting there are parallels between her argument and the ethical thrust of new materialism's treatment of both life/liveliness and death (Chen 2012: 235). Even more stimulating crossovers remain to be made. I am struck by Johnson's rejection of binary categories while still centring on identity politics, and how this echoes Achille Mbembe's approach when he asserts that successful analyses of postcolonial power relations 'need to go beyond the binary categories used in standard interpretations of domination, such as resistance vs. passivity, autonomy vs. subjection, state vs. civil society, hegemony vs. counter-hegemony, totalization vs. detotalization' (Mbembe 2001: 103). In short, Johnson's aesthetic analysis bridges ethical interests (such as those of the new materialists) with reminders of political realities (as exemplified by postcolonial theory).

Despite my admiration of Johnson's approach, I am uneasy about some of the lexicon in her argument. Taking a Lacanian perspective on the mother being personified through address (rather than treated as a person), she concludes her aforementioned article as follows: 'It is no wonder that the distinction between addressor and addressee should become so problematic in poems about abortion. It is also no wonder that the debate about abortion should refuse to settle into a single voice. Whether or not one has ever been a mother, everyone participating in the debate has once been a child' (Johnson 1986: 38). Although Johnson's findings are persuasive, the words 'mother' and 'child' are jarring when used to discuss foetal growth; further, this project is not interested in framing a debate about women's agency on the one hand and foetal patienthood on the other.[2] From the outset, then, it is important to explicate some key terminology surrounding abortion, since different activists and political groups use varying terms to normalize their own moral beliefs. Following guidelines from the BBC, Reuters and other organizations collated by the International Campaign for Women's Right to Safe Abortion, I use pro-choice to describe people who support abortion access and anti-abortion for those who are against it. Instead of a mother (to-be), I refer to the gestating figure as a pregnant woman (and/ or person) – the latter term includes trans* individuals who do not identify as women but are still capable of becoming pregnant. My reason for not using this term throughout is that all cases discussed in these fictions involve cisgender women. Predominantly I use the word foetus and, more rarely, embryo or zygote; the former is generally understood to be most developed, while the latter two are used in earlier stages of pregnancy. All three are based on scientific models of gestation rather than emotionally charged misnomers like unborn baby or unborn child. One final distinction is that some refer to any and all aborted foetuses as unwanted. Not only is this not always the case – as, for instance, when a planned pregnancy results in fatal foetal abnormalities – but it also presupposes a pregnant person's motives and erases any feelings of ambivalence, conflict or despair. To avoid the possible misinterpretation of another's agency, I use unsupportable for pregnancies that are not carried to term.

Several of the above phrases that I have critiqued are prime illustrators of natalism: the normalized view that childbirth and childrearing are an integral component of the human condition, whether this is for nationalist, eugenic or purely instinctual reasons. Queer theorist Lee Edelman interrogates this socially accepted impulse by terming it 'reproductive futurism', a concept I discuss in depth in Chapter 4; I, however, will refer to natalist ideals through the framework of repronormativity. Repronormativity was first coined by legal feminist Katherine M. Franke in a 2001 article theorizing how to frame sex positivity; Franke draws parallels between heteronormative culture and social forces that encourage or incentivize motherhood (2001: 184). Like other normative models (heteronormativity, cisnormativity), repronormative discourse operates under the assumption that sexual reproduction is a natural and desirable process. The word shows how natalism often works in conjunction with heteronormative and cisnormative ideology: by assuming that all women want to be mothers; by constructing reified models of married mothers and fathers living in nuclear families; by asserting that any and all procreation is the gift of life, even if it is the result of rape or incest; and so on. There are thus clear intersections between many forms of oppression based on one's gender and sexual identity and one's reproductive agency. For the purposes of this study, intersectionality implies that the ethical and the political are intertwined. Similar to much of the discourse surrounding abortion, and to Franke's speculative framework of repronormativity, intersectionality originates in legal theory (Crenshaw 1989: 167). Interrogating aesthetic formations of abortion, however, I use it when discussing queer triangulations between new materialist and postcolonial feminist thinking. Dorothy Roberts notes in her study of race and reproduction in the American slave trade that 'books on racial justice tend to neglect the subject of reproductive rights; and books on reproductive freedom tend to neglect the influence of race' (1997: 4). This study is mindful of Roberts' and other Black feminists' critiques of a lack of intersectional nuance in literature on 'procreative freedom' (1997: 4). Furthermore, it takes seriously the implications of her observation that books thematizing ethical issues are both political tools and aesthetic forms to be analysed. While my approach is distinctive from both Franke's and Crenshaw's, therefore, this project retains a political dimension by adapting their legalistic terms to address allegories, abortion and fiction.

Another concept emerging from African-American feminism is reproductive justice. Rejecting what is perceived as the politically conservative, consumerist and individualistic concept of choice, the Reproductive Justice Framework tends to focus on three interlinked rights – to have a child, to not have a child and to rear children in a safe and healthy environment – and it emphasizes how social factors like racism and economic status have an impact upon particular women's reproductive freedom (Bloomer, Pierson and Estrada Claudio 2019: 107–12). Throughout this book I both develop the Reproductive Justice Framework and deviate from its common parlance of reproductive freedom by favouring reproductive agency instead. There are two reasons for this. Firstly, within a rights-based framework it is sometimes unclear whose liberty is being referred to: that of the pregnant woman, healthcare providers or society in general. Secondly and more importantly, the rhetoric of freedom often contains an ironic conundrum. Even when freedom is being used to argue against choice, the fact remains that both are linked by the concept of rights: the message underlying a placard reading 'My right to decide', for instance, appears identical to another saying 'Freedom to choose'. The humanist tenet of freedom is virtually inextricable from liberal pro-choice thought, which in turn often involves more discussions about when and how to abort rather than whether this is an appropriate solution out of the various options that are available to a pregnant person. This is hardly the fault of those who support reproductive justice; given the fact that the termination of pregnancy remains a taboo topic in most parts of the world, it is important not to give the impression that one is influencing women's decisions when circulating information to raise public awareness. Yet dissociations of abortion from discussions of ethics often result in limitations of choice, per se, as people remain unconvinced that abortion really can be not only safe and legal, but ethical. Abortion is crucial for the attainment of all three clauses in the Reproductive Justice Framework: to parent, or not, *in a healthy environment.* The ecological underpinnings of abortion access are crucial and best illustrated through focusing on agency, rather than rights.

In her moral study of abortion, Ann Furedi cites several examples from Europe to argue that 'contraception does not and cannot prevent abortion' (Furedi 2016: loc. 542). This rings equally true in the context of southern Africa. Unless society reaches a utopian future where contraception never fails, we are faced with the present fact that abortion may be used as birth control, particularly in socio-cultural contexts where women are dissuaded from using condoms or taking hormonal contraception. It has already been established that South Africa is theoretically one of the most supportive environments for abortion rights, but backstreet and illegal operations remain rife in the country because of failure to regulate conscientious objections by doctors, nurses and midwives, inequalities in access to services, and misleading information on governmental reproductive healthcare (Amnesty 2017: 4). The concept of choice is thus easily co-opted by conservative anti-abortionists and illegal abortionists alike to the detriment of women's health and agency. Southern Africa has a particularly vexed history of contraceptives: birth control may be seen as a reproductive right by some, but to others it is synonymous with racist population control (see Brown 1987: 269; Kaler 2003; Klausen 2015). This is a point that antinatalists such as philosopher David Benatar fail to appreciate when discussing abortion and related procedures. Citing a plethora of pro-choice male scholars, Benatar takes the presupposed position that coming into existence is always a harm and goes on to argue that if a foetus only develops agency late into gestation, then 'the failure to abort is what must be defended' (2006: 133; original emphasis). Benatar's astonishing omission of critical perspectives by women illustrates the insidiousness of a supposed liberalism that dictates strict moral imperatives without considering women's material realities. More startling is his failure, as a scholar situated in Cape Town, to account for associations of contraception and abortion with eugenics (as they were in southern Africa during the twentieth century, a point to which I will return). The flaws in Benatar's argument demonstrate that oversimplified abstractions and moral imperatives cannot suffice in the southern African context. Women still face various hurdles to accessing reproductive healthcare, even following historical moments of democratization and independence. Southern Africa is thus a particularly useful context for demonstrating the reach of agency as an ethical and political tool. With women either being urged to procreate (by colonialists or African nationalists) or being chastised for doing so (by antinatalists or conservatives), it is undeniable that the personal is both political and ecological. Bodily forms – whether that of the gestating person or that of the developing foetus – are thus integral to discussing broader ethico-political issues.

II

She watched red blood trickle through her fingers thinking, That is my new name, baptised in blood.
          – Zoë Wicomb, *You Can't Get Lost in Cape Town* (1987: 131)

There are inevitably both discrepancies and overlaps between traditional customs and modern attitudes towards reproductive agency. This is demonstrated by a website titled 4000 Years for Choice, which features a timeline 'Celebrating the Roots of Reproductive Health, Rights, and Justice'. I am critical of the rhetoric of roots throughout this book (particularly in cases involving materials like tubers used as herbal abortifacients), and equally wary of the troubling term 'African', which risks erasing a huge amount of differences between cultural and geographical contexts. Nevertheless, it is interesting to note that only two entries on the 4000 Years for Choice timeline refer to African indigenous abortion practices: African-American slaves' use of cottonwood plants as abortifacients, and northern African exports of a plant with abortive qualities called silphium dating back to 300 BCE. Although abortion has historically been accepted by some tribes in Africa to circumvent premarital pregnancies, there are also overriding patriarchal valuations of lineage and biogenetic kinship which would resist the modern notion that the decision to terminate a pregnancy rests solely upon a woman's consultation with health professionals. It is also important to note that many national Bills of Rights, which were formed in the wake of colonial human rights violations, are designed to enshrine the sanctity of all human life. In light of this fact, it becomes easier to understand how many southern African states may utilize the World Health Organization's definition of health as a state of complete physical, mental and social wellness, while simultaneously neglecting to consider the importance of pregnant women's mental health; the anti-abortion position contends that neo-colonial violence can be prevented by imbuing each person with equal rights, regardless of their age or biological development, including zygotes and embryos that would not survive outside the uterus. Yet this perspective ignores the reality that it is ambiguous whether a foetus truly holds agency as a capacity to desire. While some frame the termination of pregnancy as morally wrong (the murder of a person), others insist abortion is a neutral action (the removal of foetal tissue).

I expand upon the legal and social histories of abortion in South Africa, Zimbabwe and Botswana in each of my chapters. Nonetheless, it is important to provide some general information about the historical contexts in question here. Social histories of abortion in southern Africa differ greatly depending on the countries, policies and normative ethics in question – yet studies of the medical procedure rarely reflect culturally situated nuances. Many articles on southern African states' abortion laws from the late 1970s and early 1980s reveal white settlers' normative attitudes towards termination of pregnancy, particularly in Zimbabwe, South Africa and Botswana. A well-cited article by Rebecca J. Cook and Bernard M. Dickens asserts that 'Commonwealth African jurisdictions display a range of laws from the prohibitive to the more liberal' (1981: 60). (Importantly, South Africa was not included in their study; although the country was formerly colonized by Britain, global controversy surrounding apartheid meant that it was forced to withdraw from the Commonwealth of Nations in 1961, and it only re-joined the Commonwealth in 1994.) It is later revealed, however, that these supposedly progressive laws may involve the inclusion of more clauses or grounds for termination but are still largely concerned with preventing abortions from being induced unless absolutely necessary. The implication here is that the provision of such services on demand would exceed the expectations of even the most liberal campaigners for women's reproductive agency, thus normalizing the stigmatization of abortion. Cook and Dickens observe that Zimbabwe is one of two Commonwealth countries to have a conscience clause (1981: 72), which allows doctors or other medical staff to refuse to assist with performing an abortion for personal reasons; the country's 'advanced' attitude towards medical personnel's ethical stances, they posit, is indicative of an 'evolution' from basic law to a more nuanced understanding of reproductive health (62). The social Darwinist undertones of this evaluation simplify the restrictive conditions which lead to such legal parameters. Another issue is presented by the term 'maternal mortality'. Characterizing the dead women as parents suggests that their foetuses had a legal status of personhood, even if they had not yet developed anthropomorphic characteristics such as a beating heart.

It is important to remember, too, that while cardiac activity is present in both embryonic and foetal tissue, the former is generally not considered by medical professionals to be a heartbeat. The classification of abortion-related deaths under the term 'maternal mortality' is therefore illustrative of a tendency for the medical profession to overdetermine the agency of zygotes from the moment of conception. Furthermore, much like the term reproductive freedom, the words maternal mortality are ambiguous: they could be interpreted as referring to the deaths of women who gave birth, women who miscarried or sought abortions, or all pregnant women (and, potentially, the foetuses they gestate).

Abortion has always been legal in some form in South Africa, even under the rule of the National Party (NP) that implemented apartheid in 1948. But in the years leading up to the drafting of the Abortion and Sterilization Act of 1975, abortion was almost completely prohibited – mostly because the current law did not explicitly state when terminations of pregnancies were permissible. The medical profession was largely responsible for publicizing this issue, because it was a common and confusing concern for doctors who were faced with the dilemma of operating upon women who approached untrained abortionists to induce incomplete miscarriages before arriving at hospitals' accident and emergency departments. Immediately, it becomes apparent that the issue of women's agency was not a major concern, so much as the legal safety of doctors who would complete the second component of a two-part operation. Not all women relied on this method. Wealthier, white women were often advised to leave the country and acquire abortion services in more liberal regions such as the UK or the Netherlands (Bloomer, Pierson and Estrada Claudio 2019: 65)[3]; poorer women, and especially women of colour, were mainly faced with the repercussions of both unclear legislature and backstreet abortionists' dubious credentials. Some South African medical professionals also argued for abortion on eugenic grounds: a fact that is hardly surprising, given the apartheid government's racist agenda. Even those who expressed seemingly progressive views about the role of Black women in modern settings remained paranoid about an impending shortage of space for living and farming. Dolly Maister and June Cope, two liberal feminists who worked respectively in Cape Town and Durban from the 1970s, were concerned with population control measures for the sake of preventing 'environmental degradation' (Klausen 2015: 99). Their views were echoed by a vocal leader in the conservationist movement named Nan Trollip who declared that Black South Africans should use birth control so as to protect the country's natural resources (Klausen 2015: 188). In this sense abortion, population control and an implicitly racist idea of ecology were intertwined in the twentieth century, a point to which I will return in both Chapters 1 and 2.

Whether southern African abortion laws were classified as basic or advanced, requirements for special circumstances, doctors or permissions meant that many faced the risk of illness or death due to complications from pregnancy during the late twentieth century. To the present day, even regions with liberal legislation face hurdles such as providing adequate healthcare facilities and sex education to the public, as access to a range of gynaecological services remains a problem. Social inequality and various privileges mean that some women have easier access to safe abortions, while others are not even aware that the procedure is legal. The divergence of moral norms and cultural attitudes does nothing to combat this problem, as proven by historian Rebecca Hodes' article surveying access to illegal abortions before, during and after apartheid (2016: 93). Hodes notes in an earlier publication that 'postcolonial scholars have [...] challenged the artificial separation of biomedicine and "indigenous" medicine' (2013: 528), and her findings in both studies suggest that researchers need to generate localized understandings of fertility and abortion in particular environments, and not merely replace imperialist or patriarchal laws with generalized rhetoric about rights.

This is a point which Malvern Chiweshe and Catriona Macleod advance in a recent article criticizing both liberal approaches to abortion access utilizing rights discourse and decolonial perspectives that homogenize definitions of 'African' culture. Chiweshe and Macleod present a grounded reproductive justice approach (2018: 57), rejecting what they view as the neo-colonial untranslatability of 'choice' that is present in the larger context of rights rhetoric. They unpack social and cultural discourse, material conditions and power relations that lead to unsupportable pregnancies, with an approach that is grounded in the traditional philosophies of Hunhu and Ubuntu. These words do not merely denote a shared humanity, but rather show that each individual's existence is connected with the collective and the environment. In a single-authored article, Macleod draws on American ecofeminist Greta Gaard's 2010 article 'Reproductive Technology, or Reproductive Justice?: An Ecofeminist, Environmental Justice Perspective on the Rhetoric of Choice'. Through Gaard, and other theorists of 'interwoven embodied and social realities' in reproduction (2019: 49), Macleod argues that we need to place less emphasis on individualistic choices when discussing abortion. Her approach and mine share many characteristics: questioning the rhetoric of choice; centring vulnerable beings through intersectionality; paying attention to geographical and historical contexts; balancing culturally and scientifically recognized knowledges; and asserting that the personal sphere is inherently intertwined with, and representative of, political accountability. Yet while Macleod continues to use the term reproductive justice, I phrase this reproductive shift as one from rights to agency.

Reinforcing moves by Hodes, Chiweshe and Macleod towards a feminist materialist understanding of abortion in southern Africa, Jane Harries' PhD thesis applies an 'ecological model' to abortion service provision in the South African context. Harries asserts, 'An ecological perspective within a public health setting emphasizes both individual and contextual systems, and the interdependent and dynamic interrelations between the two' (2010: 7). Her utilization of the environment as a metaphorical tool mirrors an informative diagram (Figure 1) developed by the International Network for the Reduction of Abortion Discrimination and Stigma (inroads).

This book is invested in continuing the aforementioned southern African scholars' feminist materialist lines of enquiry, but it differs by situating itself within the largest sphere of the social environment: that is, the cultural arena of literary-aesthetic forms. Rachelle Chadwick's sociological study *Bodies that Birth: Vitalising Birth Politics* (2018) signals the prescience of counterpointing

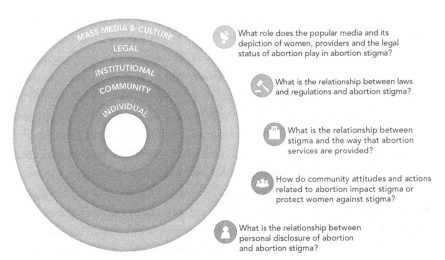

Figure 1 Ecological model of abortion stigma by the International Network for the Reduction of Abortion Discrimination and Stigma (inroads). The network circulates the model, a diagram of concentric circles, on its website and on promotional materials like fliers and bookmarks. Beginning at the level of the individual, the circles grow outwards to represent the community, institutional realms, legal spheres and, finally, mass media and culture. © inroads, 2018. Reprinted with permission.

new materialist approaches with culturally specific feminist perspectives on the politics of representation in southern Africa. There is a fascinating and moving section in her monograph where she collates South African women's birth stories as fragmented poems and narratives of resistance (Chadwick 2018: 131). Building on this provocative melding of political and aesthetic forms, I consider similar subject matter – for abortion and birth are both terminations of pregnancies – but with a literary-theoretical line of inquiry. With many who feel ambivalent towards abortion being silenced by conservative norms and homogeneously alienating rhetoric about African culture, it is apparent that the value of literary studies is to interrogate the use of metaphorical language in recent and contemporary discourse, and thereby represent the complexities of abortion ecologies in southern Africa.

The vocabularies of both new materialists and postcolonialists can rapidly become axiomatic or sanctimonious. I use them to modify and counterbalance one another, allowing room for playfulness and transgression: abortion is nothing if not a serious issue, but political grandstanding around the topic has often compromised its complexity while reducing its representational poetics to a purely moral concern. This is not to dismiss moral studies of abortion, particularly feminist monographs such as Ann Furedi's *The Moral Case for Abortion* (2016). Rather, I am interested in pursuing Jeannie Ludlow's provocative contestation that feminist discourse about terminations of pregnancy tends to centralize traumatic narratives (2008: 32), thus only normalizing one type of abortion, when the reality is that unsupportable pregnancies may occur for a plethora of reasons, falling along a continuum from the tragic to the mundane. The model of a continuum relates to the topic of abortion itself on several levels. Voluntary terminations of pregnancy are often rendered in strict terms as either immoral acts or affirmative demonstrations of women's power. The reality, however, is that abortion quite literally involves both death and life, fear and desire, refusal and affirmation. What one feels personally about the topic, furthermore, does not necessitate what one would stipulate all people should do in the case of terminating a pregnancy. Distinctions between the internal and external when discussing abortion therefore apply not only to the biological realm of the foetus and gestating figure, but also to varying ethical positions that shift according to a plethora of environmental, political and social factors. The ecological model of abortion stigma literally visualizes many ethical spheres surrounding terminations of pregnancy. My aim in this study is to further develop a continuum of abortion ecologies rooted in postcolonial feminist theory. Much like postcolonialism/s, new materialisms are wide-ranging and often interdisciplinary, but it is generally understood that the physicist-turned-critical-theorist Karen Barad is responsible for kickstarting scholarly interest in the idea that matter and meaning intersect. I discuss Barad and other well-known new materialists in detail later in this introduction when considering the role of metaphor in her writings. Crucially, metaphor is also central to the abortion scenes in the primary texts, which represent and exceed real-world equivalents of abortion narratives through experimental expressions of agency.

Agency has been used as a disembodied concept by some neoliberal campaigners for abortion law reform (Chadwick 2018: 9). New materialists such as Barad complicate agency by using it as both a verb and a noun; unlike postcolonial theorists, they often avoid the related term agent, arguing it is myopic and individualistic. As two internally differentiated fields, new materialism and postcolonialism appear to have very different understandings of agency and (human) life. Whereas postcolonial theorists are generally committed to centralizing the human agent who holds or does not hold power, new materialists are mostly concerned with moving beyond humanist constructions of personhood – and sometimes, worryingly, the political implications thereof. Yet both new materialist and postcolonial perspectives use agency in a visionary sense, arguing that it can be utilized to shape the broader ethico-political landscape and create different futures. Throughout this study the two fields counterpoint one another to create both a political and aesthetic critique of abortion and reproductive agency. To this end, I am inspired by Clare Barker's and Stuart Murray's adaptation of Edward Said's 'democratic criticism' when 'disabling' postcolonialism (2013: 62; original emphasis), exploring a critical approach that is sensitive to both the experience of disability and the histories and specificities of postcolonial contexts. Synthesizing approaches from the medical humanities and postcolonial criticism, Barker and Murray not only acknowledge how vital it is to discuss the broader environment when writing of health (2013: 70), but also gesture to the participatory possibilities of culture and critique in Said's formulation of 'democratic agency' (2013: 72). Reproductive agency is utilized throughout this book to form a shared vocabulary focusing on individual and collective desires in postcolonial environments. Within this common ground lies the potential to reorient respect for foetal agency without equivocating it with humanist definitions of personhood: in other words, interpreting serious harms to health in a woman-centric way.

This is an aesthetic project rather than a sociological study; yet, it is crucial to remember that these artistic works encompass political and social issues. This project is concerned with taking a critical approach to ethical subject matter through literary theory. To date, no one has performed an extensive analysis of abortion in this genre of literature, and specifically at this sociohistorical moment. My study also utilizes new archival findings from the papers of Bessie Head and Yvonne Vera, two authors who are taught and read as exemplary leaders in the field of southern African feminist fiction. Literature allows one to reconceive temporality, to navigate between different states of being and nodes of maturity, and thereby to challenge received wisdom about correct models of development. In literature, a beginning does not always constitute renewal or establish a marker of difference. It may also be conceived as repetition: the recurrence of a phrase, image or idea. This conception of culture as reflecting upon normative models of growth has particular resonance with the historical traumas addressed in recent southern Africa fiction. The texts in this study take a variety of forms: a translated novella; a Bildungsroman composed of interconnected episodes; a short novel; and stories that appear as both standalone tales in collections and scenes in novels. Clearly, the authors are engaging with short literary forms in their own ways. Each of the texts has a distinct materiality, but when comparing them it is important to recognize that there is an overarching tendency towards brevity, an attraction to the abrupt. In these moments of interruption, we are confronted with more than the mere imaginative function of literature. Reasons for seeking abortions in the texts revolve around questions of agency but also sustainability, poverty, biological exhaustion and more. Some of the protagonists already have children, while others have fears about racial identity and genetic lineages. The women in these stories have artistic and career aspirations that would be suspended by motherhood. Finally but no less importantly, there are some instances where no reasons are ever articulated for a termination of pregnancy. Inasmuch as each author writes at least one abortion scene, there is the sense that abortion is an absent referent that also informs the remaining pages of their fictions. Instances of brevity and ambiguity shape the political meaning of their entire works.

Just as there are many ways of achieving an abortion – medically, surgically, accidentally – there are equally diverse ways of writing the topic into literature. Interests in this study often overlap or intersect: there are recurrences of tragedy in Stockenström and Vera; iterations of desire in Wicomb and Head; experiments with intraspecies agencies in Stockenström and Head; and instances of ecological metaphors in Wicomb and Vera. All of the authors are critical of nationalism and humanism, utilizing conceptions of agency to unsettle the masculinist associations of power when discussing reproduction in postcolonial settings. Time figures in many ways in all the authors' works. First, and most obviously, there is the constant awareness that chronology determines the agentive potentiality of the foetus (and whether or not it is even referred to by that word instead of another). Narrative time is also evoked through staggered and experimental forms, the repetition of fear and trauma in discursive time, or preoccupation with supposedly feminine cyclical rhythms (and instances where these repetitions fail or are interrupted). Multiple perspectives on chronology are also evoked by Stockenström, Wicomb, Vera and Head. They evoke queer time to triangulate and temper new materialist imaginings of non-biological kinship with culturally situated understandings of belonging that acknowledge biology's importance. Finally, it is crucial to emphasize that commonalities between all these texts exist because of a shared time of writing. Yet the historical specificity of this project does not curtail its theoretical impetus. Southern African women's writing not only anticipates but also troubles current ethical issues facing feminist materialism, such as the indeterminacy of the animate/inanimate binary and (non)sentience. The geographical parameters of this study, and of the texts at its centre, reflect the ambiguity of the nature-culture dichotomy which troubles both new materialism and postcolonial theory. Instead of asserting a preference for one strict theoretical model, the texts in question exhibit points of confluence between both for what is a forward-looking conception of reproductive agencies.

The purpose of centralizing abortion is both discursive and geopolitical – opening up the possibility that colonial control extends from human bodies to broader environments. As discussed in Chapters 1 and 2, ecological anxieties were indubitably utilized by white liberal feminists during apartheid to advocate for abortion on eugenic grounds because of concerns about population growth and its impact on natural resources. This would understandably lead some to question how environmental metaphors can be applied to discussions of reproduction in southern Africa without playing into racist histories. But feminists writing in the region from the 1970s to the 1990s experimented with metaphorical formations of ecological approaches to abortion stigma, tackling material realities which women of colour faced from both liberationist and colonial nationalist regimes. It is vital, as well, to stress that the authors in this study literally crossed national boundaries, each in their own ways. Yvonne Vera moved between Zimbabwe and Canada – home to one of the largest Zimbabwean diaspora populations – several times during her adulthood. Zoë Wicomb emigrated to England and then Scotland, where she still resides as a South African expatriate. Bessie Head moved to Botswana after becoming involved with anti-apartheid activism and never returned to South Africa again (despite its exilic conditions, this was a voluntary decision, as I discuss in Chapter 4). It may be of no coincidence that the only white author in this study, Wilma Stockenström, is also the only writer to remain in her country of birth. Yet her novella clearly thematizes dislocation as its narrator, a slave, is forced into exile on an expedition from one unnamed state to the next. The term exile conveys a form of coercive separation that has connections with the nature of the topic of abortion. Throughout this book I use the exilic to encompass not only the plethora of movements on the parts of the authors – the diasporic, the expatriate and political exile – but also their experimental thematization of how nationalism colonizes both geographical and biological environments, right down to the foetal level. I use environment in the ecological sense, applying the concept to non/human animal bodies as well as broader systems wherein these agencies meet. This contrasts with the term landscape, which refers to geographical vistas (often that those that have been colonized) and implies a separation of land from non/human organisms. The concept of an empty landscape is often used to justify colonial expansion – whether this arguing for repurposing 'sterile' land, or encouraging settlers to explore a fertile (yet supposedly uninhabited) wilderness. This latter trope of fertility ironically continues to be utilized by some African nationalists when advocating for freedom from colonial powers, without considering who suffers when we continue to frame the environment as feminized. In contrast, the authors in this study consider how environments are both material *and* metaphorical, demonstrating how reproductive agency cannot be nationalized.

Metaphors abound in feminist materialist theory. They also accommodate the inextricable link between fertility and rites of passage in southern Africa: whether this is a symbolic gesture like the case of first-time mothers in Botswana being baptized with new names, which I discuss in Chapter 4, or merely the fact that some African feminisms centralize motherhood as a source of mythologized power. There are good reasons why one might believe that engaging with such metaphors may have worrying implications for abortion access. Yet there are also postcolonial feminisms that utilize elements of poststructural thought to treat 'Africa' and 'woman' as open signifiers; they focus on commonalities through material encounters and also differences through the localization of experiences (Chiweshe, Mavuso and Macleod 2017: 204). What if the metaphorical flourishes of some traditional feminisms were complemented by their counterparts in new waves of feminism? Likewise, what if the political limitations of feminist materialism were counterbalanced with women's material experiences of abortion?

III

Unnoticed as the birth of a wave an idea came into being and swelled
  – Wilma Stockenström, *The Expedition to the Baobab Tree* (1983: 62)

A common theme throughout postcolonial accounts of materiality in African sociocultural contexts is the subject of animism, or the traditional belief that nonhuman organisms, objects and natural phenomena have spiritual essences. This is perhaps particularly true since the publication of an article by Harry Garuba which argues that animist worldviews in colonial and postcolonial Africa allowed for political forms of agency to emerge (2003: 285). Yet with renewed scholarly interest in animism comes the erroneous assumption that all 'African cultures' are animist. In an article on supernatural forces in South African literature, for example, Annel Pieterse proceeds 'from the assumptions that a belief in occult powers is often central to local knowledge systems in South Africa, and that this belief should be acknowledged as a commonplace feature of life if one is to understand certain aspects of the [...] literary landscape' without establishing any evidence for or origins of these claims or, indeed, explicating what 'this belief' in spiritual phenomena actually entails (2014: 27). Writing more recently in 2018, Sam Durrant creates a rather intimidating mandate for writers situated in Africa by arguing that 'contemporary African literature must do more than simply represent the world. Its most vital role is to perform itself as a surrogate rite of re-ancestralization, one that engenders a radically expanded, trans-species spirit of relatedness' (2018: 178). There are several issues with Durrant's directive, not least its homogenization of literature from the continent (in an article studying a single literary text) and its insinuation that the act of representation is divorced from ethical or political implications. A more pressing concern, however, is the assumption that some untouched, ancestral 'African' animism exists and that one can return to its supposed purity through 'surrogacy' (a most jarring word when considering the politics of gestation). This is not a criticism of postcolonial theorists' interests in animism so much as an observation that its origins in oral storytelling mean it is constantly shifting, forming and reforming, interacting with both local and imported knowledge systems, and that this nebulous nature, this question of whose definitions are being used to which ends, must be accounted for. For as Achille Mbembe notes, the contemporary veneration of objects in consumerist cultures means that even capitalism may be understood as a form of animism (Mbembe in Blaser 2013: 6).

Since animist perspectives contend that there is spirit in all matter, one could assume that they should not tolerate terminations of unsupportable pregnancies. Yet in much southern African fiction, as in the history of the region itself, the cultures and legacies of colonizers have argued more fiercely for the supposed sanctity of the foetus than traditionalist perspectives which appear more ambivalent towards abortion. A decade after his aforementioned article, Garuba revisits the topic of animism and its 'suggestion that the boundary between Nature and Society, between the world of objects and that of subjects, between the material world and that of agency and symbolic meanings, is less certain than the modernist project had decreed it to be' (2013: 43). The writers in this study, however, are invoking both situated southern African beliefs and the so-called modernist project, often referencing and experimenting with literary Modernism in their creative expressions of reproductive agency. There are thus three primary reasons why this study does not engage with animism and related indigenous approaches to material agencies. Firstly, these novels, novellas and short stories are decidedly prosaic forms that do not emulate oral modes of storytelling; their authors make equal references to Anglo-European Modernism,[4] American con/texts and southern African myths. Second, this is not an anthropological study. In cases where tribal traditions are thematized by the texts, they are utilized to provoke aesthetic and ethical issues rather than sociological commentary. Finally, there is very little discussion of souls or spirituality in any of these narratives. The writers I am discussing are not interested in the spirit realm – nor in (the white settler's) God – but rather in how works of fiction inform political affairs as well as more literal matters. New materialism can thus gain insight not only from Western literature and science, but also from southern Africans' modes of narration which are anthropomorphizing but not superstitious.

A further point is that while the texts are political in their condemnations of colonization, they are simultaneously critical of African nationalist movements for perpetuating masculinist understandings of power and agency that privilege man. It is evident, then, that the fictions in question are not compatible with postcolonial materialisms that exclude feminist perspectives. For example, Pablo Mukherjee's eco-materialism is useful for socialist studies that attend to mapping the 'difference' of 'productive activities' (2010: 81). Yet the questions of gender and sexual difference – areas which emerging feminist and queer theories demonstrate are far from easily mapped – do not figure in his discussions of production. My biggest concern is the utilization of the word 'labor' without attending to ecofeminist theories of reproduction that exceed post-Marxist cultural geographers' works. Contra to Mukherjee, Marxist feminist Silvia Federici defines the sexual division of work as 'reproductive labor' ([1998] 2004: 14). Hers is an important theorization of all the labour that goes into producing life, whether this is parenting, housework or the physical processes of gestation and childbirth. Yet her otherwise materialist feminism does not address reproductive environments, bodily or otherwise, and is uncritical of concepts like rights, choice and related humanist categories.

In a more recent Marxist theorization of gestation, Sophie Lewis (2019) argues that all uterine labour (and particularly surrogacy) should be considered unpaid work. She uses similar concepts and ideas as those raised in the collection *Making Kin not Population* (2018). Edited by Donna Haraway and Adele Clark, the overarching argument of this volume is that with contemporary phenomena like a growing human population and ever-increasing environmental catastrophes, it is time to reconceive traditional biogenetic associations of kinship and family. Lewis' critique is remarkably self-reflexive and exciting for its many nuances, but there is still concern amongst some that the substitution of kin-making for the propagation of humankind risks erasing the experiences of those who have historically been denied reproductive agency. Jade S. Sasser expresses concerns about reproductive justice and definitions of population as purely human numbers in a recent 2019 review forum on Haraway and Clark's collection (Strathern et al. 2019: 162). Blanket antinatalist statements seem remarkably insensitive to the histories of people who have been subject to colonial violence through population control or reproductive regulations. They may also propagate the notion that some populations need to curb their fertility rates more than others, a misconception that is fairly common in environmentalist circles. There are several moments in Philip Cafaro and Eileen Crist's edited collection *Life on the Brink: Environmentalists Confront Overpopulation*, for example, where discussions of the so-called population explosion and race are dismissed as 'conversation stoppers' (Palmer 2012: 104), but perhaps the most telling is Dave Foreman's claim that 'the herd mindset of political correctness stops any unruffled, thoughtful talk about population' in the United States (2012: 65).[5] In response to the assumed incompatibility of environmental and feminist interests presented in discussions of re/production in postcolonial contexts, I am inspired by Cajetan Iheka's recent work on ecological violence in literature from Africa. Iheka argues for a distributed sense of agency (2017: 4), creating a model of 'strategic anthropomorphism' by merging concepts popularized by postcolonial critics like Frantz Fanon with the theories of feminist materialists (Iheka 2017: 14). I adapt this approach by considering queer and non-biogenetic theorizations of gestation as bridges between postcolonial and new materialist perspectives – a point to which I shall return shortly.

Gestation and reproduction also figure in many new materialist formulations of agency, where they are discussed on both literal and metaphorical levels. In her 2007 monograph *Meeting the Universe Halfway: Quantum Physics and the Entanglement of Matter and Meaning*, Karen Barad creates a semantic field which can be utilized to discuss both material-discursive issues and purely discursive matters. Barad is actively occupied by ethical questions – her classification of embodied agencies as 'phenomena' which 'intra-act' means that her theory is concerned with both organic and inorganic matter (whether this is human or nonhuman). Drawing on Niels Bohr's principle of diffraction, Michel Foucault's work on discourse and Judith Butler's theory of performativity, she is concerned with the very process of being itself. According to agential realism, 'Individuals do not pre-exist their interactions; rather, individuals emerge through and as part of their entangled inter-relating' (Barad 2007: ix). Thus Barad is interested in the ontology of how agency is made and remade in the present, as illustrated by her use of present-continuous forms in neologisms such as 'spacetimemattering' (2007: 383). Barad views new materialism as an important tool for decentring the human subject; she describes agential realism as 'a posthumanist performative account of technoscientific and other naturalcultural practices' (2007: 32). Aligning new materialist and posthumanist theory, she underlines the anti-anthropocentric and environmentalist concerns which are present in both schools of thought.

One of the most interesting chapters of *Meeting the Universe Halfway* considers ontology, agency and reproductive technologies, particularly ultrasounds. Feminist abortion activists often employ the rhetoric of choice, arguing for a woman's right to choose. Here, Barad begins to explore how associations of choice and agency are affected if one accepts that existence is not – and never can be – an individual affair: controversially, she contends that the foetus-as-phenomenon includes not only the zygote, but also the gestating body and the environment which it occupies (2007: 217). She is not, however, opposed to abortion; she is acutely aware of how pregnant people have been historically objectified and excluded from possessing political power (2007: 212). Barad opposes causing suffering on principle while also remaining open to contingencies, and without reinforcing the anti-abortion/pro-choice dichotomy. New materialism has been problematized for its tendency to focus on white philosophers' work, as well as for propagating the assumption that a focus on material reality is new when various indigenous and postcolonial knowledge systems have already been preoccupied with such questions (Hinton, Mehrabi and Barla 2015: 4). However, in this chapter Barad is at pains to illustrate how the agential realist perspective allows one to criticize not only the liberal humanist rhetoric of choice, but also concerns like infertility caused by ecological health risks and environmental racism (2007: 217). Her theories point to the shared vulnerability of each and every embodied agency, pushing intersectionality to encompass political and ethical issues.

The fact remains that although all phenomena hold agency, some have more intentional clout than others. Furthermore, the extent to which one may be said to hold agency depends upon the relationships that one shares with other beings. This is not intended as a universalist comment about familial structures (although it is generally acknowledged that a parent would be naïve at best, or neglectful at worst, to claim their infant is an equal). Rather, I am interested in a vexing question of agency that manifests in movements for social equality in postcolonial settings. Campaigns to treat autochthonous peoples with respect often appeal to a homogenized sense of identity, as noted by Chiweshe and Macleod (2018: 49). Ironically, the very notion of sameness can cause the cultural nuances and situational details of such struggles to be misunderstood or overlooked. Here I am approaching a point which is deftly articulated by Judith Butler in their 2009 monograph *Frames of War*. After defining precariousness as a 'shared condition of human life (indeed, as a condition that links human and non-human animals)' (2009: 13), Butler warns in a characteristically linguistic-discursive caveat that 'we ought not to think that the recognition of precariousness masters or captures or even fully cognizes what it recognizes' (2009: 13). Here they point to a seeming contradiction of terms: while thinking subjects are able to recognize and articulate their affinity with other beings, such intellectual knowledge is full of slippages and contradictions. A popular critique of new materialism is that some theorists appear to equate agency with material effect. A rock, for example, is readily imbued with 'agency' simply for being able to roll down a mountain and obstruct one's path. Yet if one is to truly grasp the new materialist concept that one holds no more or less agency than nonhuman materials like stone, then one has to acknowledge that in some cases such a thought can never truly be mastered. A rock, after all, possesses no intentional mind to comprehend this idea. The onus is thus on the thinking subject to be wary of what they supposedly know about material effect – while still being critical of the concept of knowledge itself.

Importantly for this discussion, Butler goes on to use abortion to illustrate their concerns about how material and social environments may make a life un/

liveable. At one point, they tangentially mention that stereotypical anti-abortion ideology is congruent with animal rights activism, as both enshrine the essential worth of every organism's life (2009: 16).[6] Butler declares that

> it is not possible to base arguments for reproductive freedom, which include rights to abortion, on a conception of what is living and what is not. Stem cells are living cells, even precarious, but that does not immediately imply what policy decision ought to be made regarding the conditions under which they should be destroyed or in which they can be used. Not everything included under the rubric of 'precarious life' is thus, a priori, worthy of protection from destruction. But these arguments become difficult precisely here, since if some living tissues or cells are worthy of protection from destruction, and others not, could this not lead to the conclusion that, under conditions of war, some human lives are worthy of protection while others are not?
>
> (2009: 18)

While the above quotation approaches a pressing question about contemporary warfare, this concern about the comparative worth – or grievability – of lives is made equally apparent in critical race theory and postcolonial studies. The discourse of entanglement risks transcending important issues like racial identity and ethnic discrimination by forging a crucible of cultural identities. Two examples from the United States are illustrative of this point. The first is the multiculturalist image of the melting pot, which implies that immigrants will (and must) assimilate to create a new national identity in their country of choice. Secondly, recent outrage sparked by the appropriative slogan All Lives Matter (in the context of my theoretical framework, the latter word appears particularly apt) is evidence of how social inequality persists despite claims to the contrary.

It is thus clear that shared precariousness does not emerge because of similar social conditions and neither is it the product of an essentialized biological sameness. One must recognize that all phenomena hold agency in an affective-material sense, while acknowledging that differential distributions of intentionality and desires mean that some play more significant roles in society or the environment than others. But if we accept that ethical parity is impossible to achieve on a microscopic level, then it may be argued that we are forced to concede it cannot operate interpersonally, either. This conclusion holds little hope for fostering empathetic exchanges. Some may remain unconvinced by new materialism and its appeal to an apparently depoliticized ethics for this very reason. For example, Mel Y. Chen is critical of what is sometimes perceived as the transcendence of linguistic and political issues in new materialist theory

(2012: 51), but conjectures that it may hold potential if it is open to the 'uncanny' tensions between variant identities (2012: 236). Other critics like Sara Ahmed remain more resolutely suspicious of what they perceive as new materialism's oversimplification of the relationship between feminism and (biological) science studies. Ahmed rigorously demonstrates how the new materialists construct a 'narrative of forgetful feminism' when they posit that older forms of feminism were not concerned by questions of biology (2008: 32). In particular, she shows how Judith Butler's work has been caricatured as 'anti-matter' when the reality is that Butler does grapple with materiality, albeit only in passing because materialization is not the focus of their work (Ahmed 2008: 33).

Butler's work has historically been concerned with how certain human animals are portrayed as grievable while others are not. Yet in the introduction to their most recent work, *The Force of Nonviolence* ([2020] 2021), Butler critiques an insufficiently articulated emphasis on individual existence as the basis for rights. Butler appears to move towards ecological theorizations of the biopolitical implications of death, particularly when arguing that 'nonviolence pertains not only to human relations, but to all living and inter-constitutive relations' ([2020] 2021: 8–9). They use reflections on destruction, desire and support from disability studies to argue against self-sufficiency ([2020] 2021: 39–41). I am interested in how Butler employs reflections from within the medical humanities – a traditionally humanist field – to support their move away from discussing human life, and their self-described 'aggressive' pursuit of nonviolence and political agency ([2020] 2021: 21–2). Highlighting agency helps to foreground the problem of social inequality which continues to impact upon women's access to safe reproductive healthcare, while also resisting the tendency towards universalism that some pro-choice activism – and new materialism – promotes. By now it should be clear that my purpose is not to discuss the potential pitfalls of pro-choice campaigns on the one hand and posthumanism on the other. Rather, I aim to explicate a feminist materialist perspective on the ecological model of women's reproductive agency in postcolonial contexts – that is, a figuration of new materialism which does not lose sight of historical frameworks that are prioritized within the medical humanities. With its emphasis on dismantling intersecting oppressions, philosophical posthumanism provides an important critical perspective on the liberal homogenization of experiences which tends to infiltrate discussions of reproductive agency, but only if it is open to discussing how and why some lives are worth more than others.

In an interview with Rick Dolphijn and Iris van der Tuin, Karen Barad notes that 'agency is not about choice in any liberal humanist sense' (2012: 54).

Elsewhere, she asserts that 'matter is produced and productive, generated and generative. Matter is agentive, not a fixed essence or property of things. Matter is differentiating, and which differences come to matter, matter in the iterative production of different differences' (Barad 2007: 136–7). This quotation highlights the duplicity of the foetus-as-phenomenon: a zygote is not only a component of a gestating figure, but also grows into a foetus which is productive (in the sense that it generates its own sex cells before birth). The word differentiating also points to the importance which stem cells play in discourse surrounding abortion. While Barad and one of her fellow new materialists, political theorist Jane Bennett, have discussed ultrasound technology and stem cells, respectively, it appears that the event of abortion is a central question at the heart of new materialism, as both anti-abortion and pro-choice campaigners often appeal to personal agency to justify their ideologies. I investigate the implications of Bennett's allegiances in my analysis of Bessie Head's fiction in Chapter 4. There are several theoretical knots that remain unpicked in her work, particularly the issue of female creativity and gender essentialism. By focusing too heavily on a woman's choice, many play into the essentialist understanding that the female sex is somehow more naturally astute at nurturing or creating new life. Paradoxically, it is only by accepting that women are not the sole creative forces – to paraphrase Butler, by declining to cognize what we recognize as reproductive – that we can create an inclusive and productive sense of agency.

Barad's theoretical intra-actions have influenced many feminist thinkers including Rosi Braidotti, a key theorist whose work I adapt in my chapter on Zoë Wicomb. Unlike Bennett, Braidotti is critical of philosophical revisitations of vitalism – that is, the belief in an inexplicable life force that charges in/animate objects – and their linkages with trends of genetic citizenship, although she elects not to elaborate too greatly on their connections with European modes of fascist philosophy (Braidotti 2010: 202). Where her thinking mostly greatly informs my readings is in her investigation of new materialism's analogies and metonyms, exploring the disjuncture between theory and reality (as well as equivalences between different contexts). During her keynote address delivered at a conference on 'Environmental Humanities and New Materialisms: The Ethics of Decolonizing Nature and Culture' in 2017, for example, Braidotti was quick to remind the audience of the 'empiricist fetishism' of some new materialist thought. Otherwise referred to as the Eighth Annual Conference on the New Materialisms, the event was hosted at the UNESCO Headquarters in Paris. Many papers interpreted decolonization metaphorically and with baffling insensitivity, discussing cancers, invasive species and other biological colonies rather than racial injustice. Postcolonial political contexts were particularly absent from discussion. That Braidotti's astute warning remained unheeded in most panels is proof that much work remains to be done in bridging postcolonial and new materialist perspectives on colonial legacies. Yet she does not abandon posthumanism as a navigational tool; the nonhuman, whether animal or environment, provides an index of empowerment for her and other feminist thinkers, even when thinking through human agency.

Braidotti's emphasis on relational and collaborative thinking when creating critical theory is shared by Claire Colebrook, although the latter is admittedly sceptical of posthumanism proper. Colebrook's reservations are implied in many of her writings but perhaps most notably by the title 'Humanist Posthumanism: Becoming-Woman and the Power of the "Faux"'. In this recent article, she exemplifies Karen Barad and Edward Said as two rare thinkers who exceed the tired dichotomy of fixed and essentialist identity categories (particularly the word woman) on the one hand, and the homogeneous category of 'we' humans on the other (Colebrook 2019: 2–4). Her evocation of Barad and Said is vital since both are formative influences in this study. Said's work on origins and af/filiation, in particular, is adapted in Chapters 1 and 4 in conjunction with queer ecocritical perspectives on gestationality, and Barad's agential realism informs concepts coined by Greta Gaard, Rosi Braidotti, Stacy Alaimo and, indeed, Colebrook herself. What is inspirational here is the collaboration between two vastly different schools of thought and her insistence that both, actually, might be utilized to embrace posthumanism's 'faux' limitations (Colebrook 2019: 17). That is, she argues for resisting 'the hyper humanism of feminist posthumanism' or 'pure becoming' that posits some feminisms are more 'real' than others and reminds the reader that poststructural thought must recognize all signifiers are inherently false (Colebrook 2019: 17). Similarly, I approach new materialism from a postcolonial feminist perspective. How might southern African literature allow for non-anthropocentric, yet politically aware, views on reproductive agency to be expressed? Can such accounts of abortion disrupt the notion that the gestating body is a mere vessel for the embryo – a body that may develop to propagate the patriarch's genes – thereby disengaging gender from sexual difference, and further challenging repronormative and nationalist lineages? These are not questions that can simply be answered with one side of a theoretical coin; neither animism nor vitalism applies in such cases. Rather, as I discuss at length in my final chapter, there is a queer vitality at play.

Queer theorist Jennifer Doyle notes that traumatic or 'tragic' abortion stories are often privileged in favour of treating abortion as a mundane and everyday reality. Doyle simultaneously provides an excellent description of misogyny-by-omission in the work of Lee Edelman, probably the most notable queer theorist to have argued against procreation. Analysing his antinatalist critique of the 'Child', which he develops from the depiction of a foetus on a billboard funded by anti-abortionists, she observes that 'the pregnant woman disappears into an amorphous and undefined background, even in Edelman's refusal of the image's ideological call' (Doyle 2009: 32).[7] Such discursive erasure is performed by those both for and against abortion, as the thought that a woman may *desire* to deliberately terminate a pregnancy remains unpalatable to many (Doyle 2009: 26). She continues to argue that

> it is one thing to frame abortion in terms of human rights – in which we discuss access to abortion as something that women of the Global South need in order to resist social, economic, and political oppression, for example. It is another to frame it as the practice of sexual freedom – to integrate abortion into a story about sexuality, desire, and the body.

(Doyle 2009: 41)

While she is deliberately presenting a false dichotomy to illustrate her point, it is telling that the example of social and political injustice turns to a homogenized notion of the 'Global South'. What emerges in the study of southern African fiction is that abortion stories often are not simple narrative arcs of women overcoming oppression. Even in cases where political issues like abortion access do inform the plot, there are multiperspectival moments where anthropocentrism is unsettled, thereby challenging humanist associations of legal personhood with power. Similarly to Colebrook's point on resisting strict dichotomies when thinking through feminist and postcolonial critical theories, my emphasis is that such abortion narratives are formations of desire; such fictions unsettle the binary of human rights narratives with linear trajectories, on the one hand, and experimental tales of sexual embodiment on the other. Aesthetic representations of abortion in southern Africa challenge normative sexual discourse to both political and ethical ends.

If one views abortion as ending a pregnancy rather than killing a foetus, then questions of finality become more apparent. The literary readings in this book do not dwell on typical associations of abortion or the abortive with failure; rather, they explore the queer potentialities that accompany reproductive agency. These potentialities are enmeshed with novel and distinctly southern African models of temporality: the narratives in question unsettle linear models of development long before the new materialists' pronouncement of a revived interest in queer time. Yet their engagement with urban and rural life, nonhuman and human forms, and Anglo-European and indigenous aesthetics demands engagement with humanism from a critical perspective.

IV

The birth of a word is more significant than the birth of a child.
                                        – Yvonne Vera, *Butterfly Burning* (1998: 68)

In what is seemingly the only existing article to date focusing exclusively on abortion in fiction from Africa, Nancy Rose Hunt names Yvonne Vera's *Butterfly Burning* alongside four other feminist novels which she reads for social and historical traces of terminated pregnancies (2007: 279). There is a tendency for comparative collections or area studies of 'African' literature to employ the 'anthropological fallacy' (Huggan 2008: 50); many lack cognisance of sociological specificities, failing to pay attention to individual novels' forms, ironies or ambiguities. Trained as a historian, Hunt counterbalances the anthropological view by providing an overview of social scientific literature. She proceeds to read the five novels as artefacts, arguing that the point of her approach is not to create a window on the real Africa, but rather 'to show how much the novels *tell*, while implicitly posing a set of questions that the social scientific literature has not even begun to *ask*' (Hunt 2007: 281; original emphasis). Hunt reads the culmination of Vera's novel as the protagonist's decision not to repeat the process of seeking an abortion (2007: 297), a point with which I disagree; I present an alternative reading of *Butterfly Burning*'s themes, and particularly the novel's final scene, in Chapter 3. Yet Hunt's conclusion is remarkably insightful and invites further investigation: 'If we read – and teach – [such novels] *not* as reflections of the social, but as constitutive objects, we will necessarily devote more attention to their formal and structural elements and thus to *how* they pose selves in formation' (2007: 302; original emphasis). Her utilization of the word formation here is particularly striking, given the emphasis on forms which I read in other southern African women's writing about terminations of pregnancy. While our frameworks differ – mine, for instance, avoids associating agency with the individualist subjectivity of 'selves' – I agree that fiction seems closer to developing critical approaches to abortion than social theory itself. I would go further and argue that the novelists in this study ask questions which literature and theory informed by the hard sciences (biology, genetics, physics) routinely avoid.

The first section of this introduction intimated how those who support abortion access have, historically, had to refer to the procedure in cryptic terms due to various stigmas and conservative censorship. Yet terminations of pregnancy recur in novellas, novels and short story collections from South Africa, Zimbabwe and Botswana, none of which were banned at any point during southern Africa's liberation struggles of the twentieth century. That these abortion narratives escaped censorship is quite remarkable, especially since enforcers of South Africa's 1974 Publications Act targeted many writers who challenged their political views including Nobel Prize winner Nadine Gordimer. Even children's classics were subject to scrutiny in the late twentieth century, as demonstrated by the apartheid government's misinterpretation of Anna Sewell's *Black Beauty* ([1877] 2012). Their reaction to this novel's title – and ignorance as to its contents – demonstrates how censorship evokes tensions between silence and desire. It also points to fascinating slippages between the nonhuman and human in literary texts, particularly when they are read in post/colonial contexts. I have organized the sections of this book into four vectors of metaphorization surrounding abortion: animal, plant, mineral and human. Yet it would be reductive to suggest that the authors in this study were simply veiling abortion through ecological metaphor in order to avoid censorship. Not only is abortion discussed with frankness and detail in the texts that form the heart of this study, but it is also reconceptualized as an ethico-political issue rather than a moral conundrum to be resolved in the legal sphere. The distinction between ethical frameworks that rely on analogy and Karen Barad's approach to philosophy is that while the former compare subjects as being like one another, the latter method reads them through each other. All the authors in this study are preoccupied by the fact that nationalist discourse has metaphorized the female reprosexual body as environment, or vice versa, whether this is through colonial tropes of the mother country or liberationist rhetoric about Mother Africa. Nevertheless, their fictions move past equivocations and analogies, viewing non/human subjects through a diffractive lens.

Some may argue the simple fact of the matter is that ecologies cannot possess the same level of agency as a human subject. However, nonhuman materials in these texts come to figure for, and even influence, social matters; they embody a new and critical form of humanism that does not revere repronormative roles (particularly that of the *mater*), but rather views both agency and abortion along situational continuums. The term 'critical humanism' has been popularized by Martin Halliwell and Andrew Mousley with the publication of their 2003 monograph *Critical Humanisms: Humanist/Anti-Humanist Dialogues*. As its title suggests, their study argues that elements of post- and anti-humanist thought may be located within humanist thinking, and vice versa. I similarly do not argue for a complete break between humanism proper and more-than-humanist thought (posthumanism, anti-humanism or critical humanism). While Halliwell and Mousley focus almost exclusively on European and North American contexts, my study is interested in critical humanisms forming in southern African texts.[8] Each author demonstrates a unique approach to writing abortion, but their focuses on reproductive agency are representative of a broader anti-nationalist trend. As its many epigraphs suggest, this book is thus designed to evoke an ongoing conversation between these voices and other southern African authors who thematize human embodiment through ecological metaphor: Olive Schreiner, Ingrid Jonker and Tsitsi Dangarembga, to name a few. The concept of a conversation also extends to the vectors of animal, plant and mineral metaphorization that are shared and refracted through these critically humanist tales. Chapters 3 and 4, in particular, demonstrate how Black women may write abortion ecologies without playing into nationalist discourse.

The chapters that follow investigate a range of intersecting values that are mirrored and repeated in southern African fiction from the 1970s to 1990s. My first chapter focuses on J. M. Coetzee's English translation of Wilma Stockenström's Afrikaans novella *The Expedition to the Baobab Tree* (1983), which I refer to as an interpretive translation. The novella is set in a vague area of southern Africa and features an abundance of domesticated species and wildlife. Adapting several ecofeminist perspectives from literary and critical theorists, and focusing particularly on the ethics of listening, I read Stockenström's fictional slave narrative in both the original Afrikaans and Coetzee's highly popular translation. The novella uses beastly riddles instead of the technique of analogy upon which the animal fable traditionally rests. I argue that *Expedition* paints a complex picture of social parasitism in southern Africa: both in terms of its thematization of slavery and its form as a text 'co-parented' by two white writers. Stockenström's formations of gestation and parasitism queer the figure of the human that informs much discourse surrounding abortion. This chapter also contextualizes indigenous histories of abortion, and how discussions of genetic and birth origins in southern Africa are inextricably linked with legacies of slavery and racial discrimination.

Chapter 2 analyses Zoë Wicomb's *You Can't Get Lost in Cape Town* (1987), a Bildungsroman of semi-autobiographical stories set in several very specific areas of South Africa. Developing associations of gestation with parasitism from the previous chapter, I wade deeper into the realm of metaphors, particularly plant life.

Wicomb presents a perverse take on abortion under apartheid with references to literary Modernism, as well as African and feminist Bildungsromane. Utilizing the concept of autopoiesis as developed by scholars ranging from science studies, critical race theory and new materialism, I analyse several story-segments from this text, including the titular story's abortion scene. I further consider how Wicomb's academic writing reinforces this text's suspicion of both the apartheid government and masculinist African nationalisms. Formations of agency and desire intersect with anxieties surrounding genetic roots and miscegenation, resulting in deviation from what both repronormative cultures deem as natural.

Yvonne Vera's *Butterfly Burning* (1998) is a novel with short chapters that thematizes the rural/urban divide in colonial Zimbabwe. In Chapter 3, I explore how the novel weaves organic and inorganic elements through two abortion scenes, creating a nuanced vocabulary for discussing reproductive, among other, agencies. This is inarguably the most posthumanist novel in the study, as shown by my analysis of how human and nonhuman bodies are exposed to and enmeshed within one another through Vera's literary form. Elemental forms in *Butterfly Burning* include water, fire, lightning and rocks. The melding of organic and inorganic imagery signals a move from formations to transformations: Vera metamorphoses the tragedy of lost personhood that is supposedly inherent to abortion narratives. Yet her querying of sexual and racial politics in literal and figurative birthings means that the text is also witness to very human matters.

The final chapter affirms this transition to the human realm (and to an earlier period of southern African history) by focusing on Bessie Head's oeuvre of short stories and novels, particularly *The Collector of Treasures and other Botswana Village Tales* ([1977] 1992), *Maru* ([1971] 2008), *A Question of Power* (1973), *Tales of Tenderness and Power* ([1989] 1990) and *When Rain Clouds Gather* (1968). I consider how Head's writing style resonates with a wealth of literary traditions: from African folklore to European Modernism, the vibrant and political work of both contemporary feminists and postcolonial theorists. Instead of focusing on gestating beasts, as in Stockenström, Head queers non/human agencies through what I term 'creative ferment': individuals in her work possess a queer vitality that continues to be demonstrated in and by the broader political landscape. Head's fiction traces abortion as self-formation and challenges not only normative models of personal development, but also narrative time.

The very structure of this study thus illustrates its circular logic: there is a move from nonhuman animals to less familiar environmental agencies, before an ultimate return to questions of personhood and agency in the human realm. While Stockenström and Head are preoccupied with questions of intraspecies allegiances, Wicomb and Vera thematize ecological phenomena. Narrative form is another notable ground for comparison, particularly in the first two chapters. Stockenström and Wicomb both reformulate the novella by using fragmentary styles: the former is co-creator of an interpretive translation, while the latter writes an African feminist Bildungsroman. There are striking formal similarities between Wicomb's writing and Head's queer collection of stories, too: their shared experimentation with brevity and shame, owing perhaps to shared Modernist influences discussed at several points. Finally, Vera's complication of the tragic form has ramifications for all the other narratives in this study and, indeed, broader associations of abortion with catastrophe. It is true that the political left needs to acknowledge difficult or traumatic abortions in order not to silence people who have suffered. At the same time, we must resist seeing abortion as synonymous with disaster. A person's reasons for terminating a pregnancy may range from the practical to the profound. Through their metaphors of parasitism and plant life, of nonhuman elements and queer sexuality, these authors demonstrate the power of situating such reasons and scenarios on a continuum.

The birth of a wave: an idea. The birth of a word or a child. A new name, baptized in blood. Each in their own ways, the authors in this study are preoccupied with how discourse is created, particularly when it involves the idealization of motherhood and reproduction. For women who reconceive abortion narratives defy nationalist teleologies, whether they are expressed by the racialized political violence of colonizers, or through the insidious sexualized control of the traditionalists who follow in their wake. These authors are narrators of vitality. In their words, in their fictional worlds, women are never simply victims. Abortion does not signal southern Africa's demise, but rather a plethora of new possibilities.

Notes

1   The title in question was of Helen Bradford's (1995) article 'Olive Schreiner's Hidden Agony: Fact, Fiction and Teenage Abortion'.

2   The term 'foetal patienthood' does not necessarily equate to legal personhood, but may be used to advocate for prioritizing the rights of the foetus; for more on this, see Elizabeth Chloe Romanis et al. (2020).

3   For more on the phenomenon of 'abortion tourism' across a range of geographical and historical contexts, see Christabelle Sethna and Gayle Davis's edited collection *Abortion across Borders: Transnational Travel and Access to Abortion Services* (2019).

4   Their preoccupation with Modernism is particularly interesting in light of
    work on abortion in Modernist literature: see Christina Hauck (2003) and Fran
    Bigman (2016). The scope of my study does not allow for extended discussions
    of transnational Modernisms and their legacies, but this is an exciting avenue of
    crossovers for postcolonial and Modernist studies, as evidenced by the ongoing
    project 'South African Modernism 1880–2020' led by Jade Munslow Ong.

5   For a critique of such insidious attitudes towards immigration and race in the
    environmental humanities, see Timothy Clark (2016).

6   For a more detailed – if subjective – study of this linkage, see Sherry F. Colb and
    Michael C. Dorf's vegan theorization of reproductive agency in *Beating Hearts:
    Abortion and Animal Rights* (2016). The authors point out that many contemporary
    arguments for abortion pose the medical procedure as a form of self-defence,
    raising interesting questions about the supposed innocence and benevolence of
    new life. In cases of unsupportable pregnancies, the foetus may be characterized as
    dangerous or even parasitic (as discussed in Chapters 1 and 2), despite the fact that
    it has not deliberately chosen to jeopardize the woman's health.

7   For further critique of Edelman, see Nicole Seymour's (2013) discussion of
    anti-futurity's complicity with hyper-capitalism (as discussed in Chapter 4).

8   My definition of critical humanism is outlined further with respect to emerging
    queer posthumanisms in Chapter 4.

1

Animals

Pregnancy as parasitism in Wilma Stockenström's
The Expedition to the Baobab Tree

The first novella in this study, *The Expedition to the Baobab Tree*, is something of an anomaly. First published in 1981, Wilma Stockenström's *Die kremetartekspedisie* was translated into English for British publishers Faber & Faber by J. M. Coetzee in 1983 (to date, this is his only Afrikaans translation).[1] Stockenström's text grapples with what many would perceive as unusual subject matter for Afrikaans literature, particularly in the years leading up to the 1985 State of Emergency: it is a fictional slave narrative set during the advent of European colonial expansion in southern Africa (historical dates, along with geographical specificity and other details, are deliberately obscured by the novella). In spite – or perhaps because – of its controversial content, the text succeeded in reaching a sympathetic audience without being banned by the apartheid government. In 2014 the English version was reissued in the United States, receiving a resurgence of interest and critical acclaim from publications including *Asymptote* and the *LA Review of Books*. The moral impetus of the novella is generalized in contemporary reviews by critics such as Lily Saint (2017) and Cory Johnstone (2014) as overtly feminist with anti-racist undertones. Yet there is danger in summarizing a text which emerges from such a complex moment in history without contextualizing its origins and, particularly, the thematic and literary concerns of its original author. This chapter therefore deviates from many reviews and critical articles on the English text – both those that were written soon after its publication, and more recent pieces – by considering the long history of the novella, particularly ethically ambiguous elements which are opened by reading *Expedition* as what I term an interpretive translation. As translator Coetzee 'listens' to the original text, but the very act of interpretation reinforces Stockenström's preoccupation with narrative, cultural and biological origins.

Wilma Stockenström was born in the Western Cape of South Africa in 1933 and currently lives in Cape Town. She has worked as a translator, actress and writer, and has received prestigious awards for her Afrikaans writing including the Hertzog Prize (for poetry and fiction), the CNA Prize for Poetry and the SALA Literary Lifetime Award. *Uitdraai* (*Turn-Off*), Stockenström's first novel, was published in 1976. The text conforms to the thematic preoccupations of the Afrikaans *plaasroman* – that is, a pastoral narrative set on a farm, usually revolving around a white patriarch – but is distinctive in its use of sexually explicit imagery. For instance, Gerrit Olivier summarizes the novel's transgressive elements by focusing on the scene of 'a sordid backroom abortion, dramatically visualised by one of those present vomiting up the figs she has consumed' (2012: 319). It is quite remarkable that such frankness was not targeted by apartheid censors, given that abortion law was extremely strict at the time of publishing. Stockenström's sarcastic and distanced technique is further reinforced by the fact that the pregnancy is a result of miscegenation, which Olivier correctly identifies as a prominent theme in Afrikaans writing at the time (2012: 319–20). One of the most famous examples of such a narrative is Etienne van Heerden's *Toorberg*, which was translated into English as *Ancestral Voices* ([1986] 2011). Van Heerden's novel charts four generations of two families who are complexly sired, shamed and united by a chain of patriarchs named Abel. Immediately it is obvious how *Uitdraai* simultaneously adheres to and departs from the conventions manifested in this exemplary *plaasroman*: Stockenström also utilizes imagery with heavily religious connotations (figs represent fertility and prosperity in the Bible; a fig tree which does not produce fruit is cursed by Jesus), but is less concerned with male lineage and genetic anxieties than women's labour. Christianity is an important component of both traditional Afrikaans writing and culture, as illustrated by the fact that Biblical passages were often quoted by the conservative NP to promote social segregation and ideas of racial purity. Furthermore, the fruit mentioned here recurs in southern African women's fiction.[2]

This chapter is concerned with understanding abortion during colonial expansion across southern Africa, contextualizing the slave trade's legacy of gestational violence. Yet we must remember that Stockenström's fictional slave narrative was written during the height of apartheid. As such, it is helpful to begin with the historical context under which the novella was written, before considering the histories that it represents. Canadian historian Susanne M. Klausen's monograph *Abortion under Apartheid: Nationalism, Sexuality, and Women's Reproductive Rights in South Africa* (2015) traces the discrepancies between Black and white women's access to health services between 1948 and 1991. Klausen refers to Zoë Wicomb's novel *You Can't Get Lost in Cape Town* to illustrate how women of colour under apartheid could not (or did not) necessarily approach abortionists of their own race (2015: 39) – a clear indicator of fiction's capacity to document material realities of the vulnerable, particularly during times of political extremism and censorship. She notes that, while the ANC urged women to be wary of contraceptives and abortifacients, white men simultaneously encouraged settler women from the supposed motherland to procreate so as to ensure that they were not outnumbered by the Black majority; the result of autochthonous Africans' and Afrikaners' paranoia was that 'both expected women to reproduce for the sake of the nation' (Klausen 2015: 194). Unequal power relations between different racial groups thus allowed misogynistic discourse and law-making to flourish. Klausen's analysis is outstanding in its dedication to discussing a range of racial identities; however, there are a few instances demanding more complex considerations of intra-ethnic agendas and literary allegiances. The characterization of feminist abortion law reform supporters as 'white, English-speaking, and middle class' (2015: 90), for instance, fails to account for the writings of prominent Afrikaans activists like Ingrid Jonker. Daughter of a conservative politician, Jonker had at least one illegal abortion, which she addresses in her poetry and journals. Together with André Brink and others, she was involved with an experimental writing group called *Die Sestigers* (the Movement of Sixty), which Klausen describes as a 'group of male Afrikaner writers' (2015: 60). Not only was Jonker an active member of the group but, as an author writing in Afrikaans from the 1970s onwards, Wilma Stockenström's work was indubitably influenced by *Die Sestigers*. These complications involving aesthetic treatments of terminations of pregnancy show just how challenging it is to create comprehensive portraits of abortion in the southern African context, where the politics of choice are staged across intersecting spheres of representation and reproduction.

Die kremetartekspedisie is Stockenström's third, and undoubtedly best-known, fictional work; a postscript in the Afrikaans Kindle edition records that following its publication in English, it has been translated into French, German, Dutch, Italian and Hebrew ([1981] 2013: loc. 1562). Unlike the generic *plaasroman* and her earlier novel *Uitdraai*, *The Expedition to the Baobab Tree* is different in that the pregnancies and sexual violence which form its thematic centre are not relayed from the perspective of a white narrator. Rather, the protagonist is a woman of colour who becomes a victim of colonial expansion and slavery. The narrative is set during the establishment of the Portuguese sea-route to India and it is implied that the nameless protagonist is first captured on the East Coast of Africa ([1981] 2013: loc. 1552–4). She recounts her life story in achronological fragments as she travels inland to an area which is both unidentified and untouched by modern civilization. After seeking an abortion and escaping her third master, she ruminates on the lives of sharks, baboons, birds and bats, before arriving at the titular baobab tree.

The novella is remarkable not only for its poetic rendition of sexually and biologically graphic scenes, but also for the boldness of its narrative situation. For though we are never given explicit indicators of the narrator's racial identity – or, it must be added, the markers of miscegenation, which recur in tell-tale descriptions of the 'brown-skinned, blue-eyed' Riet family in van Heerden's *Ancestral Voices* – it is implied that she is not speaking from the privileged position of whiteness. For an Afrikaans woman to write a slave narrative during the height of apartheid, and in the language of the oppressor, may be interpreted as either the ultimate renegade act or the pinnacle of ventriloquism. If one considers the state of censorship at the time of writing, then one is inclined to interpret it as the former; this is certainly what most, if not all, reviewers have tended to do, as the aforementioned pieces by Saint and Johnstone illustrate. However, there is something unsettling about seeing the novella named alongside writings by people of colour who were really forced to live as slaves, like Phillis Wheatley or Janet Lim, as an example of a 'modern' slave narrative (Fister 1995: 284). Jennifer Fleischner notes that slave narratives are most notably characterized by an autobiographical account of one's birth and childhood, and the escape therefrom (1996: 1–2). The importance of authorial positionality is explained by titles such as *The Interesting Narrative of the Life of Olaudah Equiano* ([1789] 2020); *The History of Mary Prince* ([1831] 2004); and *Narrative of the Life of Frederick Douglass, an American Slave* ([1845] 2014). *Expedition* obviously lacks this layer of personal authenticity. Yet the novella is preoccupied with similar themes to these transnational slave narratives, particularly issues relating to genetic origins and agency.

It is already clear that Stockenström is less interested in birth than in gestation: that is, the process of potentiality which precedes childbirth without necessitating it. But if her oeuvre charts a growing resistance to clichés of male birth rights and inheritance in Afrikaans writing, then it is worth noting that to date, most readings of her third fictional work follow something of a formulaic mould. Firstly, these readings synthesize large blocks of quotations from the text which are assumed to 'do the work' for an underlying feminist message. Secondly, and related to this last point, such readings overemphasize a particularly gendered aspect of social justice which they deem to be its central focus. While Louise Viljoen usefully points out that both 'thematically (in its focus on a slave woman) and stylistically (through its lyricism, complex chronology, gaps and silences), the novel questions male-oriented representations of the past' (Viljoen 2012: 461), I believe critics should be cautious about reading too heavily into dichotomous gendered messages simply because of the narrative situation. For example, Stephen Gray goes so far as to describe Stockenström as a 'poetess' with a 'particularly female' mode of expression (1991: 52; 51) – an outdated means of referring to a female author and an ambiguous assessment of her writerly skills. A greater problem with Gray's interpretation is that it typifies Stockenström's feminism as synonymous with a universalizing humanism. When analysing *Expedition*, he argues, 'In reading this work one is invited to be a child again, to marvel, and to listen to the maternal voice of a past which can always become accessible again. Stockenström sees no border between South Africa and Africa, and brings Africa back to us as a whole experience' (Gray 1991: 57). The notion that one can experience an entire continent by reading a single novella – which, despite its multiple settings, still originates from one country – seems essentialist at best. Although no national borders are specifically referenced by the text, there are other geographical markers that are evident by mention of specific species of fauna and flora, immediately disproving that the text utilizes the homogeneous Mother Africa trope. Ironically, the author's use of a female narrator has led some to patronize both her and the text; they equate the use of what Gray refers to above as a 'maternal voice' with a comforting but oversimplified presentation of post/colonial African countries.

This is not to say that second-wave feminist readings are the only apparent responses to the text. One of the more interesting studies of the novella is Cecelia Scallan Zeiss's comparative study of the 'boundary-state' in Samuel Beckett and Wilma Stockenström (1991: 57). Hers is not an overtly materialist reading, but the in-between state alluded to here is remarkably similar to the new materialist theory I discuss in my introduction in its emphasis on liminality as figured through natural elements. Astrida Neimanis' *Bodies of Water: Posthuman Feminist Phenomenology*, for instance, argues much like Zeiss that human and more-than-human agencies all flow together both metaphorically and literally by conceptualizing their shared origins in a 'watery' commons (Neimanis 2017: 12). The latter critic does not use water as a philosophical tool, but her reading is also grounded by references to nonhuman and nonanimal agencies, specifically in her sustained comparison of intersecting circles of oppression with rings of a tree (Zeiss 1991: 76). Zeiss is so interested in the materiality of the titular baobab that she provides an extensive quotation from a reference book titled *Trees of Southern Africa*, which accounts for 'several authentic reports of dead trees bursting into flame by spontaneous combustion', and suggests that Stockenström's evocation of such a phenomenon is strengthened by urban myths about old baobabs similarly catching fire (Palgrave 1984 in Zeiss 1991: 77). The event of self-immolation serves as a central theme and plot device in Yvonne Vera's *Butterfly Burning*, as I discuss in Chapter 3; it is fascinating to consider that an oral history with similar associations surrounds the symbol of the baobab tree. Here Zeiss is cognisant of the fact that gender-based discrimination is one of many forms of violence in Stockenström's text and that ecological issues should also be addressed.

In this chapter, I am interested in how Stockenström conceives of gestational relationships and the organisms which surround or encompass them. I argue that she deliberately thematizes wildlife during the height of apartheid in order to express the complexities of utilizing ecological analogies to advocate for the intersecting ideals of national independence and reproductive agency. Stockenström writes from the perspective of a slave to foreground both the roots of racial injustice and African abortifacients: natural remedies, made from tubers and seeds, that moved with women across national borders during colonial rule. Simultaneously, she queers the tradition of animal fables through questions and riddles, showing how focusing upon freedom as the primary precondition for personhood causes certain individuals to remain precluded from ethical considerations. The text's localized understanding of literal and metaphorical fertility – including gestation, the 'birth of a nation' or the creation of art – is strikingly similar to emerging new materialist theories about the interconnectedness of all subjectivities, such as Neimanis's 'posthuman gestationality', a term maintaining that pregnancy involves but also exceeds the human female reprosexual body (2017: 68–9). Stockenström's use of a slave woman as a narrator certainly foregrounds sexism as a unifying concern for all women in southern Africa. Nevertheless, it is important to *question* her utilization of a Black woman's body not only for comparing human and animal agencies, but also in light of what Greta Gaard terms 'the practice of attentive listening' (2017: xvi).

Contemporary interventions in materialist theory commonly create neologisms to address feminist concerns within science studies; some of these coinages are arguably limited in their originality or depth. Yet Gaard foregrounds in her latest monograph one such word which is useful for both my project and broader materialist literary studies: 'restor(y)ing'. Perhaps counter-intuitively, the word is used to refer to not only the creation, but also the *reception*, of stories; the author is invested in a 'rich community of indigenous, feminist, and trans-species listening theory' which is 'our birthright as earth citizens' (Gaard 2017: xviii). She argues that more fiction, in particular, needs to focus on the material implications of interconnected oppressions. While I certainly would not challenge the demand for more creative narratives, this chapter is an analysis of an exemplary fictional work which hears and answers Gaard's call. My argument is that *Expedition* spans the interspecies implications of pregnancy and the negation thereof through such an ethics of attentive listening. Gestation emphasizes an unfinished, Deleuzian process of becoming that supersedes supposedly finite chronologies of birth and death.[3]

Listening to beastly riddles

Relayed in an achronological manner, Stockenström's novella commences towards the end of its narrative arc: having already travelled south from a nondescript northern African region, the protagonist begins her narration by describing the 'bitterness' with which she has decided to commit suicide (1983: 7). Interestingly, the Afrikaans word which Stockenström uses initially is *wrewel* ([1981] 2013: loc. 6), which literally translates as resentment, rancour or spite (Kromhout [1952] 1992: 167), but is interpreted by Coetzee as bitterness. It is significant that Coetzee chooses to use a more colloquial term – one which also recurs in Stockenström's use of the equally informal Afrikaans words *bitter* ([1981] 2013: loc. 568) and *bitterheid* or bitterness ([1981] 2013: loc. 590). There are both literal and metaphorical connotations of this word, which I will return to later in this chapter. Early in the narrator's description of the baobab tree and its surrounds, she recalls a riddle that she and other slaves used to ask each other in their youth: 'What carries its life in its stomach?' (8). Perhaps puzzlingly to the reader, an answer is not overtly suggested; moreover, it is unclear exactly whose life is in question here. Firstly, the phenomenon of gestation in the abdominal cavity is a defining characteristic of mammals, meaning that there could be an inestimable number of solutions. However, if the word 'its' is to be taken literally, then the riddle must be referring to any being that contains its *own* heart and stomach in a singular body cavity (thus precluding mammals from the discussion, but bringing most other vertebrates into consideration). So far, so vague. Yet one must remember that this puzzle has been translated into English. Combined with the ambiguous 'What' at the start of the riddle, this fact is most useful in considering how to read both the question and the text. After narrowly avoiding being crushed by a herd of elephants, the narrator describes how 'an elephant swallows a pebble down, and the pebbles rattle around in their tremendous bellies all their lives' (9). The Afrikaans for elephant is *olifant*: this word contains, at its centre, the Old English *līf*, which forms roots of both the English word life and the Afrikaans *lewe* (body, life). Thus, just as the belly of the real animal may harbour foetal forms or rattling stones, the heart of the word *olifant* signifies, etymologically, two bodily concepts. The intertwined notions of corporeal and ecological life are what inform my reading of Coetzee's translation of the text. I begin, therefore, by considering the proliferation of non/human bodies and analogies of 'questioning', before moving onto matters of gestation, narrative form and negation. This chapter concludes with a discussion of the ways in which Coetzee's interpretive translation listens to, but also deviates from, Stockenström's interspecies and materialist understanding of human reproductive health.

While lying nervously curled in the aforementioned passage, the narrator likens herself to a beetle the size of her little finger. In a sense, her enactment of a 'sham death' calls to mind how popular pregnancy discourse often measures the moral worth of a foetus by its size (9): zygotes may be compared to any organic materials from kidney beans to pea pods, depending on their stages of growth, and the larger an embryo or foetus, the more likely it is to be seen as living. Most interesting is that while the protagonist mimics the form of a human foetus, the metonyms and metaphors used to describe her remain situated within the animal realm. Although she wishes to 'stand up like a human being and look around' (9), she is forced to remain on the ground – implicitly, the same level as non-bipedal animals – for the sake of her safety. Simultaneously rendered as a developed zygote, a crawling infant and an animal, the moral worth of the slave is immediately foregrounded as a central thematic concern. When she recalls her earlier life in northern Africa, she remembers a slaughterhouse full of hearts, livers, lungs and other bodily parts. Although the cacophonous sounds of 'lowing and bleating' merge with the butchers' suggestive comments whenever the woman is forced to buy meat by her owner – in what Carol J. Adams would describe as the sexual politics of meat (Adams [1990] 2015: 23) – this does not deter her from cooking and sharing the food with the other enslaved women (Stockenström 1983: 22–3). Yet it is imperative to consider what immediately follows the scenes in the slaughterhouse: a description of the slaves' quarters. In the Black women's dwellings, they are forced to share everything from their food to parenting duties; for the sake of simplicity, lactating women breastfeed any and all infants. Implicitly, then, the protagonist is aware that 'we women fertile and rank' are treated with the same level of respect as livestock (23) – not only because they are capable of bearing children who will be sold, but also because they themselves are owned by white men. There is thus a second interpretation of the word rank which is relevant here: that is, a position in a hierarchy. The narrator gradually realizes uncanny similarities between herself and nonhuman animals as she recalls her former life and attempts to survive in the veld.

Yet the narrator verbalizes an exchange with domesticated animals which point towards an interspecies understanding that is aware of the complications which racial and class prejudices present. An interesting sentiment about interspecies exchanges is displayed when the slave remembers speaking to a cock about their 'mutual owner' in the yard, reminding him that 'your crowing and shitting and our chatting and our excretions and secretions, our babies, our ornaments of pod-mahogany seeds and our body-cloths, and the house and the warehouse full of baskets of spices and the rats there', are 'all his' (Stockenström 1983: 44). This passage is particularly striking because of its synthesis of animalistic noises with scatological and inanimate imagery. Postcolonial studies has, from the outset, been acutely aware of the fact that the colonization of Africa relied on reducing people of colour from human subjects to beastly objects: 'discourse on Africa', Achille Mbembe notes, 'is almost always deployed in the framework (or in the fringes) of a meta-text about the *animal*' (2001: 1; original emphasis). This is a fact which is crucially omitted in Mary Midgley's *Beast and Man: The Roots of Human Nature* ([1978] 1995), one of the best-known modern studies of human behaviour as contextualized within the animal kingdom. Midgley does repeatedly emphasize how beastliness is a false construct that denies the orderliness of both the 'animal within' and nonhuman animals ([1978] 1995: 49), but her philosophy lacks sensitivity to the historical oppression of certain racialized and exoticized bodies within this framework. Perhaps sensing racialized connotations of the 'beast', the 'creaturely' has become something of a buzzword in critical animal studies in the last decade, with researchers such as Anat Pick (2011) and Tobias Menely (2015) discussing its potential in highlighting the shared vulnerabilities and experiences of human and nonhuman animals. Donna Haraway correctly identifies the term's religious etymological roots (all organisms as creations), opting instead to refer to all living beings as 'critters' (2008: 330). I use the term beastly to resist the transcendentalist and universalizing associations of both 'creatures' and 'critters', respectively. Furthermore, by using a word which is not associated with the politics of victimhood and is thus more adaptable to discussions of agency, I foreground how *uneven gendered relationships* underlie racist animalization or dehumanization. To adapt Jacques Derrida, the 'beast' (whether human, animal or any other living being) is that which both submits to and resists the whims of an 'anthropo-theological' sovereign (2009: 14), whether this authority is a (male) human figure, a metaphorical conception of the law or the homogeneously 'harmonious' construct of the creaturely itself. Together with unresolved intraspecies injustices in the human realm, the phenomenon of animalization is one of the major reasons why postcolonial studies as a discipline is generally reticent to address the animal question, and particularly the 'dreaded comparison' between nonhuman subjects and historically dehumanized peoples (Spiegel 1988: 3). Yet in moving immediately from a description of human infants to objects which form part of the slave-owner's household, *Expedition*'s narrator implies that all these material beings exist on a similar ethical terrain (and not only from the colonizer's perspective). This is not to say that she endorses the objectification of humans that animal analogies may justify; rather, her positionality as an oppressed person causes her to reflect upon the potentially interconnected agency of all matter, and what interspecies analogies would mean for ethics.

Such concerns about dehumanization were prescient at the time of publishing, during the height of apartheid. It is important to remember that *Expedition*'s subject matter was highly unusual for South African literature, but simultaneously that the novella cannot resist being read as a product of its time. That is, in thematizing the slave trade, Stockenström risks the accusation of harking back to comparatively 'worse' times instead of addressing injustices in the years leading up to the State of Emergency. Yet there is also the possibility that her narrative takes the historical long view in order to contextualize the origins of apartheid South Africa's racial injustices, and, particularly, the gendered elements of this oppression. Here I am referring to the colonial project's feminization of the natural environment. Fertility is a duplicitous term, serving as the basis for growth but potentially also exploitation; in colonial contexts, pastoral images of fertility often masked patriarchal violence, for slaves' lack of agency meant the constant possibility of sexual abuse or rape. The majority of births by slaves in America took place during the late summer or early fall (Roberts 1997: 41); reproductive cycles therefore tended to align with the yearly harvest of crops. Slavery is a perennial condition, and those babies that survived delivery would often face perilous infancies, as their mothers would be forced to return to work soon after childbirth. It is difficult to quantify exactly how similar conditions were for slaves in southern Africa as most studies of abortion and slavery focus on African-American and Amerindian women – see, for example, the work of

Jennifer Doyle (2009), Loretta J. Ross (2005) and Londa L. Schiebinger (2004). However, Nigel Worden records that Khoisan women in Dutch South Africa 'deliberately induced abortion' ([1985] 2010: 59), meaning it is not unreasonable to assume that slave societies shared repronormative pressures due to enforced sexual labour.

Slave women rebelled against reproductive roles through abstinence, contraception and the use of abortives (mechanical methods of external or internal manipulation, or medicines). Dorothy Roberts argues that the last of these methods was by far the most popular and originates from a root geographical location, as herbal remedies using the roots and seeds of cotton plants, camphor, cedar gum and other plants were 'techniques slaves probably brought with them from Africa' (1997: 47). In a literal sense, the abortifacients are 'natural' elements which are easily accessible to Black women, and that can be utilized to exert control over their bodily involvement in repronormative, racist environments. These traditional ingredients and herbs form an important sense of cultural identity from a shared source: an origin that remains crucial, but nevertheless *unknown*, as the homogenizing usage of 'Africa' proves above. In her study of culturally induced ignorance surrounding Merian's peacock flower, a plant used by slaves to induce abortions in colonial Suriname, Londa L. Schiebinger asks how and why this indigenous knowledge was obscured even when the flower was transferred to colonial Europe (2004: 153). The unknown history of Merian's peacock flower points to both the political potential of nonhuman elements in creating safer abortion ecologies, and the parasitic relationship between colonizer and colonized. Why, after all, does Schiebinger conclude her fascinating study of culturally induced ignorances by speculating how *European and American* women could have benefitted from indigenous abortifacients (2004: 241)? By extension, how do white women profit from Black women's power or from writing about the supposed lack thereof?

These are uncomfortable questions that speak to the positional limitations of my very project. Yet critical race theory complicates the dichotomy of parasite and host. First appearing in the year between the novella's publication and its translation into English, Orlando Patterson's *Slavery and Social Death: A Comparative Study* (1982) conceptualizes social slavery – colonialism's simultaneous root and by-product – as a cyclical enforcement of 'natal alienation' upon certain peoples by treating them as material property. This phrase refers to a particular sense of isolation which slaves feel: one which consists of both the literal loss of ties with one's kin, and damage accrued by a lack of birth rights and more symbolic elements of one's identity (Patterson 1982: 5–7). Patterson stresses that slavery strips people of their cultural heritage, which is vitally distinct from history. '[A] past is not a heritage', he asserts, since '[e]verything has a history, including sticks and stones' (1982: 5). One is reminded of Derrida's discussion of worlds; if history refers to the factual past of an object or subject, then heritage differs in that it signifies the symbolic interpretation of previous events. Slavery, then, is typified by Patterson as a process wherein people are denied the opportunity to extract meaning from their material circumstances, their being-in-the-world. Unlike animals, they are not even considered as 'poor in world', because they are relegated to the status of objects (below the realms of human and nonhuman organisms). Yet Patterson cautions against conflating one's treatment as property with a lack of legal status (1982: 23), and he is also wary of speaking to the private lives of slaves because 'it is the height of arrogance, not to mention intellectual irresponsibility, to generalise about the inner psychology of any group' (1982: 11). It is fascinating – and not coincidental, I would argue – that both he and Stockenström's narrator resist the temptation of imaginative positioning. Rather, we are urged to consider slavery as a 'continuum' of social 'parasitism', wherein the dominator and dominated may be either dependent or independent, equal or unequal, depending on a variety of complexities (Patterson 1982: 336). Similarly to Patterson, the narrator limns dehumanization beyond mere animalization, approaching her degradation as a scalar phenomenon which is inevitable under the logic of colonialism. That is, she considers parasitic relationships as representative of broad social structures in colonial southern Africa.

The animalistic term of parasitism, borrowed from biology, is crucial to my study, especially considering Michel Serres's *Le Parasite* ([1980] 2007), a philosophical study that uses fable to compare human relationships to parasitic symbiosis. In his introduction to a recent English translation of the text, Cary Wolfe notes how '"noise" (for the English reader) forms the third and unsuspected meaning of the French word parasite: 1. biological parasite; 2. social parasite; 3. static or interference' (2007: xiii). Wolfe goes on to explain that for Serres, noise is a sign of *difference* and *multiplicity*. Sound as a phenomenon involves both creation (noise-making) and reception (listening). Yet much like the parasite-host relationship, it is uncommon to encounter 'noisy' scenarios where one is purely an active or passive participant, even in cases where only two actors are involved. Here we may imagine the undergraduate student who questions their tutor or an opera enthusiast humming along to a symphony. Even in the case of a singular organism, the actor always creates noise: its guttural rumblings (eloquently evoked by Stockenström's riddle of the elephant) and its beating heart mean that the body is never truly silent. It appears, therefore, that *listening* is once again a crucial term in helping to explain the differences and similarities between the dialectics of internal and external, creator and receiver, and parasite and host. Symbiosis signifies interdependence between two organisms, and in the case of parasite and host, their relationship may be deadly. Yet in Stockenström's novella, the symbiotic relationship is rendered indeterminate through an ethics of listening. This queer switching of positions is explored not only in her contemplation of gestation and abortion, but also by framing the narrator's journey and her body in the 'belly of a baobab' (Stockenström 1983: 14).

Literary critic Godfrey Meintjes (1996) has discussed how *Expedition*'s aesthetic elements express growing and generalized ecological anxieties during the late twentieth century, while Susan Meyer provides an overtly ecofeminist reading by concentrating on the scenes in which the slave-narrator is presented as the Self in 'Othered' nature, arguing that these more pastoral passages show her 'reaching the core of humanness [...] self-respect, pride, and dignity' (Meyer 2013: 311). I take issue not only with the uncritical insertion of such humanist terms into an ecocritical reading, but also with the fact that Meyer appears to be relying here on the very process of imaginative positioning that Patterson warns against. To date, a significant lacuna in scholarship is a consideration of how specific wildlife in the novella marries both nonhumans' *and* humans' struggles for agency in colonial settings. Scholars have not accounted for the congruence between the unnamed woman's horrific handling by slave owners, the multifaceted exploitation of megafauna around her and her treatment of autochthonous peoples as she explores the veld. This seems a crucial omission, given that interactions with nonhuman animals not only thematize the protagonist's origins, but also influence the plot and her predicament as she is abandoned near the baobab tree. When her last owner comes to his end 'in the belly of a reptile' (Stockenström 1983: 63), she appears to be more indifferent than distressed. His death is described as 'silly' and 'ridiculous' as she reflects on the arbitrary nature with which humans decide what is killable and edible,[4] and what is not (63). In contrast to the opening riddle which renders an elephant's belly as a fertile birthplace, here the crocodile's body cavity signifies random violence and death. It is important to iterate that the narrator's story – and Stockenström's text – is not an animal fable. Rather, the author *questions* the fabular tradition by creating beastly riddles that provoke answers to the internal/external dialectic of the parasite through attentive listening.

Although she is selected as his favourite, the slave only refers to the leader of the expedition aloofly as 'the stranger', even after entering an intimate relationship with him. Her treatment of the man on these terms highlights the text's thematic indeterminacy and, in particular, its focus on unknown origins. The slave goes on to recall words uttered by her unnamed owner which directly resonate with moral indifference: after trying (and failing) to entertain the narrator with mystical fables of the afterlife, the colonizer comments, 'I think one can be ridiculous with dignity. Or try to' (74). Ironically, his death proves his own hypothesis: it illustrates the fictional nature of humanist constructs like dignity, as he is easily outwitted and devoured by a reptile which is purportedly lower on the great chain of being. In one of the few instances when the untimeliness of his demise appears to upset her, the narrator chides herself that it is no 'less ridiculous to be buried and eaten by worms' (64). Here Stockenström questions the bizarre anthropocentrism that is involved in narrating the beastly. Further, she queers the very idea of analogy on which the animal fable rests: its assertion that human and nonhuman agencies are exactly alike while still imbuing the latter with familiar and wholly anthropomorphized traits. This dramatic moment in the narrative shows, rather, that there is an asymmetrical relationship between both humans and animals, and between analogies and materiality. There is an equally non-identical connection between the beast fable and the origin myth; Westerners typically understand the former to be synonymous with the latter in indigenous contexts, whereas Judeo-Christian lore about the beginnings and ends of life is more strictly humanist (or, rather, insistent that the narration of animal lives is literal rather than analogy). The death of the slave-owner thus marks a further progression in the protagonist's thinking about agentive exchanges.

This is not to say, however, that such recognitions of humanity's precariousness completely alter the character's preconceptions about power. If anything, her thoughts about 'tedious humans' develop into a subtle form of misanthropy (78), particularly when regarding the lives of other and, in her mind, lesser slaves. Recalling again how the members of her expedition party appeared to collude before the stranger and his son died, she asks, 'What prevented the slaves from overpowering the two of them, doing away with them, and making off? Were they then so unmanned? I thought I detected a glint in the slaves' eyes. They were watching like the crows were' (78). Distancing herself from those who carry her through the veld on a litter, she simultaneously objectifies and emasculates them by suggesting that to be without an identifiably elected leader is to be like an 'unmanned' vessel. In his aforementioned monograph, Patterson proves otherwise: although most civilizations did not have a word for freedom until slavery arrived, he notes, many still conceived of power and domination through metaphors such as the Ashanti proverb, 'If you have not a master, a beast will catch you' (1982: 27). The implication of this phrase is that all people – even those sovereigns who 'own' others – are subject to being treated as property, and that it is unwise to define slavery as a lack of legal personhood because even material objects may be imbued with legal powers. The proverb suggests that it is entirely possible to understand violent acts of domination without adhering to (typically Western) vertical models of leadership, governance and power. Yet the narrator is reluctant to recognize agency as a scalar phenomenon. Furthermore, her comparison of the other slaves to the scavengers that clean her owner's carcass shows that she is suspicious of both their motives and their cognitive capabilities. Thus while the narrator comes to display some nuanced understandings of the wildlife on her journey, her attitudes towards other colonized humans are not so forgiving. At this point, it is worth pausing to read the narrator's internalized prejudices through her interactions with the Khoisan people who visit her once she has been abandoned at the titular baobab tree. Through tripled associations with childhood – learnt behaviours and biases, literal pregnancies and instances of infantilization – I will return to the narrator's attitudes towards racial identity and argue that she ultimately presents a flexible but imperfect conception of reproductive agency.

Slavery, gestation and infantilization

At surface level, *Expedition* is illustrative of a slave's natal alienation and subsequent internalization of her supposed inferiority. For example, early in her narration the protagonist remarks, 'I have no idea what my value must have been or what it ever was' (Stockenström 1983: 13); this may be read as indicating that she has come to 'buy into' the dehumanization of Black women in her society. Yet I would argue that the woman's estrangement from her origins leads to a more overtly feminist and intersectional reading of natal alienation than Patterson articulates.

During her childhood and adolescence as a slave moving through various households, the narrator lacks both privacy and a supportive network to smooth her transition from puberty to adulthood. Soon, sexual abuse results in the first of her many pregnancies. She notes, 'I was still a child when I carried a child inside me' (14), later reflecting that she was a 'mother-child' who 'played at swelling for nine months' (41). Although she is fixated on age, it is clear the narrator's naïveté is not merely a result of her youth. Forced away from the village where she was born, she attempts to forge a new identity and retain some semblance of self-respect; the easiest means of doing so is by divorcing herself from reality and denying the similarity of her subjugation to that of other indigenous peoples. When she is abandoned in the wilderness following the death of her master, she tries to convince herself that she has imposed a sense of order on the world to ward off 'the danger of timelessness' and that she is not merely 'a subordinate beat in the rhythm' (17).

Yet this gestational imagery of major and minor intertwined lifelines reveals the truth underpinning her fears: even once she is free she remains childlike, relying on 'little people' (a dysphemism for the Khoisan community) who bring her gifts. Protected only by their interventions and the bark of the baobab tree, she is barely capable of looking after herself – the opposite of a stereotypically caring maternal figure. There are multiple ironies at play here: the former ingénue was forced into early maturity and adulthood, but still views herself as lacking agency; she has cared for children and adult slave-owners since her youth, yet struggles to sustain her own life; and internalized racism means that she is prejudiced against those who attend to her (perhaps, also, because such actions confirm the fact that she is vulnerable). Immediately we can see how a scalar conception of slavery and agency might apply to such a scenario. Particularly, it is implied that enslaved motherhood may lead to a form of social parasitism, whereby a (girl or) woman is faced with the paradox of caring for another life while simultaneously relying on the kindnesses of others. Returning to my earlier discussion of symbiotic relationships, a further complication is that parasites may be said to 'care' for the hosts they prey on, sometimes killing by degrees through sustained dependence. If a parasite appears harmless due to its size, it is likely to be viewed as a pest, or, worse, it may even evoke a caring response if the harm it causes is initially undetectable. This has many ramifications for Gaard's theory of reciprocating care through listening (or, more broadly, for adopting the ethics of care which underlies much ecocritical and ecofeminist theory). It also alters one's perspective on the supposed innocence of the embryo, which is interpreted as a foreign body in the uterus. An embryo's fight for a nurturing environment and sufficient nutrients is often to the detriment of the gestating body.

In the Afrikaans version of the text, an afterword informs the reader that the narrative is relayed from the perspective of an *ou slavin* or old slave (Stockenström [1981] 2013: loc. 1553). Reading the novella with age and comparative stages of growth in mind further intensifies the complexity of the narrator's internalized oppression. Marius Crous performs a nuanced analysis of the original text and its translation, homing in on the importance of poetic word-choices and little-known irregularities, such as the fact that *moederkind* (mother-child) is an archaic word (Crous 2013: 6). In a sense, the narrator's very vocabulary contributes to a disjointed and uneasy narrative situation; her antiquated phrasing is verbose but uncommon, implying a lack of ease with the language of the colonizer. We can easily imagine her attempts to appear educated and mature while being surrounded by men who simultaneously infantilize and sexualize her. Crucially, Crous does not discuss the prevalence of diminutives in the Afrikaans language; it is a general rule that the suffix *-ie* refers to a small entity. The proliferation of such words throughout the text, however, is somewhat missing in the English translation. For example, the word *paadjie* literally means little path, but it is simply interpreted by Coetzee as path (Stockenström [1981] 2013: loc. 26; 47; 53). Other diminutives which are lost in translation include *stroompie* or stream (loc. 26); *wyfies* or females (loc. 73); *mannetjies* or males (loc. 74); *praatjies* or little talks (loc. 160), translated as the talk, and so on. Instances where the translator does denote a sense of littleness are notably marked by double diminutives in the original text, such as the repeated phrase *klein mensies* (loc. 564; 880), interpreted as little people. Thus, while the thematic preoccupation of growth, or the inversion thereof, is not as explicit in the English version of the text, the moments where it is most apparent are when the narrator is considering the lives of other autochthonous peoples, and their comparative worth in a colonized landscape.

The narrator's many pregnancies confirm and further complicate this understanding of subjugation and objectification. Indeed, her very descriptions of her own children display a sense of indifference. She recalls: 'I could kneel in waves of contractions with my face near to the earth to which water is married, and push the fruit out of myself and give my dripping breasts to one suckling child after another. My eyes smiled. My mouth was still' (Strockenström 1983: 24). The slave is both unsmiling and unvocal. Importantly, at no time are the metaphorical fruits of her labours described in much detail: just like the narrator and her home country, they are never assigned names. We do not even learn what happens to these children once they grow older: whether they dwell at the same location, or are sold to a different owner, or even manage to escape remains a mystery. Her emotional distance from her progeny is further reinforced when she specifically recounts her very first birth, remembering that afterwards, 'from my young mouth the rotten laugh of the fruit-bearing woman sounded' (42).

This association of her voice with overripe produce evokes a sense of both decay and depravity. Having initially refrained from moving her mouth, her delayed laughter is coded with *bitterness*. As mentioned earlier, this word appears in the opening paragraph of the novella: 'With bitterness, then. But that I have forbidden myself. With ridicule, then ...' (7). With their short clauses and paratactic structure, these sentences are what Derek Attridge would characterize as typically 'Coetzean' (2004: 52); lacking a subject or object, it is difficult to decipher what exactly the protagonist is referring to. It is worth noting, however, that both the words bitter and forbidden have a rich history of association with fruit, from the book of Genesis to Abel Meeropol's poem 'Strange Fruit'. The latter protests racist lynchings in the American South, a region which is infamous for its history as a slave territory; it is also referenced in Yvonne Vera's *Butterfly Burning*, as discussed in Chapter 3. I have already elucidated how the weight of pregnancy is manifold, and the protagonist's narration confirms this: 'I carried myself', she records, 'I grew tired from the carrying' (42). She thus grows exasperated with her children for the burden they cause her to carry (their literal heaviness appearing almost parasitic), and correspondingly with herself for birthing them and conforming to a gendered script (a more esoteric weight to bear).

When her eldest child's skull appears during his birth, the narrator lets out an inarticulate 'scream back' to her 'place of birth', which she imagines to still be echoing at the time of narration (42). One reads the text with this incoherent cry for help resonating as a constant reminder of the narrator's inescapable fixation on birth origins: that is, both her personal history and the heritage of those who surround her. Once again, it is important to stress that her biographical 'beginnings' are indeterminate; here I follow Edward Said in differentiating between 'beginnings' or linear historical activities and 'origins', which he defines as more passive and 'sacred' and thus open to being manipulated for ideological purposes ([1975] 1985: 357). While it is clear that the slave is not indigenous to southern Africa, her country of birth is never named. With no indication of the narrator's true cultural or biological beginnings, both she and the reader must explore her origins instead by reworking references to creation myths. Natal alienation may fascinate the narrator, but this does not mean she merely accepts a passive role or that she is even fixated on the 'passivity' which Said identifies in the discourse surrounding origins ([1975] 1985: 6). Even after her horrifying handling by slave-owners, she describes herself as 'a lucky, privileged person, without rights but not wholly without choice' (Stockenström 1983: 57). Again, one is reminded of Patterson's observation that treating a person like property does not necessitate the absence of their legal rights. Nowhere in the text is this capacity for choice more apparent than with regard to reproductive agency: 'When I was expecting my third,' she states, 'I visited an abortionist' (44). In a sense, this simple sentence epitomizes the polar opposite of Yvonne Vera's elaborate literary style and approach to reproductive agency which I discuss in Chapter 3, as the slave's decision is condensed to a mere declarative statement. By treating abortion as a fact of life – and, unapologetically, the negation of it – the narrative normalizes the desire to possess agency over one's reproductive capacity. However, not all of the characters in Stockenström's text display such a liberal attitude. Similarly to Fumbatha in *Butterfly Burning*, one of the slave's friends is scandalized by her attempt to abort, scolding her and calling her a whore after she confesses that she paid for medical help with sex. The woman even throws away the abortifacient (violet-tree roots), meaning that it is uncertain whether the abortion is achieved or not. Together with favouritism from one of her owners, this disagreement is one of the major factors which leads to her isolation from the other slaves: when she visits the same friend later in the narrative, the woman refuses to speak to her, and then throws sand at her back as she leaves (49).

A recent study of abortion in the United States shows that more than half of reported abortions are performed on women who already have at least one child,[5] indicating that the desire to abort is not merely symptomatic of antinatalism or a callous disregard for ethics. While it is inevitable that such a statistic would not be the same in colonial southern Africa, it is important to remember that women's reasons for terminating pregnancies transcend temporal and geographical barriers. In other words, it is conceivable that a woman in the protagonist's position would visit an abortionist for a similar reason. Dorothy Roberts notes how property laws under slavery meant that women were seen as separate from the zygotes they carried from the very moment of conception. Yet this taxonomy of bodies did not apply to slave-owners or their legitimate children: 'The notion that a white mother and child were separable entities with contradictory interests was unthinkable, as was the idea of a white woman's work interfering with her maternal duties' (Roberts 1997: 39). The problem of acknowledging reproductive agency was thus compounded by the fact that women's labour was subject to interpretations which were based not so much on the quality of work as the bodily markers of the person who was performing it.

The narrator's peers in *Expedition* are not sympathetic to her use of abortifacients and other preventative measures, but she remains unperturbed and does not apologize for her actions. In fact, she becomes so accustomed to giving birth that she longs for 'grown children' and mourns the fact that she struggles to connect with prepubescent and adolescent people (Stockenström 1983: 58). It is implied that the narrator would not have been able to parent any of her children up to significant developmental milestones, and here we are invited to contemplate the distinction between abortion, adoption and other losses – a point to which I return in Chapter 4. What, for example, is the definition of a grown child? Does this phrase refer to a legal minor who has reached a certain stage of biological growth, or to the point when a young person gains full bodily, legal and social agency? To appropriate Patterson, do such fixations on legal personhood really matter when the construction of slavery through its absence is nothing but a 'fiction' (1982: 22)? Another possibility is that the narrator is referring to the fact that children become fully formed persons in a sentimental sense, as their emotions and personalities develop. In a more vulnerable moment she recalls burying a stillborn foetus behind the slaves' childbirth hut and uses this memory to prove 'that it is innate in woman to have a spontaneous approach to atrocities, is a lie' (Stockenström 1983: 105). Religious epithets such as 'God's plan' and 'Heaven's babies' are often used to comfort women who have not brought pregnancies to term (more often in cases of involuntarily terminations than abortions), and to insinuate that they should not feel upset. This, however, is another fiction which Stockenström exposes: it is clear that the protagonist would be far happier if she could eventually engage with her children as grown subjects, rather than facing the cyclical course of conception, gestation, birth and loss.

Underlying the slave's anxiety is the racialized association of growth (or its lack) with maturation (or its delay). These terms are both utilized in medical discourse when describing the growth of a foetus; further, and more troublingly, they are used in colloquial discussions of puberty, particularly in women's bodies. I isolate the female sex here because their maturity is most often and overtly visualized in a teleological progression towards child-bearing potential, from the development of secondary sexual characteristics to the swelling of a pregnant belly. In a sense, then, gestation is the underlying fascination which propagates many essentialist constructions of womanhood and/or motherhood. Repronormative markers of sexual growth are even more apparent in the discourse surrounding Black womanhood; women of colour are triply threatened by negative bodily associations because their sex, race and position in the legacy of slavery cause them to be viewed as exotic, bestial beings. Thus while the colonizer may be fascinated and aroused by a 'grown' slave's bodily curves,[6] she is simultaneously degraded and denied her own desires and agency. In fact, the instrumentalization of Black women's bodies has its own larger history in the context of slavery and reproductive rights (or the lack thereof), as elucidated in Dorothy Roberts' aforementioned study of Black women and reproductive liberty in the United States. Roberts identifies not only tropes from American history such as the hypersexual Black Jezebel and the maternal (yet powerless and desexualized) Mammy (1997: 13), but also stereotypes in the more recent cultural imaginary, such as the fact that in modern America, poor and/or 'Black mothers are portrayed less as inept or reckless reproducers in need of moral supervision, and more as calculating parasites deserving of harsh discipline' (1997: 18). The animalistic undertones of such prejudices recur as a theme throughout Roberts' study: from the practice of 'slave-breeding' to the fact that young slaves were often sold like livestock (1997: 27; 34). When critiquing the patriarchal 'slavery of reproduction' (de Beauvoir [1949] 1956: 142), therefore, it is imperative to remember the coterminous processes of racialized sexualization and infantilization which further complexify the comparative worth of child-bearing women and the infants they are forced to raise.

Roberts' evocation of parasitism above brings us back to Michel Serres' philosophy. His work is not without problematic elements, particularly its reduction of women in terms of their reproductive capacities and its suspicious treatment of the foetus: 'Is mammalian reproduction an endoparasitic cycle? What is an animal that can reproduce only by another animal, inside it? What is a little animal that grows and feeds inside another? It seems to me that it is a parasite, the one who finds a milieu of reproduction and development in another animal, though this other be the same' (Serres [1980] 2007: 216). If the 'other' truly is the 'same', then why is the male human excluded from these rhetorical questions? Why does the second question seem to encapsulate misogynistic insecurities about the female body's role in conception and its overall primacy in gestation? Nevertheless, it is intriguing that Serres argues that fables help hosts and parasites to metamorphose ([1980] 2007: 216) – in a chapter notably titled 'The Proper Name of the Host/Masters and Slaves'. Consider my earlier discussion of how Stockenström both queers and queries the animal fable. Although the slave is frank about how she views men to be perpetually parasitic in their treatment of women, her narration is once again complicated by a sense of complicity when she equates agency with power instead of desire.

White male slave-owners are consistently rendered as immature throughout the narrative, whether this is because of their reliance on women as caregivers or their 'childish dreams' of dominating hitherto untouched landscapes (Stockenström 1983: 60). Even the narrator's favourite owner is problematized for this reason, as illustrated by her memories of their intimate encounters. When he mysteriously falls ill, she recounts,

> I let the invalid nestle between my drawn-up knees with his head on my breast. In his language I whispered lewd stories which made him smile blissfully in my arms. Shrunken baby, what an easy delivery for me. I fed you with the deathsmilk of indifference, for it could do your dried-out body no more harm and perhaps it was your way out, this being set free of any charitableness.
>
> (20)

It is no coincidence that she pulls the man's head onto her breast, an organ which is simultaneously representative of sexual objectification and maternal functionality. Her positionality as his favourite slave means that she has catered for his every need, whether domestic or sensual in nature. And yet, despite their physical proximity and shared history, the narrator feels neither platonic nor romantic warmth for him. Instead, we are told that she approaches him with a great indifference, which is so potent that it is rendered into a metaphorical milk that she imagines inducing his death. If we entertain her infantilization of the slave-owner, then in a perverse sense, this too is a termination: we are encouraged to imagine the induction of death as the ultimate act of charity. Charitableness and charity are firmly situated in the humanist tradition, appearing in both secular and religious (Old or New Testament) rationalizations for beneficence as a key factor for the utilitarian betterment of society. I return to these words in the next section of this chapter, by considering Coetzee's subversion of similar Christian concepts such as mercy, sacrifice and (dis)grace. The above quotation contains a remarkable reworking of a word that is the root origin of many religious origin myths and of some anti-abortion campaigns. Here abortion is not the negation of new life (or the absence of social conscience, as argued by some conservative religious groups), but rather the creation of a new chapter.

The men whom the protagonist knows less intimately are described as looking 'so funny, like disappointed children, when they lose control of something but dare not openly acknowledge it' (79). This prompts not merely a condescending attitude, but also problematic and manipulative behaviour on her behalf. She openly declares that she holds a 'peculiar position as a parasite' on the expedition and attempts to use her sexual attractiveness to her advantage by blossoming 'for them to admire my orchid-like nature for its colourfulness' (79). On a superficial level, this association is evocative, but not particularly apt: as epiphytes, many orchids attach themselves to trees but do not require assistance from these organisms to survive. If one pauses, however, and remembers Patterson's assertion that parasitism is a complex web wherein both dominated and dominator may act dependently,[7] then the metaphor seems far more appropriate. Although the woman is 'utterly dependent like a parasite' (79), the very men that she relies on are also dependent on *her*, whether this is for practical assistance, sexual gratification or merely emotional fulfilment. Such a symbiotic relationship is further conveyed by another memory of her favourite master. She reminisces:

> When I put my arms around him it was like protecting a child. Crazy, when he was the possessor, but it was so. He propped his head against my shoulder like, and with the innocence of, a child. And in the wink of an eye he changed [...] and when we had intercourse he was both father and son and I both mother and trustful daughter.
>
> (52)

In this passage the male slave-owner – who was typified earlier as a helpless child – is simultaneously powerless and commanding. The heterosexual dynamic between the two characters is queered in a power-switching process of paraphilic infantilism, as he allows the young slave to assert her dominance and then subverts her power just moments later. Considering their intricate relationship, which is only revealed after his death, one may revisit the earlier scene and wonder: has the narrator truly offered him nothing but indifference? And can the same be said for him? The exploitative dynamic of slavery is undeniable, but in this passage, sex becomes an agentive exchange and an imaginative space for the protagonist to explore all elements of her natal alienation. In the other avenues of her life, she has been forced to act as a responsible adult, and as a literal or metaphorical mother. Here, however, she experiments with youthful desire and agency which relies on the very *negation* thereof.

It is apparent that *Expedition* and *Butterfly Burning* utilize vegetal, natural materials to approach fertility and its negation, and to experiment with narrative form and time, as I shall elucidate in further detail in my third chapter on Vera. Yet in Stockenström's novella, it is the possibility and metaphorical import of abortion which is addressed with frankness, rather than the actual procedure itself. Like the wordless scream that permeates the entire narrative, terminated pregnancies are evoked in order to highlight the narrator's ruminations on gestation and childishness: her literal children, her infantile owners, but also her own weaknesses. The following section takes as a point of departure the translation's ambivalent treatment of gendered oppression, and goes on to consider how narrative time and negation form the novella's particular ethical take on new materialist concerns.

Translating negation

In the previous sections of this chapter, I stressed how beastly riddles and images of gestation are utilized in *Expedition* to complexify the uneasy positioning of Black women in colonial contexts, particularly the broad area of southern Africa. Yet it is worth repeating that the text is often read in an oversimplified manner, especially when critics linger on the fact that it was translated into English by the 'father' of contemporary white writing in South Africa (aside from his extensive oeuvre of creative work, J. M. Coetzee's *White Writing: On the Culture of Letters in South Africa* (1990) makes him a literal authority on the topic). Coetzee's own fiction features the de/construction of Christian concepts such as charity, hospitality and (dis)grace, which has led many to view his characters and novels as nothing more than allegorical commentary on 'the heart of the country' of South Africa (Stockenström 1983: 20). The very appearance of this phrase in Stockenström's text – which was published after Coetzee's *In the Heart of the Country* (1977) – shows that those who see similarities between the two writers' political concerns are correct. I take issue, however, with reductive readings that are reliant on the assumption that Stockenström utilizes similar thematic preoccupations to Coetzee for the same ethical or allegorical ends. Coetzee's mixing of New and Old Testament vocabularies interrogates the ethics of care in post/colonial southern Africa, particularly through the symbiotic intermeshing of seeming antonyms such as mercy and sacrifice, forgiveness and punishment. Most readings of *Expedition* are heavily invested in deciphering what Coetzee's translation means, at the expense of analysing what it shares with the original novella: that is, narrative form, time and length. The result is that the female author-figure recedes to the background, as those who respond to the text engage in a seemingly endless conversation about the role of zoologically and biologically specific terms in Coetzee's allegories (Crous 2013: 2; Saint 2017: 11), the literary implications of political analogies, and generalizations about white positionality in apartheid South Africa. I believe the only truly productive solution to such a conundrum is to move beyond clichéd associations of the white writer with allegory and language games. This is not to neglect the importance of Coetzee's status as translator, but rather to focus on the ethical implications of Stockenström's chosen narrator and narrative form.

On one level, the colonial setting comes to serve as a metaphor; the 'virgin territories' that the narrator enters with her owner, his son and their slaves are representative of the woman's body in colonial and postcolonial contexts. The land is dominated by men and defined by the ways that they exploit it. As the narrator observes this process of degradation, she sees that she has come to be infected by similar greed and self-preservation: 'I knew the fear of bloodthirstiness and of isolation and of ignorance and of punishment and of bewilderment. I knew him' (Stockenström 1983: 55). By personifying these violent states as male, she implies that aggression and masculinity are inextricably linked; yet, the fact that she, as a woman, 'knows' such feelings means that this observation is not meant to be interpreted as an essentialist typification of the gender binary. Indeed, as she goes on to imagine time as a figure who 'squats continually before my tree' (66), she continues to subvert and complicate gendered archetypes. Crouching not only lowers one's position, but is also an act that is associated with primal acts like defecation or childbirth: squatting during labour is very common in rural southern Africa. In this case, then, she queers the image of a sexless and disembodied Father Time, imagining him as passive, fleshly and feminized. Queer time – in the sense of both identity formation that defies gendered scripts, and creativity that exceeds linear chronologies – is integral to all the readings in this book, but particularly my analysis of Bessie Head's fiction in Chapter 4.

Later the narrator observes that the names for everything created by Western society all pertain to power relations, such as forced labour and slavery (100). In contrast to the inventors of these names, the slave and her associated water spirit are 'not listened to' (100). Some may take the juxtaposition between these violent images and the passive nymph to suggest that women are inherently gentler than men, or more aligned with supposedly sanctified nature; literary critics are quick to associate Stockenström with ecofeminism or second-wave feminism. Michael du Plessis, for example, reads *Expedition* through the lens of French feminist theory, arguing that the text ultimately privileges 'flows of the female body/language' (1988: 125). I have already demonstrated, however, that such simplistically pro-female readings are unproductive. They are founded on ironically limited understandings of female embodiment, and they detract from the complex gender and power dynamics which are tested throughout the novella. I maintain that to reduce the text's agenda into a neatly gender-oriented message is to not listen to the very voice from which Coetzee's translation originates. As Greta Gaard suggests, if one is to be critical of ecofeminist analogies, then one must attentively listen to a range of voices, regardless of their class, gender, race, sex or species identities.

Essentializing *Expedition* as nothing more than a feminist fable means losing sight of one of its most important thematic and formal elements: temporality. This is a point Derek Attridge raises when writing against allegorical inter-pretations of Coetzee, as he argues, 'To allegorize is to translate the temporal

and the sequential into the schematic: a set of truths, a familiar historical scene'
(Attridge 2004: 46). It may seem ironic that I am utilizing Coetzean criticism
in order to argue against centralizing Coetzee; yet, Attridge's study is a ground-
breaking intervention in the general field of South African literary studies,
because it is aware of the paradoxical landscapes of political metaphor in,
and literal elements of, a text. Furthermore, there are other understandings of
allegory; Paul de Man, for example, performs Benjaminian readings in *Allegories
of Reading: Figural Language in Rosseau, Nietzsche, Rilke, and Proust*, arguing
that 'genuinely dialectical minds' understand the allegorical to encompass
indeterminacy and untranslatability (1979: 81). Moving away from the overly
trodden territory of Coetzee's writing, and focusing instead on the novella he has
translated, it becomes clear how uncertainty emerges as a possible outcome of
allegorical storytelling. Tellingly, Stockenström's text manifests the *unfamiliar* in
multiple guises. From a lack of proper nouns in the narrative to the protagonist's
literal separation from her family (resulting in a loss of personal history), the
author is less interested in the generations and legacies exemplified in the typical
plaasroman than in writing against the association of progeny with identity, or
perpetuation with inheritance. The most sequential passages of the text narrate
how the woman spends her time as a slave, whether this is learning how to please
her owners or raising their children. Yet these relationships do not contribute
to her sense of identity; rather, they are constant reminders of 'the nuisance of
a body and the time-consuming needs thereof' (Stockenström 1983: 98). That
is, the most familiar moments in her life are merely representative of the never-
ending labour – whether this is physical or emotional – which Black women are
forced to perform. To some extent, then, abortion does not simply constitute the
decision not to prolong a life, but rather the desire not to perpetuate a system of
inheritance that does not care for the work of female progenitors.

Complex shifts in tense are particularly interesting elements of temporality
which merit further investigation. The original Afrikaans text is based largely
in the present tense, whereas the English version is more duplicitous about the
narrator's chronological positioning. For instance, the Afrikaans *is* (is) recurs
in the original text (Stockenström [1981] 2013: loc. 250; 252), whereas the
translation relays these sections in the past tense. Some of the most obvious
sections which have been adapted are passages where the narrator discusses – or
rather remembers – children borne by her and other slaves, such as when the
words 'Ons kindertjies is' (loc. 474) are translated as 'Our children were' (39).
The progression of chronology is further disrupted when *Ek praat* (I talk) is
translated in the past tense (loc. 1294). In this instance, the distancing of the

word 'spoke' foregrounds the oxymoronic positioning of the supposedly illiterate slave's voice (94): we are reminded that this is a written text, and that the author's positionality is vastly different to that of the narrator's. Still, Stockenström remains dedicated to the narrative present, and the word *nou* (now) is dutifully translated even when Coetzee chooses to adapt her ruminations into the past tense (37), creating an ambiguous sense of narrative positioning. In some respects, Coetzee's interpretation adds a further layer of nuance – he uses m-dashes to disrupt lengthy clauses and differentiate between temporal points in the narrative. Yet the sense of immediacy and urgency in the original text points away from schematic understandings of time and, more broadly, history.

As her isolation grows, the narrator chooses to abandon not only man-made language but also chronological conventions (92). Gesturing to the arbitrariness of units of time, the narrator implies that it is irrational to attempt to exert control over natural processes such as ageing and the inevitable, immeasurable progression of history. Language, particularly names, and time are both constructs that are used by humans to make sense of the world around them, but the narrator avoids naming the people and places she encounters, resisting nationalist logic and eventually reverting to making beastly noises. Here noise performs again as a marker of difference while simultaneously signifying a common origin between the supposed parasite and host. The protagonist also loses track of time. Instead of using the Khoisan people's handmade black and green beads to mark her days, she turns to 'the grey dream' of a world that does not rely on binaries to construct meaning (92). She inhabits the limbo of a baobab tree where she is removed from both colonial society and the Khoisan community that provides her with food. The liminal space of the tree is the discursive site where the narrator simultaneously addresses her past and present. It is also where she commemorates the lives of the Khoisan people who are murdered towards the end of the narrative: 'if death is life', she reasons, 'then they still live. Here. Right here' (98). The tree – and, by extension, the text – accommodates an interspecies sense of gestation, as the narrator negates teleological understandings of time's progression and death's finality. With its upside-down trunk, the baobab is the antithesis of a typical tree's shape. It is no coincidence, then, that the narrator gradually addresses the tree and identifies with it (30); it is the physical manifestation of her desire to subvert stereotypes and expectations, such as the chronological linkage of gestation to birth. The baobab is simultaneously the narrator's destination and her undoing, as it is both the discursive site and the thematic summation of the narrative. The novella thus self-reflexively challenges traditional narrative forms which privilege 'anthropo-theological' storytelling as described by Derrida (2009: 14). Further, it reverses the processes and associations of gestation: the narrator is preparing for death, a new type of potentiality or becoming.

Discussions of aesthetics and materiality on the expedition further reinforce this self-reflexivity. Remarking upon the bizarre ecologies depicted in some rock paintings the group encounters, the narrator says that they appear to be artworks (Stockenström 1983: 85). The stranger dismisses them as nothing more than 'The work of adult children' (87): 'Who in the name of the creator of all things', he asks, 'would have come here to immortalise himself, and in so unfinished a way?' (87). But with the knowledge that this man is himself no more than a grown child, we are encouraged to entertain the narrator's interpretations of art, rather than the stranger's trivialization of non-mimetic and abortive creativity. The very fact that such a painting could have been created by a woman seems impossible for him to fathom. Yet within the paintings are three figures: a female person, a snake and an ancient elephant. Both a woman and a serpent feature in the creation myth of the Abrahamic traditions. Here, however, we find a triumvirate of beasts. As Jonathan Saha notes in his overview of the role of elephants in imperial contexts, British colonizers relied upon indigenous knowledge to utilize the animals as instruments (military or commercial), ornaments or both (2020: 56–7). African elephants, in particular, represent the origins of several intersecting and ongoing challenges to environmentalist discourse. There are two species – the bush/savannah elephant and the forest elephant – that transform the landscape in different ways, each competing for resources as human societies continue to expand and construct houses, roads and fences across their territories. Saha observes that, in the historical context of racial and class privileges that tended to classify white people as hunters and Black people as illegal poachers, 'The history of African elephants' interactions with humans has involved conflict – in many ways exacerbated by empire – but also coexistence and cohabitation, although finding an equilibrium among the needs of the three species remains an ongoing problem' (2020: 59). Given Saha's meditations on the relationship between these particular (human and nonhuman) species, it is telling that Stockenström chooses to pair two traditionally Biblical figures with the image of an elephant, a figure which appears and reappears throughout her fictional slave narrative. The tri-species assemblage in *Expedition* gestures beyond typically anthropocentric explanations of humankind's origins (and other species' beginnings).

Together with the beads which the Khoisan villagers leave for the narrator, the rock painting is a materialist form of 'Humanware' (96); conveying a narrative without written words, such artistic objects represent humanity's inseparability from nonhuman environments, or nonverbal means of understanding the world. It is possible that, through its engagement with Khoisan artefacts, Stockenström's novella may be experimenting with this autochthonous group's myths and folklore explaining time (including the life-death continuum). However, I am reticent to draw any hasty comparisons for several reasons. One issue is that the protagonist mostly views the Khoisan people from a literal distance and they are never centralized as speaking characters. Another concern that is argued astutely by Michael Wessels in an article on /Xam stories is that such oral narratives 'cannot be treated as timeless examples of mythology or traditional folklore. This not only because narrative participates in the multivocality of discourse but also because there is no point outside history from which a /Xam narrative could be viewed as a stable artefact' (2013: 2). Together with the plethora of languages and ethnicities constituting Khoisan identity, this means it is virtually impossible to identify any typical characteristics of traditional origin myths. Another artistic element that the slave encounters towards the end of the narrative is a collection of golden nails that she addresses as 'you' while she waits to die (111). Moments later she imagines that she will be commemorated as 'a mistress and mother and a goddess. Enough to make you laugh' (111). The second-person pronoun acts here as a marker of material equivalence: the narrator addresses inanimate objects and the reader as similarly reactive elements of the text. The act of interpellation is clearly foregrounded as the protagonist confronts mortality, pointing to her preoccupation with upending human hubris. Listening is, once again, analogized by the works of art that she both listens to and addresses in this moment of tactility and audibility.

Literary scenes like this appear to resonate with both materialism (in this case, Serres's philosophy, which I have already problematized) and postcolonial theory (particularly, Patterson's conceptualization of parasitism as a continuum). Yet reading fiction with an ethics of attentive listening calls for considering more than two perspectives. It would be too easy to claim that Stockenström's fiction is both new materialist and hyperaware of postcolonial politics. The implication of this move is that one camp – the one that was established first, whichever that may be, or that which is more new and ostensibly updated – is the host and the other remains a subsidiary, a parasite. What if, instead, we were to read such scenes with an openness to noise, attuned to beastly similarities but also mindful of human differences? For even the slave is far from immune from the logic of colonization and domination. She admits that she has been educated to value division, counting and classification upon her journey (92). The very expedition she undertakes to the southern tip of Africa is thus symptomatic of 'anthropo-theological' discourse. Particularly, the teleological progression from familiar lands to exotic spaces is a common trope which she occasionally endorses in her quest for a safe, untouched space. Yet when she eventually breaks free from her owners and shelters in the baobab tree, she is confronted with her own ethical shortcomings: 'I soon had to conclude that my way of thinking did not slot in with that of other beings here. And I searched and opened a way and found. Found, I say. Terrifying' (10). What is frightening is not a new, more-than-humanist way of understanding the world, but rather the fact that she believed that found terrain could somehow save her from repressed trauma – the very same logic used by both colonialists and liberationists in order to justify repronormative demands placed upon Black women. This realization of the pervasiveness of asymmetrical analogies (particularly those which associate landscape with womanhood) causes her to search for a more materialist understanding of relationality. And indeed, it is when narrating her life in retrospect that she advises any 'remedies against being empty' should mix 'a judicious application of old and newly acquired knowledge' (13). In other words, she does not profess to abandon all her preconceptions and prejudices, as I have shown by critiquing her attitude towards autochthonous peoples in the veld. Rather, she takes her former ignorance as an opportunity to explore identity formation through material encounters, a narrative process which I discuss in further detail in the following chapter on Wicomb.

The formation of the narrator's reproductive agency is strengthened by multiple interactions with the natural environment. As she recovers from the ordeal of the expedition, she notes,

> Every time I step out from the protecting interior of the tree I am once again a human being and powerful, and I gaze far out over the landscape with all its flourishes of vegetal growth and troops of animals and the purple patches of hills that try to hedge it in on the horizon. Reborn every time from the belly of a baobab, I stand full of myself. The sun defines my shadow. The wind clothes me.
>
> (14)

To be full of oneself is a colloquial expression for egotism, a characteristic which is found in much nature-writing that hubristically presents the landscape as an entity to be empirically measured and observed. Here, however, the common interpretation of these words is disrupted by the trope of regeneration; in continually returning to and emerging from the baobab tree, the narrator interacts with the very same vegetation that she observes. Crucially, she only describes herself as being human when *outside* the baobab. This both foreshadows and complicates her decision to drink poison inside the belly of the tree, a most ecological metaphor for abortion. If the precondition of personhood is being (re) born, Stockenström's text suggests, then a termination of pregnancy cannot be conceived as murder. Schiebinger notes that the terms miscarriage and abortion were used interchangeably in Europe to refer to any loss of an embryo until the eighteenth century, when cases of miscarriage in animals began to inform much discussion of accidental or intentional terminations; the words took on their current legal connotations in the nineteenth century (2004: 114–15). Here we are confronted by different forms of death – killing and murder, miscarriage and abortion – and how society often uses animalistic imagery, with racially and sexually charged undertones rooted in histories of slavery, to differentiate between them.

In order to escape supposedly rational scientific discourse, and its reliance on gendered and racialized dichotomies, the narrator chooses instead to sleep and finally to commit suicide by drinking poison. That her sleep is described as greyness is highly relevant. Grey is a combination of black and white, or a liminal shade between two ends of a continuum; it is also used to refer to ethical conundrums as suggested by the phrase 'morally grey'. Her slumber thus illustrates how she desires to embrace the indeterminacy which permeates her riddles and narrative style. By removing herself from society, language, time and finally from her own narration, she seeks 'an ecstasy of never being', 'equilibrium' and 'the perfection of non-being' (105). The slave believes that it is better to never be exposed to the inequalities of society – much like an aborted foetus – rather than to be born as a human with no sense of agency. During her journey, she observes a hammerhead shark that 'chose the total nothing of seeing nothing more' by dying on a shore (35). The hammerhead is stuck between two ends of a continuum: birth and death. Significantly, most hammerhead sharks are either grey or brown in colour. We are told that 'in uncertainty the poor thing struggled' (35); and 'like a baby laid on its stomach, curling its spine as it tries to curl upright, so the hammerhead shark had struggled' (36). Her commemorative act of burying the animal in a small grave foregrounds its almost foetal vulnerability. Similarly ending her own life at the end of the novella, the slave aligns herself with the literal 'water-spirit' of the dead shark (111). Yet it would be overly simplistic to suggest her suicide is merely a choice to reject superior humanity and connect with some beastly underlying origins. The fluid symbolism of greyness – and, indeed, of queer gender fluidity – suggests a more layered understanding of gestation and terminations.

Greyness is, in fact, the most prominent tone in Stockenström's metaphorical palette. The shade appears in a prophecy of 'huge grey breakwaters' that signal 'extermination over and again' (89); it is used to describe both a landscape of 'Grey cloud. Stones. Lichen. Wet and grey' and 'Grey phantoms' who 'must surely have lived there looking for their slave bodies' (70). This latter quotation is followed by the protagonist's anxious attempts to 'limit myself to within myself and resolve against dissolution into the attracting all-swathing grey' (70). Yet we know this will result only in failure. That is, even when the narrator tries to isolate herself, her positioning in the baobab means that she is merely one embodiment of agency in a larger environmental system. She has been taught to keep herself to herself, but in the words of Karen Barad, she is both part of and parting from that which exceeds her physical body. This is further reinforced when she commemorates the deaths of childless women, or 'women convicted of witchcraft and shunned because they could not prove they had not let loose the mysterious deaths among the cattle and caused the bad harvests' (92); she imagines sleep as a 'smaller death', a grey composite of 'good and evil, the inseparable pair, the twins who defy death' (92). Greyness appears throughout the novella, and particularly in this passage, as a marker of ambiguity and dissolution. Here I am referring, again, to Neimanis's Deleuzian 'amniotics', which aims to dissolve the gender dichotomy by showing how 'gestationality extends beyond the human reprosexual womb' (2017: 49). Like the witches and spinsters before her, the slave has been found wanting: by society's standards, and even the values of her friends, she is evil for desiring not to behave as a normal mother should. Yet here, and indeed throughout the novella, she *questions* such repronormative ideology by analogizing her fate with that of an indeterminate beast, the twinning of life and death (whose species, importantly, is never disclosed). I discuss the links between sterility, queer theory and ecocriticism further in my final chapter on Bessie Head; in the interim, it is worth noting how Stockenström's narrator refuses to repent for exercising reproductive agency.

Her act of refusal is further reinforced by repeated instances of negative phrasing. This is something that is admittedly more apparent in the Afrikaans version of the text, as the language normalizes the use of double-negatives like *niks nie* (nothing) and *niks meer nie* (nothing more) (loc. 460; loc. 1533). Nevertheless, the translated text still retains a sense of denial, particularly when the narrator considers her species identity. When she first discovers she is truly alone in the wilderness, she verbalizes her unease as follows:

> I opened my mouth and brought out a sound that must be the sound of a human being because I am a human being and not a wildebeest that snorts and not a horned locust that produces whistling noises with its wings and not an

ostrich that booms, but a human being that talks, and I brought out a sound and produced an accusation and hurled it up at the twilight air. A bloody sound was exposed to the air.

(65)

Birthing a violent shout, here the narrator is defined markedly by what she is not. In fact, if the word bloody were to be excluded from the above passage, it would be virtually impossible to determine the exact nature of the sound she emits, since more precise words are used to describe the vocalizations of other animals. The human form is displaced and decentralized by beastly noise.

Considering these repeated ruminations on both refusal and negation, one may be confused when reaching the final page of the novella. As the narrator drinks her poison, she urges, 'Quickly, water-spirit. Let your envoy carry out his task swiftly. Yes' (111). At first glance, this conclusion takes exactly the opposite approach to what I have just described. Not only is Stockenström's narrator enthusiastic about her approaching death, but she is also choosing dissolution through water (rather than self-immolation with flames, as discussed in my chapter on Yvonne Vera). Yet all is revealed if one returns to the original text: the concluding pages of the novella are the most glaringly different passages in translation. In fact, Coetzee inserts the word Yes; *Ja* does not appear in the Afrikaans version, providing a contrast to the negation which precedes this scene, both thematically and linguistically.[8] This is not even a case of stylistics: elsewhere in the same section he pares down Stockenström's prose by deleting the word *in* (in) and translating *'n vrug* (a fruit) as merely fruit (111). Yet I would argue that this final paradox does not detract from Stockenström's project; rather, it adds to the sense of indeterminacy that permeates both versions of the text. *Expedition* utilizes the very text itself as a gender-defying phenomenon, a fact which is further reinforced by Coetzee's role as the male interpreter, and in some regards co-creator, of an intersectional text. In new materialist conceptualizations of gestation, both parents play an important role in the formation of a life, but the person who gives birth holds more agentive clout because their body is the site and origin of the event. However, this interpretive translation holds far less reverence for myths of origins. We must therefore listen to the text with an attentive ethics and with openness to queer potentialities.[9] These potentialities include the possibility of gestation without birth, or of alternative futures and identities that are not weighed down by normative systems of inheritance and progeny. This is why I have focused on both the Afrikaans and English versions of the text, especially since both Stockenström and Coetzee make certain (at times, conflicting) stylistic choices.

A human being and powerful

By now it should be clear that the puzzling 'rattle and rattle' that resonates through Stockenström's novella is evocative of multiple formations (9). By formations I am referring not only to the bodies of elephants that wander through the text (107), foregrounding the empire's fascination with both race and species – and to more, too, than the 'bestial death-rattle' of the baobab (105). I am naming these elements, and the figure of the human who holds the narrative's centre, but also the process of nomenclature itself. For as the slave writes, even when she has the names, 'I am not listened to. There is nothing I can do with the names. They are nothing but rattles' (100). Yet again, Stockenström anticipates the importance which materialist feminists such as Greta Gaard place upon listening to situational nuances, as the very literal audibility and recitation in the above quotation suggests. Words become playthings to the writer; yet, her very experimentation with narrative forms is indicative of a fascination with creativity, desire and agency. In lingering on stillbirths, abortions and deaths, the novella is undoubtedly concerned with human injustices: a fact which is true for all the texts in this study, but is most manifest in Head's oeuvre (as I discuss further in Chapter 4). Yet Stockenström's novella is distinct in that the protagonist's reversion to unconventional and beastly narrative techniques emphasizes the impossibility of creating feminist accounts which are truly independent of gendered expectations – at least, not without foregoing humanist norms and forms.

Feminist texts typically promote gender equality by advocating for anthropocentrism in favour of androcentrism.[10] This has already been illustrated by the protagonist's rejection of patriarchal discourse in favour of feminist narrative modes. However, *Expedition* seems to suggest that to merely concentrate on human life is irresponsible, as nature and animals remain inferior in comparison. The narrator decides to ignore humanist ideals like reason and drinks the poison that will end her life. In this defiant act, she reconciles herself with her generative potential and the animality which is coded into the female form by patriarchal and repronormative discourse. Instead of attempting to write, and thus redefine herself through traditionally male creative forms, she embraces the silence that has so often been ascribed to women. As the narrative process ends, she abandons the male-dominated art of storytelling and is compared to both a bird and a bat (111). Her association with the bat is of particular relevance; these wild animals pollinate baobab trees. In being unified with a pollinator while ending her story, then, the protagonist is both provider and recipient, both parasite and host. Choosing to resist the urge to assert either her national or species identity, her death inside the tree is a voluntary and paradoxically constructive affirmation of humanity's position in nature. At the same time, it is also a materialist reflection of the termination(s) that she had chosen to undergo earlier in the narrative. By dying in the baobab-belly, she disrupts the external/internal dialectic of mother and foetus, while also very literally showing how this simplistic binary is naturalized by much discourse surrounding abortion.

The conclusion of the novella suggests that it is futile to attempt to exert mastery over nature or to assume that one is more powerful than other forms of life. *The Expedition to the Baobab Tree* contemplates the limits of uprooting discrimination through an anti-anthropocentric materialism by deconstructing binaries and challenging traditional notions of power. The slave's voluntary death is a powerful ending to the non-linear narrative; it suggests that agency can be used to symbolically protest against sexist, racist and repronormative displays of political control. The text certainly does not omit some problematic elements, particularly when read with the positionality of the author in mind. It is worth pausing to consider, however, to what extent the discomfort the text generates is because it is reflective of an unjust society which misunderstands the conditions necessary for reproductive agency. This is a matter of collective agency rather than individual choice, as many pro-choice campaigns would misleadingly suggest. It also involves more than a dichotomy between life or death within the human, however that beast is defined, and life or death outside. What carries its life in its stomach? Both Black women and white men, the text answers. Either a tree or an animal. An adult slave and a child. All of these beings, or none at all. These are not contradictions.

Notes

1 Coetzee has translated two texts from Dutch (the formative 'parent language' of Afrikaans): *A Posthumous Confession* ([1894] 2011) by Marcellus Emants and an edited collection titled *Landscape with Rowers: Poetry from the Netherlands* ([2004] 2016).

2 For an extensive discussion of the implications of the fig as autopoietic symbol, see Chapter 2.

3 Here I am referring to poststructuralist philosopher Gilles Deleuze's interest in open systems of ontological 'becoming'. For further discussion of this concept, as well as Deleuze's collaborations with Félix Guattari, see Chapter 2.

4   For a posthumanist analysis of the 'economies of death' involved with edibility and killability/grievability, see Patricia J. Lopez and Kathryn A. Gillespie (2015).

5   The figure for this particular study from 2008 was 61 per cent (Jones, Finer and Singh 2010: 1).

6   There are countless recorded instances of sexually charged experimentation upon Black women's bodies, but two pertinent examples would be the display and dissection of Sara Baartman's genitals and the cultivation of cells from a cancerous growth in Henrietta Lacks's womb. For more on Baartman, see Sadiah Qureshi (2004); a popular account of Lacks's case and legacy is Rebecca Skloot's *The Immortal Life of Henrietta Lacks* (2010).

7   For an extensive discussion of analogies of parasitism in abortion narratives, and an analysis of Deleuze and Guattari's wasp–orchid rhizome as a synonymous figuration in materialist theory, see Chapter 2.

8   Here Coetzee may be referencing Molly Bloom's famous final word in James Joyce's *Ulysses* ([1920] 1987), a textual moment of affirmation which is also highly sexualized. As I discuss at length in later chapters (particularly on Wicomb and Head), it is not unusual for southern African writers to operate in the wake of literary Modernism, particularly referencing moments of corporeal disruptions and excesses in such narratives.

9   Although I am not referring to utopian visions so much as a multiplicity of futures, an illuminating collection of essays edited by Angela Jones titled *A Critical Inquiry into Queer Utopias* (2013) provides further insight into such potentialities.

10 For a comprehensive and ecofeminist overview of this phenomenon, see Val Plumwood (1996).

2

Plants

Uprooting desire and deviance in Zoë Wicomb's
You Can't Get Lost in Cape Town

I was young then and able to banish things, but seeds do grow.
— Tsitsi Dangarembga, *Nervous Conditions* (1988: 203)

The second writer in this study to have been raised in – and the first to emigrate from – South Africa, Zoë Wicomb is one of the most significant literary voices from that country. I use the term emigrate here since Wicomb and Bessie Head left South Africa under significantly distinct conditions, a fact I discuss when distinguishing between the diasporic, the expatriate and the exilic in my introduction. Wicomb was born in 1948 (the same year that apartheid officially started) in the rural Western Cape and moved to the UK in 1970. Writing mostly from Scotland, and drawing on autobiographical anecdotes as a self-identifying coloured woman, she has since published multiple works of fiction and academic pieces on the state of post/apartheid South Africa. In South Africa, the term 'coloured' is used to refer to people of mixed ethnic descent – particularly those whose ancestors were South and Southeast Asian slaves. Even in the post-transitional democracy, such groups mostly embrace this term, viewing it as a source of 'mythologised' pride (Wicomb 1998: 363). As suggested by the titles of papers in a programme for a 2010 conference entitled 'The Cape and the Cosmopolitan: Reading Zoë Wicomb', many literary critics tend to foreground notions of race, miscegenation and genetic roots as indicators of oppression in Wicomb's work. A notable example is Abdulrazak Gurnah, who writes on travel, 'the value of rootedness' and cosmopolitanism (2011: 261), ultimately arguing that 'Wicomb's figures are not "heroic" enough' to achieve self-liberation and self-knowledge fully, and 'none are by any means liberated' (2011: 275). While acknowledging the importance of earlier analyses, this chapter, in contrast, considers racial injustice alongside multiple vectors of prejudice: those based on one's gender, sex, class and other signifiers. Analysing *You Can't Get Lost in Cape Town* (1987), I explore how Wicomb utilizes desire, disgust and deviance through incidents involving the pubescent or pregnant female body. Deviance is typically defined as the shameful departure from socially normalized behaviours (including, particularly, sexual practices), but Wicomb's novel exceeds such associations by representing the seeds of supposedly obscene desires. These concepts represent the intersecting obstructions to reproductive agency which women of colour face in southern Africa. The inextricable link between racial and gender equality means that one cannot speak of race as a social construct without discussing problematic repronormative values.

First published in 1987, Wicomb's literary debut contains ten vignettes that chronologically catalogue the childhood, adolescence and early adulthood of a young woman of colour named Frieda Shenton who seeks an abortion in the city of Cape Town after entering a relationship with a white man. There have been many conflicting characterizations of the text's material nature, as Andrew van der Vlies' collation of critical responses in a scholarly article shows (2012: 22). His article is unique in that it discusses the material history of the publication in its multiple forms; due to the historical parameters of my study, I am only discussing the original (1987) version. Although the text features chronologically ordered incidents, its elements are rarely discussed as a composite literary system. Rob Gaylard writes in an article focusing on racial identity in the titular section that 'while the stories collectively constitute a *kind of bildungsroman*, they remain *fragments* of a whole' (1996: 178; emphasis added); his comments echo verbatim an early review of the text by Barend Torien, who alludes to Wicomb's debut as 'episodes of a novel, *a kind of Bildungsroman* and a carefully structured one at that' (1988: 43; emphasis added). Despite the shared allusion to the novel form in these responses, the text continues to be described – and taught – as a group of short stories. This seems particularly strange when one considers an early feminist response to the text by Sue Marais, in an excellent article titled 'Getting Lost in Cape Town: Spatial and Temporal Dislocation in the South African Short Story Cycle'. Marais argues that while the text is a 'short fiction cycle' (1995: 31), its experimentation with irony and metafiction means that it is more novel than short story collection (1995: 33). Her analysis features varied references to the abortion scene (which occurs in the eponymous section, 'You Can't Get Lost in Cape Town', but is also referenced in later sections of the text). By way of contrast, Gaylard only refers to abortion in one elliptical instance, when describing the figure of the abortionist. It is disappointing that Torien and Gaylard briefly entertain the notion that Wicomb engages with a predominantly masculinist, long-form genre (the Bildungsroman),[1] before ultimately classifying her debut as a story collection. Such *fragmentary* responses – deciding that abortion is a topic of impropriety, or only briefly drawing parallels to the novel form – trivialize the text's ethical impetus and its experimental form. Viewing it as collection of short stories, critics assimilate it to a pre-established normative form rather than allowing it to be something ungainly.

Recent scholarship, however, has destabilized such reactions by foregrounding the feminist significance of *You Can't Get Lost in Cape Town*'s structure. An article by Kharys Laue is refreshing for its focus on gendered oppression in one segment from Wicomb's earliest text alongside two of her later stories (Laue 2017: 19); more readings would do well to focus on all the sections of Wicomb's debut, as gender performativity is one of the central concerns of her oeuvre. Andrew van der Vlies' aforementioned analysis is significant in that it is interested in the *material* history of the text, and in sustaining its narrative indeterminacy by referring to segments as 'chapter-stories' (2012: 21). Van der Vlies' use of such language endorses Marais' reading of novelistic elements in Wicomb's metafictional work. I take Marais' reading as a formative influence on my study, and Laue's approach as an encouraging step in discussing miscegenation as one constitutive element of broader intersectional and political concerns; my analysis differs, however, in that it explores how the author experiments with the literary form of the Bildungsroman to expose the erasure of female (and foetal) human forms in patriarchal environments. In particular, Wicomb creates a contrapuntal relationship between hybridity and linear growth, thereby challenging contemporary notions of personal development. Throughout this chapter I favour the term development over growth, due to its relevance in both narrative and scientific theorizations of formation. There are instances, however, where a synonym is preferable; in cases where the latter term is used, I am referring to strictly biological processes. The text advances a biological sense of identity formation: it contains progressions from vegetation and animal life to the scatological and deviant, resulting in a conception of creativity which is not associated with naturalized and feminized fertility, but rather with an artistic and agentive form of autopoiesis.

The previous chapter on Wilma Stockenström intimated how many people of colour simply refused to engage with abortion law reform in apartheid South Africa because of suspicions of ethnic cleansing. Some, however, were more openly critical of the activist movement's problematic undertones. In an address to delegates at a 1974 conference on abortion, a Zulu presenter named Dr H. Sibisi repeatedly registers her concerns about how birth control is perceived by Black South Africans: 'family planning in order to avoid population explosion,' she says, 'is often seen as one of the lines taken by the dominant imperialistic societies calculated to keep down the number of those they want to dominate' (Sibisi 1974: 57). Other sections of the conference proceedings approach abortion with reference to Judaism, Free Churches, Islam, Hinduism, the Dutch Reformed Church, the United Congregational Church of South Africa and Roman Catholicism. As the only Black presenter at the conference, Dr Sibisi is expected to represent all of 'African' cultural attitudes (1974: 53), despite the fact that there is a multiplicity of ethnic groups – with correspondingly divergent religious beliefs – in the country. Her views, however, are trivialized by the final speaker at the conference; not only does he condescend to her by expressing surprise that 'all these things which afflict all organised and technologically developed societies, also involve the African people' (Shapiro 1974: 233), but he further dismisses Sibisi's suspicions of state collusion with the medical profession as unsubstantiated (1974: 233).

At surface level, he is partially correct. Already under significant scrutiny by international audiences for their segregation of Black and white citizens, the NP was careful to emphasize that it would not use abortion as a method for population control lest it faced further sanctions (Klausen 2015: 155). Yet the majority of conservative Afrikaners in government positions, fearful of liberal values, became increasingly aware that they needed to revise legislation on the termination of pregnancy in order to clearly iterate their ideological positions to voters. Passed during International Women's Year, the 1975 Abortion and Sterilization Act was ironically designed 'to discipline the body, both literally (the individual women) and symbolically (the social body)' (Klausen 2015: 133). In comparison to the strict and simple prohibition of the previous law, its verbose clauses about conditions under which access was acceptable did little to help those who were most at risk. Much like Zimbabwe's Termination of Pregnancy Act (which I discuss in further detail in Chapter 3), South Africa's new law was technically permissive of abortion in certain circumstances. However, it included a range of access barriers, including a conscience clause and the requirement for certification from at least two doctors, one of whom, in applications for abortion due to mental health, had to be a psychiatrist. The latter condition proved to be one of the most difficult problems to overcome; even if medical professionals agreed in principle with the voluntary termination of pregnancy, mental health care was a luxury that only the wealthy and white could afford (Klausen 2015: 168). Yet in the wake of the passing of the Act, medical professionals increasingly came to view abortion more flexibly: three out of three psychiatrists who responded to a questionnaire said that the legislation should be liberalized; seventeen out of twenty-four responding gynaecologists echoed this sentiment; and seventy-one out of ninety GPs answered that the new Act was not lenient enough. This was particularly true in the case of doctors treating Black patients (Westmore 1977: 48).

Another issue which Black women faced – and which the government was reluctant to challenge – was exertion of control over their bodily autonomy by both patriarchal men in their communities, and by African feminist ideologies grounded in the sanctification of motherhood. Alongside the stipulation in Zulu and other Bantu languages to use the term *mama* as a signifier of respect when addressing any woman who is elder than the addresser – whether she is a mother or not – veneration of the maternal figure is also expressed by Motherism,[2] which emphasizes the importance of maternal caregiving and identity when fighting for women's rights. Motherist values were adopted by some in the BCM in order to encourage women to join the struggle against apartheid. Yet, paradoxically, as women moved from rural homesteads to the city in search of work, they threatened to disrupt traditional values. In the case of Zulu ethical principles, for example, Dr H. Sibisi highlights 'the value of human life i.e. the value of life more than material things' (1974: 53). With urbanization, however, women increasingly began to view their political positions – and the occupations which brought them a modicum of wealth and social status – as important. Pregnancy came to be seen as an inconvenience for some who risked being fired if they had children out of wedlock. Thus while many South African tribes share kinship terminology which refers to multiple members of the community as mother or father, women in both urban and rural settings began to challenge the duties of an 'integrated personality' which had hitherto been enshrined by repronormative scripts (Sibisi 1974: 58).

Men of colour, meanwhile, were preoccupied by the thought that the white population planned to precipitate a Black genocide by controlling women's fertility. Both the BCM and the ANC were hostile towards talk of reproductive agency for this reason (Klausen 2015: 195). It is important to note that there may be other reasons for Black men's reluctance to grant reproductive agency to women; denied political autonomy, many men were only able to assert power fully in the domestic sphere. Many Black South Africans would (and still do) see abortion in a hostile manner, associated with killing and colonialist involvement in rural people's lives (Bloomer, Pierson and Estrada Claudio 2019: 67). Patriarchal folklore, such as the persecution of witches for supposedly spoiling crops by menstruating or miscarrying, may have also played a role in these beliefs.[3] Even the ANC's Women's Charter of 1955 did not support abortion (thanks to the work of women in the party and the influence of speakers at international conferences, the ANC reformed abortion law after apartheid).

Susanne Klausen argues repeatedly throughout *Abortion under Apartheid* that the 1975 Act was predominantly passed in order to control the white population's reproductive agency and ensure the supposed racial purity of future generations. Due to the aforementioned structural inequalities of the health system, however, most of the women who received lawful abortions were white (Klausen 2015: 210), and the majority of those treated for complications from unsafe abortions were Black (2015: 212). Women of colour were consequently forced to respond inventively to the limitations placed upon their reproductive capacities by finding new contraceptive methods or means of inducing abortions. Helen Bradford's exemplary 1991 article 'Herbs, Knives and Plastic: 150 Years of Abortion in South Africa' charts a detailed movement from traditional abortifacients like plant roots in rural settings to more contemporary methods,[4] while Fiona Bloomer, Claire Pierson and Sylvia Estrada Claudio note that herbal concoctions were commonly used for inducing abortions throughout the twentieth century (2019: 65). In response to this focus on ecologically minded creativity, I am interested in exploring how women of colour used artistic resources to express frustration with restricted reproductive agency in an age of heightened political paranoia and censorship. As a coloured author from the Western Cape, Zoë Wicomb obviously does not reflect every southern African woman's experience of abortion through her writing. Yet, as the case of Dr H. Sibisi demonstrates above, it would be remiss to suggest that any singular Black woman should act as a representative for others' lived realities. Wicomb's novel uproots multiple forms of repronormativity through a Bildungsroman that unearths both the dominant NP's racist fears of white genocide *and* African nationalists' appeals to Motherism to curb eugenic population control. Through the vegetal imagery of its many vignettes, *You Can't Get Lost in Cape Town* experiments with abortion ecologies as formations of self-creation.

Autopoiesis and the Bildungsroman

Emerging from the scholarship of biologists Humberto R. Maturana and Francisco J. Varela, autopoiesis literally refers to the self-making process wherein any living system (such as a cell or organism) creates and sustains its own existence. The concept of autopoiesis is a key illustrator of the overlaps and differences between postcolonial and new materialist theories. It has been adapted in conjunction with the philosophy of Frantz Fanon by anti-colonial writer and critic Sylvia Wynter, as Max Hantel notes in a fascinating essay on the anti-anthropocentric potential of 'revolutionary humanism' in Wynter's work (2018: 71). Simultaneously, Maturana and Uribe's framework has been contested by well-known scholars like Donna Haraway and M. Beth Dempster, who reactively coin the neologism 'sympoiesis' for a contrastingly monist and new materialist understanding of living systems' intra-actions. While both Dempster and Haraway are concerned with the connectedness of all life, they ironically invented this term entirely independently of each other. Directly evoking Dempster, Haraway writes in *Staying with the Trouble* that 'many systems are mistaken for autopoietic that are really sympoietic' (2016: 33). Sympoiesis is intended to refer to collective creations or organizations of living cells. Yet in an article by Varela, Maturana and Uribe, the concept of more organizationally open systems is already discussed when they distinguish autopoiesis from allopoeisis, or 'systems in which the product of their operation is different from themselves' (1981: 8). Dempster and Haraway establish a term to distinguish more open living systems from the biologists' study, without acknowledging that the scientists already coined another word for the very same types of systematic processes. Allopoeisis or reproduction is a 'moment in autopoiesis' (Maturana and Varela 1980: 101), but not the primary focus of autopoietic studies. I have only encountered mention of allopoeisis once in Dempster's work (2000: 8), in a passage which does not acknowledge the origins of the term.

This is only one of many inaccuracies surrounding the topic in materialist circles. Bruce Clarke states that the term is primarily used in one of two contexts: either in the hard sciences, to describe units of both biological and artificial life, or to define social and artistic systems (2011: 222–3). His summary is largely correct, especially when one considers how many scholars in the humanities have tended to base their often convoluted understandings of autopoiesis upon illustrative scenarios from biological studies. Yet the history of the concept is not so easily reduced to a binary model. In his introductory notes to *Autopoiesis and Cognition: The Realization of the Living*, Maturana reveals that the term was invented after a discussion with a friend about Miguel de Cervantes Saavedra's *Don Quixote* ([1605] 2003), whose titular character's personal development is marked by a choice of praxis over poiesis (Maturana 1980: xvii). The Quixotic figure is unsurprisingly emblematic in discussions of the Bildungsroman, and the fact that Maturana's scientific theory was formed in response to *Don Quixote* indicates that autopoiesis holds potential theoretical clout for new materialist studies in the humanities. This is particularly true for literary scholars, provided that one prefaces any aesthetic applications of autopoiesis with two caveats. Firstly, one must stress that although literal reproduction and intersubjective experiences are not of interest to autopoietic studies, this is not to say that it negates the existence of more collective and undefined structural organizations. Those who study autopoiesis are interested in the continual *process* of sustaining a singular life rather than intersubjective moments of creation, but they do not deny that such broader patterns exist. The second disclaimer may operate with this last point in mind, and react as a direct retort to Haraway's phrasing: many texts are mistaken for sympoietic which are really autopoietic. This is particularly true in the case of the Bildungsroman.

A Bildungsroman is a novel which follows the development or socialization of an individual from immaturity to adulthood. In his 2002 monograph *Modernism, Narrative and Humanism*, Paul Sheehan outlines a history of the European Bildungsroman as being informed by humanist philosophies. He argues that in reducing the world to anthropocentric meaning, the Bildungsroman creates the figure of the human – yet he notes there are 'seeds of philosophical uncertainty' germinating within such narratives of 'integrated selfhood' that later give rise to the experimental Modernist novel (Sheehan 2002: 5). The Bildungsroman's focus on physical growth and personal development has many implications for postcolonial literature and the manner in which Wicomb's semi-autobiographical text has been received: particularly, how many critics have avoided sustained discussions of its experimental overlaps with both this literary form and Modernist aesthetics. According to Joseph Slaughter, Bildungsromane are remarkably similar to human rights laws in that both are preoccupied with the tensions between collective, social desires and personal freedom (Slaughter 2007: 10). Although Slaughter focuses on world literature, the same is arguably even truer in postcolonial novels featuring settings where human rights have historically been violated in particularly brutal and systemic manners. Yet as Slaughter notes towards the end of his study, 'the effective limitations of human rights are related not merely to the institutional frailty of the international legal regime but to the historically nationalist limitations of our literary imaginations' (2007: 324). That is to say, even a narrative which strives to promote personal agency will often fail to reconcile such an ideal with the legal and political clout of the nation-state. There is a fundamental difference between acting and having the freedom to act. One's pursuit of agency is therefore largely dependent on the rigidity or flexibility of meta-narratives of liberty, and often prone to failure. Lack of success may apply to anything from physical growth to a more metaphorical

Bildung and even to the very formation of the literary text. (*Bildung* also does not merely denote education, even though many Bildungsromane are at least initially focalized through a protagonist of school-going age.)

This preoccupation with success and/or failure is expressed by Ralph H. Austen in a 2015 article titled 'Struggling with the African Bildungsroman'. Austen argues that in contrast to portraying a tropified journey from childhood to maturity, most African Bildungsromane conclude with the hero suspended in a state of 'frozen or promising youth' (2015: 220) – in other words, such narratives often terminate before even personal agency has been attained, still less political freedom. Failure to achieve any sense of agency means that the protagonist is incapable of adopting a role in adult society. Importantly, Wicomb's protagonist is still childless at the end of *You Can't Get Lost in Cape Town*, with no mention of a job, a partner or other social responsibilities. Although she has made her journey to the UK independently, she still visits her family in South Africa frequently and appears to rely on parental support from either her father or mother, depending on the section in question. This is the portrait of the writer as a young woman: privileged in comparison to her peers, Wicomb's self-styled narrator follows the same upwards trajectory as seen in novels such as James Joyce's semi-autobiographical *A Portrait of the Artist as a Young Man* ([1916] 1993). Here I take seriously Gaylard's reading of Frieda as embodying 'the (Joycean) desire to escape or overcome whatever is limiting or constricting in the environment and society' (1996: 178), but without losing sight of the situated differences between Wicomb, as a South African experimental writer, and Joyce as an Irish Modernist. I am interested in exploring commonalities without essentializing either the texts or their authors, as the questionably 'off-colour' wording of André Viola's (1989) article title, 'Zoë Wicomb's *You Can't Get Lost in Cape Town*: A Portrait of the Artist as a Young Coloured Girl', threatens to do. But while Wicomb is clearly indebted to what Austen describes as 'the "modernist" (and largely British or German) late nineteenth- to early twentieth-century return to disillusionment', he states that Tsitsi Dangarembga's *Nervous Conditions* is 'the only African bildungsroman I have found that cites "classical" European exemplars of the same genre' (2015: 220–1). His omission of *You Can't Get Lost in Cape Town* from his analysis is particularly puzzling when one considers that Wicomb's oeuvre holds repeated references to Joyce (as I discuss later in this chapter), Thomas Hardy, George Eliot and other canonical European writers. Austen even goes on to quote Franco Moretti's assertion that only George Eliot knew how 'to deal with the major theme of the [continental] European bildungsroman: failure' (Moretti 2000: 216 in Austen 2015: 221).

The appearance of intertextual references to Eliot and other authors in Wicomb's – and, indeed, Dangarembga's – writing suggests there is a recurring interest in failure in both European literary styles like Modernism and the so-called African Bildungsroman, a commonality that he sporadically highlights but fails to interrogate in a sustained discussion.

The same curious omission holds true for critics who have focused specifically on South African fiction rather than on African literature at large. When writing on modernity in South African literary history, David Attwell argues that in contrast to European Modernism, which frequently concentrates on the subject in exile, Black writers tend to focus on the displacement that they feel in their country of birth (2005: 176). Given his emphasis on natal alienation, one would imagine Attwell's study to feature an analysis of Zoë Wicomb's fiction, particularly for its focus on genetic roots and racial hybridity (this reading is only expected and by no means desired; as I have already stated, the theme of miscegenation is oftentimes overemphasized by critics, eclipsing other potential avenues of discussion). Yet he only mentions Wicomb – and Bessie Head, an influential writer with similarly experimentalist tendencies – in passing:

> Undoubtedly, their work is both modernist and postmodern in specific ways, some of which have to do with gendered modes of representation and their implied subject-positions. However, I would argue that the case I am making can be formulated all too easily with respect to Head and Wicomb, whose gender-positions and whose exilic relation to their material weighs more heavily than it does with writers such as Ndebele and Mda.
>
> (Attwell 2005: 178)

I take issue with the assertion that the former women writers are not worthy of discussion, or not as committed to a 'South African epistemology' as writers such as Njabulo Ndebele or Zakes Mda (Attwell 2005: 178), simply because they chose to leave their country of birth. To categorize writers by their geographical locations (and by the degree of their interest in gender) seems to me to invest too heavily in gendered and nationalist constructs of home. It is worth stressing here that both writers speak frankly of sexual reproduction and are central to my study of abortion in southern African literature. Furthermore, Zoë Wicomb mentions Bessie Head in several of her writings including 'To Hear the Variety of Discourses' (1990: 43) and 'Setting, Intertextuality and the Resurrection of the Postcolonial Author' (2005: 152–3). In the latter essay (and in contrast to Attwell), she describes Head first and foremost as a 'South African writer [...] who moved to Botswana' (Wicomb 2005: 152). Unlike

Head's, Wicomb's departure from South Africa was not final; this is reinforced by the fact that almost all her fiction to date has been set in that country. It is ironic that Attwell emphasizes the importance of agency in African literary experimentalism (2005: 175), but then chooses not to examine how feminist experimentation with exilic states (and autonomous rejection of the nation-state) might complicate his thesis.

Yet this is not to say that there is nothing to be gleaned from either David Attwell's or Ralph Austen's discussions. As should be evident in my analysis, I read Austen's article as too categorical, particularly as he does not account for experimental approaches to the Bildungsroman. Overall, however, I agree with the thesis that the genre represents 'individualistic development, especially through autonomous reading and personal mentorship, but one that, in both its African and "canonical" European forms, always has to confront larger social contexts' (Austen 2015: 228). The Bildungsroman resists nationalist discourse by projecting identity-formation as a self-led but global project. It does not – or should not – render the creative individual as allegory for a patriotic identity to be mindlessly reproduced. This rejection of naïve nationalism is evident in Wicomb's article 'To Hear the Variety of Discourses' (1990). Writing in the years leading up to South Africa's transition to a democratic state, she questions how the ANC has subjugated Black women while fighting for racial equality, by observing the objectification of female bodies during a celebration. In such instances, Wicomb argues, even womanism 'reveals itself to be more *desired state* than theory. By its own definition, it must meet the spectacle with *silence*' (1990: 35; emphasis added). There are echoes here of the ethics of attentive listening discussed in my previous chapter on Stockenström. Wicomb suggests that many South Africans of colour are so preoccupied with racial inequality that they tend not to notice the interrelated material conditions of women and that this perpetuates cyclical censorship. Indeed, silence is precisely the response that Frieda chooses when her body is viewed as either an exotic being or a grotesque hybrid. Continuing her analysis, Wicomb goes on to state that 'Apartheid laws, the notions of home, motherhood, and the family have become constructs characterised by desire. Analogies with slavery are clear and in black women's writing [...] these issues can be traced as tropes of desire that adapt and transform received ideas of womanhood, manhood, motherhood [and] dominant domestic ideologies and gender relations' (1990: 39). If home and the home country are nothing but constructs of desire, then how can we make sense of readings such as Austen's and Attwell's, which ultimately neglect to explore feminist issues like embodiment and reproductive agency? Furthermore, how can we serve justice to Black southern African women writers without essentializing them as nothing more than products of a very specific environmental and political climate?

At this point one may turn to a highly influential theorist on the intersections of sexuality and racism: Robert J. C. Young. In *Colonial Desire: Hybridity in Theory, Culture, and Race*, Young draws on Gilles Deleuze and Félix Guattari to focus on 'the historical material procedures of colonialism and its ideological operations', such as 'the severing of the body from the land' ([1994] 1995: 170). Yet this fails to consider the fact that the woman's body *is* the land in colonial discourse, a point that remains underdeveloped in Young's study. His analysis of fantasies involving desire and fertility is undeniably important for the field of postcolonial studies, but lacking in intersectional scope. Young uses almost exclusively cerebral concepts like the 'colonial machine' and terms from economics ([1994] 1995: 97), without considering how women and the land are embodied in colonial and nationalist rhetoric. Bearing in mind the silence of various critics around intersectional experimentations with personal formation, and interpreting Wicomb's description of narrative suppression as an integral preoccupation of southern African women's writing, I am interested in exploring how the above extracts from 'To Hear the Variety of Discourses' interact with *You Can't Get Lost in Cape Town*. Following Rosi Braidotti, we can take the desired state to signify 'not just libidinal desire, but ontological desire, the desire to be, the tendency of the subject to be, the predisposition of the subject towards being' ([1994] 2011: 124–5). In this way we can conceive of desire as both a bodily form of craving – whether this is sexual, epicurean or otherwise – and a more philosophical state of not-yet-being, of wishing-to-be.

Braidotti operates, like Young, in the legacy of Deleuze and Guattari, but is far more attentive to feminist embodiment when discussing agency, domination and desire. Mine is not a Deleuzian approach (I prioritize formation as development over 'becoming'), but it is important to emphasize how both Young and Braidotti formulate their models of desire in the wake of Deleuze and Guattari's work, especially since Braidotti normalizes the conception of the assemblage when writing about the collective nature of desire. A curious symbolic overlap with Deleuze and Guattari will become more apparent, too, in my textual analysis. Braidotti utilizes the concept of autopoiesis at several points in her oeuvre; in her theoretical model, autopoiesis is both a biological and ontological process that recognizes the simultaneous self-sufficiency and interconnectedness of all living organisms (Braidotti 2010: 210). What is integral to one's identity formation is, ironically, depersonalization (particularly the recognition that the self constitutes one part of a larger whole). Immediately we can see how such a model relates to new materialist theory: in this understanding of autopoietic growth, the self-styling subject may be either a single-cellular organism, a non/human animal or a more metaphorical corpus such as the nation-state. Braidotti is invested in both the personal and political ramifications of this biological process, as she emphasizes that subjectivity involves 'complex and continuous negotiations with dominant norms and values and hence also multiple forms of accountability' (Braidotti in Dolphijn and van der Tuin 2012: 31). Considering that *You Can't Get Lost in Cape Town*'s central plot device is an abortion – a most poignant and taboo matter of life and death – I deem it necessary to analyse the text with this materialist model of political and reproductive agency in mind.

It is apparent when reading Wicomb's non-fiction that agency, creativity and failure are significant avenues of ethical and aesthetic experimentation to the author. As she discusses J. M. Coetzee's *Foe* (1986), for instance, she is consumed by the way that the character Friday dresses in the author's cloak, 'a moment marked both by the impossibility of reproducing the story of the colonised and by indeterminacy', and the resultant fact that 'our aspirant author's strategy of impersonation does not father a text' (Wicomb 2005: 148). Analysing a story by South African author Ivan Vladislavić in the same article, she admires how his 'ideas are stillborn' (Wicomb 2005: 148); his text does not have a traditional teleological trajectory but rather 'proclaims its failure' (2005: 149). Even when discussing the authorial self in African-American modernity, the writer is consumed by reproduction and its negation. Moving on to a critical appreciation of Toni Morrison's *Jazz* ([1992] 2001), she pays particular attention to intertextual references to T. S. Eliot's 'Prufrock' and 'The Waste Land', two famous examples of Modernist spiritual sterility (Wicomb 2005: 150). All of these writers share an experimental approach to literary aesthetics, but Morrison is one of Wicomb's formative influences; she is even quoted in an epigraph in one of her most recent novels, *October* (2014). Similarly to Morrison, the author is experimenting with symbols of displacement and barrenness – which I have argued can be found in both European and southern African modernity – but her aim is not to entirely negate the narrative trajectory of development found in a typical Bildungsroman. I thus build upon ideas broached by Wicomb's non-fiction, and Braidotti's feminist formulation of autopoiesis, by contending that the preoccupation with racialized reproduction in Wicomb's first fictional work is not merely literal. Rather, it also symbolizes the problem of feminist self-formation in autocratic, nationalist political climates. In his study of Modernism, colonialism and the Bildungsroman form, Jed Esty argues that anglophone Modernism and anti- or decolonial critical frameworks are both suspicious of Western models of development (2012: 201–2). Esty's is an important intervention in the field of global Modernisms, and it is particularly relevant to this study for noting how developmental allegory is complicated in the writings of feminist authors including Olive Schreiner, Virginia Woolf and Jean Rhys (all of whom have thematized abortion in their fiction).[5] I, however, am eager to move beyond colonial writing and consider how the southern African Bildungsroman further complicates patriarchal forms and nationalist norms.

Alongside its exploratory interactions with modernity and Modernist disillusionment, there are various other aspects of *You Can't Get Lost in Cape Town* which suggest there is much to be made of viewing it as an experimental Bildungsroman. This proposition gains credibility when one considers the bodily *Bildung* which Frieda undergoes throughout the narrative. In the first few sections, she does not describe her figure (or her feelings about it) in any great detail. When narrating her childhood in retrospect, for example, she observes that she had no idea that she was overweight (Wicomb 1987: 28). It is also during this period that her mother is completely present within the narrative, as well as in the family home. In 'Bowl Like Hole', the reader is introduced to Frieda as a passive child who curls up in the foetal position. This arrangement of the child's body symbolizes that she has not yet exited the domestic realm and interacted with the outside world, and therefore has not yet encountered others (who will, it is later revealed, be prejudiced against her because of her appearance). Instead of speaking to, or even seeing, Mr Weedon (the white man who owns and visits the gypsum mines near her home), Frieda chooses to curl next to a familiar maternal presence. Once she reaches puberty, however, two changes occur: she becomes deeply uncomfortable with her body, and her mother is almost exclusively written out of the narrative.

Gypsum is a soft, pale sulphate mineral which may be used as a construction material, fertilizer or as an additive to food and cosmetics. All of these utilizations literally relate to development: of buildings, of plants or of a human's bodily form. From the outset of the text, concrete elements of the literary environment symbolize a deeper concern with identity and narrative formation. In the following sections, I begin by discussing literally autopoietic environments and systems which recur throughout *You Can't Get Lost in Cape Town*. Next I analyse how Wicomb redefines desire through various corporeal developments, particularly with reference to vegetation, food and the female body. Lastly and most importantly, I argue that the text's very formation evokes an extended abortive metaphor that is autopoietic in its scope. The supposed resurrection of Frieda's mother in the final section of the text is what informs my reading of Wicomb's experimental literary form. It is of the utmost importance that the narrative closes with two coloured women speaking freely, without interruption from repronormative discourse. In communicating with her mother, Frieda navigates the territory between her genetic identity, her bodily desires and her agentive potential. She is no longer yearning nostalgically for her roots, but rather looking promisingly at the mountain in the presence of a female role model whom she, in turn, has come to mother.

Apartheid's abortive environments

In the first section of *You Can't Get Lost in Cape Town*, Frieda recalls how she used to lie curled in a ball beneath a kitchen table whenever Mr Weedon came to visit her village: 'At an early age,' she narrates, 'I discovered the advantage of curling up motionless in moments of confusion, a position which in further education I found to be foetal' (1). The reference to learning here is more than literal, as later she will not only go on to attend university (an unusual opportunity for women of colour under apartheid) but also experience an unplanned pregnancy. Yet in childhood, with no premonitions of her future, lying in this position appears to alleviate anxiety about the white man's visit and the 'topsy-turviness of the day' (4). 'These topsy-turvy days' which so vex the narrator are, in a sense, redolent of the very presentation of a foetus before birth (1): babies are typically born head-down, unless they are in the breech position. Frieda recounts that 'the flutter inside' subsides when she draws up her knees to 'became part of the arrangement of objects, shared in the solidity of the table and the cast-iron buckets full of water lined up on it' (2). Thus from the outset of the novel, the distinction between the animate and inanimate, or organic and inorganic, is subject to imaginative reinterpretation. The young girl's empathy with the system of objects that surrounds her is indicative of a subversion of anthropocentricism. Yet, as various inequalities between human and nonhuman agencies in the text suggest, the protagonist is not renouncing humanist models of development so much as experimenting with them. There is no universalizing gesture here to making kin with collective social desires. Rather, Wicomb's political priority is to imbue coloured female embodiment with a sense of autopoietic agency.

In the foundational years of her schooling, Frieda has two female friends called Sarie and Jos who are also intellectually gifted. When the latter spies on a woman giving birth, she is disgusted; she tells the others, and 'with an oath invented by Jos we swore that we would never have babies' (28). By the conclusion of the narrative it is revealed that Frieda keeps this promise, but it is unclear what happens to the other two girls: their friendships end when they are forced to leave school and help provide for their families, since their names are never mentioned in later sections of the text. Yet Wicomb is not simplistically suggesting that working-class women have no choice when aligning with repronormative values. The story of Tamieta, a poor woman who works in the university canteen, demonstrates how reproduction and motherhood are not necessarily bound together, and that women may desire only some – or none – of the stages found in heteronormative narratives of personal development. The cook is delighted to adopt her cousin's baby after it is revealed that the mother cannot adequately care for her: 'She who adored little ones would have a child without the clumsiness of pregnancy, the burden of birth and the tobacco-breathed attentions of men with damp fumbling hands' (45). Tamieta's decision to 'witness the miracle of growth' without falling pregnant challenges heteronormative scripts surrounding fertility (61), such as the assumption that people only adopt children if they are physically incapable of conceiving. Women may simply not desire to be pregnant, or to give birth, and yet still display stereotypically maternal qualities. This character's agency represents non-reproductive parenthood, complicating repronormative/antinatalist and pro-choice/anti-abortion dichotomies.

Similarly to Tamieta, Frieda is reluctant to give birth, although her reasons are less to do with an aversion to sex than with the ethical consequences of bringing a child into the world under apartheid. During her undergraduate years, she conceives a child with Michael, the white student whom she is secretly dating, and decides to have an abortion. Although her friends are aware of the relationship, she is reluctant to tell her family, but not because interracial sexual activity is illegal under apartheid law: she fears that her parents would press her to settle down with Michael in the hopes of raising their social status. Tamieta and Frieda thus embody two transgressive, if not entirely compatible, attitudes to the institutions of marriage and family. When one considers the title of the text and the chapter featuring the abortion, it is clear the latter woman is exercised by the potential shame of being exposed, of being unable to keep a secret in a society where everyone is invested in monitoring and judging each other's actions. Frieda's fears of being shamed for supposed deviance involve both what is inside her body (the unsupportable foetus) and external appearances: although the abortionist ignores her skin tone and assumes her 'English' accent means she is white (78), there is the implicit recognition that the foetus would also develop to carry markers of miscegenation. The inside-outside dialectic is central to both new materialist theory (which challenges such binarized distinctions) and my final chapter on Bessie Head, whose own indeterminate racial identity informs much of her fictional writing on individual desires and collective social issues in rural Botswana.

Sitting on the bus with Michael's wallet clutched in her handbag, Frieda internally recounts the story of Jesus's betrayal and crucifixion and visualizes how Judas 'howls like a dog' with his 'concealed leather purse' (72). On the surface, the parallel between her material situation and Judas's in the parable is suggestive of her disloyalty to the foetus in her womb. She even imagines that other people in the bus suspect she is pregnant and intending to terminate. Yet a few moments later, there is a shift of their two metaphorical roles, and a struggle for dominance ensues: 'The foetus betrays me with another flutter, a sigh. I have heard of books flying off the laps of gentle mothers-to-be as their foetuses lash out. I will not be bullied. I jump up and press the bell' (72). It is Michael, not Frieda, who contemplates bringing the pregnancy to full term; in contrast with 'gentle' women, the protagonist does not even entertain the notion of being a 'mother-to-be'. This repronormative wording – which frames pregnant women in the future tense, assuming they will want to be parents – foregrounds how choosing education over motherhood is usually perceived as a disloyal act. Yet, as she recalls stories of gestation actively interfering with the intellectual lives of women, Wicomb's narration subtly begs the question: if embryos really are fully formed persons, with all their legal rights, then should they not, also, be held accountable for contravening their responsibilities? In short, if both the woman and unsupportable foetus are embodied agencies, then who is betraying whom?

It appears Frieda is herself uncertain how to respond to this possibility. Even when imbuing the foetus with the immaculate more-than-personhood of Jesus – his 'sad, complaining eyes' – she resolves to 'resist' all guilt (72). Moments later she deviates from revering the foetus as divine (and framing it within Judeo-Christian spirituality) by evoking animal imagery. Recalling the words Michael told her (the quote which informs both the title of this section and the text), she confesses, 'I am lost, hopelessly lost, and as my mind gropes for recognition I feel a feathery flutter in my womb, so slight I cannot be sure, and again, so soft, the brush of a butterfly' (67). The sensation that the narrator is describing here is known colloquially as quickening, a word that for centuries has referred to the stage of pregnancy when a foetus's movements are first felt (*OED*).[6] Quickening, in other words, is a traditionally recognized indicator that the baby has not been lost in utero – a compelling further complication of the text's title and its associations with (birth) origins, deviance and exposure. This experimentation with the butterfly-wing trope is taken to even further extremes by Yvonne Vera's engagement with tragedy in *Butterfly Burning*, as I discuss extensively in Chapter 3. Comparison of foetal kicking with 'fluttering' is one of the most common tropes in the discourse surrounding pregnancy (Wicomb 1987: 73); while Wicomb is creating a three-way relationship between the human, the nonhuman and the divine, the animal is not necessarily symbolic of animist spiritual beliefs. As Frieda walks to the abortionist's and feels another flutter, however, she thinks of 'moth wings struggling against a window pane' (77). In this moment, she braces herself for the termination by reimagining the foetus-butterfly as its stereotypically drab, nocturnal counterpart. The foetus, which is not the product of a miracle but ordinary sexual intercourse, develops through a range of animalized associations while remaining one autopoietic form. This transspecies metamorphosis negates any associations with sunshine, colour and (re)birth which may have been evoked earlier. It also dissociates the phenomenon of foetal kicking from the formation of legal personhood. Importantly, both of the animalistic metaphors render the foetus as a living subject, but the image of the shapeshifting moth is suggestive of ambiguity and transformation, thus continuing one's suspension of moral judgement.

The section preceding 'You Can't Get Lost in Cape Town' is titled 'A Clearing in the Bush'. It opens with Tamieta fixating on an itch on her back, an embodied urge which she interprets as 'something ominous', and ends with her marching 'chin up into the bush, to the deserted station where the skollie-boys dangle their feet from the platform all day long' (37; 61). I read the section's conclusion as a premonition of gender-based violence inflicted upon the woman's body by *skollies* (hooligans) for several reasons. It is of particular importance that Tamieta meditates that she is tired of things 'creeping up on her, catching her unawares, offering unthinkable surprises' (61), since sexual violence is commonly committed against women in South Africa. Particularly, those who are perceived as lesbians may be victims of corrective rape, a hate crime perpetuated by men who purportedly attempt to cure women of homosexual desire (Di Silvio 2011: 1470). Although Tamieta's choice to remain chaste is not necessarily indicative of queer identity, her rejection of sexual advances may be perceived as such by predatory men. Further, 'Home Sweet Home' (the section following 'You Can't Get Lost in Cape Town') describes a raped woman's corpse that is found in the river (Wicomb 1987: 91), offering an ominous potential conclusion to this scene. The narrative develops, in these sections, to contemplate a trinity of killings: of an adoptive mother, of a foetus and of a mule. Here the notion of killing is problematized not only since Tamieta's rape and/or murder in the clearing is unnarrated, but also because of moral and narrative ambiguities surrounding the three deaths.

I have already explored how both the pregnant woman and the foetus are likened to betrayers in the titular section of the text, and how this challenges the apartheid regime's classification of most abortions as murder. In the case of 'Home Sweet Home', the narrator is similarly preoccupied with questions of moral personhood and classifications, particularly when she sees a mule that is endangered by a landslide at the riverbank. Importantly, she is visiting the river to escape her extended family, who remain unaware that she terminated a pregnancy from an interracial relationship. Frieda is also reluctant to tell them she lives alone and so invents a communal living situation with her fictional landlady Mrs Beukes: her relatives 'are pleased at the thought of a family, comforted at the Beukes's ability, in common with the rest of the animal kingdom, to reproduce themselves' (86). This scene highlights two recurring thematic tensions in Wicomb's oeuvre. The first, and perhaps most obvious, is the paradox of coloured identity, as shown by the family's simultaneous pride and internalized prejudices, and their desire for Frieda to transcend the racial classifications imposed upon them. Second, Wicomb is acutely aware here of how racist animalization often underlies antinatalist discourse (as exemplified by Frieda's sardonic tone). This is indicative of a trend throughout her writing: she frequently foregrounds humans' animality, but chooses to 'cling, if periodically, to the humanist notion of a core self that is essential to the possibility of resistance' (Wicomb 1998: 367). The idea of a core self implies a certain allegiance to fixed definitions of personal identity that operate under the same logic as the anti-abortionist position that any and all human forms should be granted legal personhood. Yet complications remain in the periodic nature of Wicomb's humanism, which appears at times to parallel the 'revolutionary humanism attuned to nonhuman landscapes' that Hantel reads in Sylvia Wynter's formulation of autopoiesis (Hantel 2018: 64). I am interested in exploring the tensions between the human and the nonhuman presented in this section of the text, and not only (or even primarily) because mules recur throughout Judeo-Christian spiritual imagery. The body of the mule is a most autopoietic form: as the offspring of a horse and a donkey, it cannot reproduce due to an uneven number of chromosomes.

Although they are proud of her academic ambitions and creative success, Frieda's working-class family are puzzled by her interest in political activism, calling her stubborn as a mule (Wicomb 1987: 86). Through this cliched comparison, she is immediately aligned with the animal that struggles against quicksand. As she watches from the riverbank on which she 'theoretically' stands (90), the mule appears to shapeshift: 'Transformed by fear its ears alert into quivering conductors of energy' (103). Here new materialist theories of vibrant intra-actions are not sufficient to help the animal; only a benevolent and fully autonomous organism can assist in such a scenario. The fact that the feminist narrator chooses not to act is of particular significance. Like the mule, Frieda and the terminated foetus are construed by society as hybrids (as revealed by the etymology of *mulatto*, a term used historically to refer to mixed race persons). Her decision not to tell anyone about the animal's death is thus not only illustrative of her reticent character – contrary to her family's beliefs, she is not as tenacious as she seems, as she chooses to let them remain blissfully ignorant of the constant exoticization of women of colour – but is also symbolic of her earlier decision, that 'guilty secret' (101). Important, too, is her disgust with the mule's 'grotesque dance', 'like an ill-trained circus animal', and subsequent 'lack of desire' to search for the water-spirits of her childhood (103). Disgust and (its negation of) desire feature in various other sections of the text, as I shall discuss further in this chapter. The mule's death serves to thematize the cyclical inevitability of gendered crimes committed upon human subjects, whether this is the mulish narrator or the rape-murder victim. As in 'A Clearing in the Bush', Wicomb sets a fatal scene, but the section ends abruptly, before we are sure of what exactly has been witnessed. The reader is only left with ambiguous allusions to environmental actors like bushveld, quicksand or 'water spirits' that may or may not signify death (103). Read together, the three killings challenge the reader to consider which lives are assigned the most value, and who (or what) suffers as a result.

Another section set in the narrator's hometown, titled 'Behind the Bougainvillea', experimentally subverts the infantilization and exoticization of women. In this section Frieda's father pleads with her to visit the local doctor to have a cough examined; when she finally agrees, he smiles like 'a child placated by a parent's exasperated, Yes, all right' (110). As I discuss at length in my previous chapter on Wilma Stockenström's *The Expedition to the Baobab Tree*, the inversion of gendered power dynamics – particularly between father-figures and young women – has the potential to queer reproductive expectations. Without being overly optimistic about the potential of gender non-conformity in challenging patriarchal authority, there is the sense here that Frieda's succumbing to his wishes is indicative of experimentation with a non-reproductive sense of parenthood and agency. While the older man is infantilized, the woman acts in an authoritative capacity: Frieda is no longer the pathetic, foetal figure who hugged her knees behind her old school door, the place where her childhood sweetheart Henry Hendrikse left her love letters (115). This fact is reinforced when she accidentally meets Henry in the queue for the doctor's waiting room. In his previous letters he had written that Frieda's 'breasts were two fawns, twins of a gazelle, that feed among the lilies' (116). The young Henry's words are inspired by the romantic tradition which portrays men as explorers and women as docile environmental actors. In adulthood, however, *she* is compared to a Swiftian conqueror of terrain: 'an awe-struck Gulliver' surveying his 'great caverns' of 'flared nostrils' and 'distorted mountain of flesh' (111). Frieda's relationships with both of these male figures from her childhood are transformed as she starts acting on her desires and comes to reject the passive, repronormative roles which are so often reserved for women. In a development not free from problematic implications, she mimics masculine structures of power to attempt to attain agency. Yet queer ecological scholarship shows the logic of patriarchy is so lacking in coherence and rigidity that it does not allow for a simple inversion and occupation of two opposing positions; in other words, it remains dubious whether displays of (hyper-)masculinity are truly affirmative or expressive of 'natural' femininity (Sandilands 2015: par. 3), whatever that expression may mean.

The last few segments of the text reveal that interactions between people of all genders are pivotal in reimagining reproductive agency. In the penultimate section, Frieda visits the house of an old university friend called Moira who has since married and had children with Desmond, a political activist from their student days. It is telling that Desmond, who is representative of both African nationalism and so-called liberalism, expects his wife to perform all the labour in their household (Wicomb 1987: 153). In the kitchen, something catches Frieda's eye; she describes it as 'a curious object on the windowsill from which the light bounces frantically. It is a baby's shoe dipped into a molten alloy, an instant sculpture of brassy brown that records the first wayward steps of a new biped' (153). One cannot but think here of the famous six-word story, 'For sale: baby shoes, never worn', which is often attributed to Ernest Hemingway (with whom the protagonist, a graduate of literary studies, would presumably be familiar).[7] Although Moira's baby lives and learns to walk, the reproduction of the baby's shoe is just as unwearable and useless as the pair in the above short fiction. The metal object thus has no function other than serving as a sentimental, aesthetic signifier of procreative achievement – a feat which Frieda critiques by viewing Moira and Desmond's child in cynical economic and evolutionary terms.

Even in the last section of the text, the narrator's views on childbirth do not appear to have changed significantly since her decision to have an abortion in early adulthood. An older Frieda opines on a visit to her mother, 'Such a poor investment children are. No returns, no compound interest, not a cent's worth of gratitude. You'd think gratitude were inversely proportionate to the sacrifice of parents. I can't imagine why people have children' (171). In the economy of desire, Frieda believes, sex is not worth the risk of parental responsibility. It is worth noting that here, as earlier, she is using a distanced vocabulary to hypothesize about human reproduction. Yet this time the *mulish* and *childless* Frieda is detailing the disadvantages of bearing children to her own mother. The issue, in short, is personal. There is much irony to be found in the narrator's attitude, particularly when she has a dream during the same visit to her mother that she is in the UK once more, and that her neighbour is pegging up nappies in the freezing English weather. The mention of the so-called Mother Country is particularly fascinating and foregrounds what may be perceived as contradictions between the protagonist's rationalization for antinatalist views and her own ungrateful actions. Frieda has forsaken her biological family by moving to England, severing her ties with the lower-class community from her childhood. She also decides to kill off her real mother in her stories (172). Yet her repeated returns to South Africa in adulthood, and her final visit to her childhood home – where it is implied that her mother is her only surviving parent – complicate the traditional narrative trajectory of a young scholar from the colonies who finds personal freedom in the English academic environment. If there is any *Bildung* to be found by the end of the text, it is her growing realization that repronormative culture and colonial expansion share rhetorical nuances, embodying the patriarchal urge to control women's reproductive autonomy.

Frieda's desire to tell her neighbour that 'she's wasting her time' is thus symbolic of the female subject's deepening misgivings with repronormative and nationalist values (174). Her recurring contemplation of gendered violence – perpetuated by men of all races – causes her to suspect that the birth of a new, democratic nation will remain nothing more than fiction. But before I interrogate how Wicomb experiments with killing off patriotic discourse in her literary treatment of abortion, it is necessary to further explore literal and symbolic connotations of disgust and desire that are apparent in the text.

Seeds of disgust, roots of deviance

In adulthood Frieda grows averse to Afrikaans due to its gendered and 'babyish diminutives' (90).[8] Her rejection of the language may be traced to an experience earlier in life when, disgusted with the traditional signifiers of coloured identity, Frieda's mother scolds her child for speaking Afrikaans and playing with other children. When Mr Weedon visits the village, Mrs Shenton is impressed by – and eager to emulate – his enunciation of English words. She is particularly struck by the way he pronounces 'Bowl like hole, not bowl like howl' (9), a fact which she reports to her husband, who is ironically the local English teacher. Hidden in the parents' incorrect pronunciation is a real word, which remains hitherto unaddressed by reviewers and critics alike: bowel. I believe the digestive system is alluded to here for several reasons, and that it signifies more than the mere butt of a linguistic joke. Taking this emergence of the obscene in the early stages of the text as my point of departure, I will explore how literal and metaphorical figurations of craving and disgust are central to understanding Wicomb's transgressive formations of sexual desire and reproduction.

Nourishment appears as a central thematic motif from the first section of the text. One of the few instances where Frieda and her mother speak involves the use of a milk separator, and it reveals how internalized prejudice operates on not only racialized, but also sex- and species-based, models of oppression. Frieda's mother takes a cow's milk to test the device which divides the white liquid into 'yellow cream' and 'thin bluish milk' (5). The young narrator accuses her mother of stealing food from the baby calf, to which she responds with eyes that 'beg as if she were addressing the cow herself, as if her life depended on the change of routine' (5). Milk is the most defining element in the inherent mammalian connection between mother and infant – an assemblage that is severed in dairy production, as the liquid is consumed by human adults instead of young cows.[9] Unlike the 'deathsmilk of indifference' which I discuss in my analysis of *The Expedition to the Baobab Tree* (Stockenström 1983: 20), the milk in this instance is undeniably real, the product of a maternal animal. Yet its rendering through the separator means that it loses its nutritional value for the calf, and is transformed into two unnatural products that are, according to Frieda's mother, designed for human consumption. The young girl's disgust with her mother's actions, and her decision to sympathize with the (young and/or female) animals, foreground what will later develop into indifference displayed towards childbirth. In other words, the homogenized labour of milk churning is only one of many gendered roles which she views with suspicion.

As Frieda grows older, the twinned threats of domestication and paid domestic work – fates common for most women of colour under apartheid – loom in the imaginations of both herself and her father. When waiting for the train which will take her to the so-called white school, the pair's fixation on her future is perhaps most apparent. As he passes her a bag of raisins, a 'terrifying image of a madam's menstrual rags' that she would have to wash 'swirls liquid red' through her mind (24). The transition from food to female embodiment here is particularly interesting. On first reading, it appears bizarre that the thought of blood does not evoke disgust in Frieda, or at least cause her to lose her appetite. Yet seconds later, her father hands her a stick of biltong and she confesses, 'I have no control over the glands under my tongue as they anticipate the salt' (24). Anxiety about his daughter's bodily and personal development is repressed by Mr Shenton into stress-eating, a coping mechanism that is then transmitted to Frieda and with which she struggles for the rest of her academic career. By studying hard and attending university, she does escape the role of housecleaner; yet, gendered servitude is still coded into Frieda's dietary habits (given her father's influence and constant interference, to use the word choices here would seem ill-judged). With this word one is reminded again of how the rhetoric of choice fails to encompass the multiple complex reasons why a woman may feel that a pregnancy is unsupportable. Accordingly, Frieda's relationship with food serves as a further symbol for women's struggles for bodily autonomy.

Even when Frieda tries to form self-assurance and agency through learning, her uncomfortableness with sexual maturity remains. For example, it is the narrator's father who lectures her about childbirth on her fourteenth birthday with a quotation from Gen. 3.16; 'in pain you shall bring forth children', he says, before mentioning in passing, 'Your mother was never regular' (22). He goes on to literally feed her unhealthy relationship with food by equating good nutrition with high social standing. Instructing her to clear her plate, he says, 'we are not paupers with nothing to eat. Your mother was thin and sickly, didn't eat enough. You don't want cheekbones that jut out like a Hottentot's' (24). This section is the first instance in the text where Frieda's mother is referred to in the past tense (with a derogatory term for the Khoisan, from whom many coloured people are partially descended). In the wake of the maternal figure's apparent disappearance, it is important to note that Wicomb is engaging with a common trope in feminist Bildungsromane: that of a working-class young woman attempting to improve her perceived social standing by feeding her body in accordance to the values of an older, male character. Readers of postcolonial fiction may be familiar with examples such as the anorexic Nyasha in Tsitsi Dangarembga's *Nervous Conditions*. Clare Barker provides a compelling analysis of this novel, arguing that Dangarembga's feminist fiction not only 'generates its own theoretical intervention into feminist postcolonial cultural politics' (2011: 63), but also provides a culturally situated model of disability and illness in Zimbabwe. As I stress in my introduction, I am similarly interested in investigating how theorizations of materiality emerge through southern African feminist fiction.

Yet here Wicomb is also engaging with a longer history of feminist fiction that finds its roots in Modernist experimentation. A notable illustration is Esther Greenwood in *The Bell Jar*, who expresses a similar attitude towards food once she is introduced to fine dining as a young adult; she eats a whole jar of caviar when reminded of her grandfather's reverence of the delicacy (Plath [1963] 1971: 22). This attitude to food is not the only similarity between *You Can't Get Lost in Cape Town* and Sylvia Plath's novel. Both protagonists, for example, are intelligent young women who use education in order to escape their working-class upbringings. Another commonality is that both Esther's and Frieda's *Bildungen* are decidedly gynaecological; the former suffers abnormal and excessive bleeding after sexual intercourse while the latter undergoes an abortion. The authors' shared interest in, and indebtedness to, such influences is indicative of a broader preoccupation within Modernism: figurations of sexual sterility as metaphor for the failure of one's identity formation.[10] It is also no coincidence, I would argue, that both writers allude to the writing of James Joyce: Esther's thesis proposal concentrates on *Finnegans Wake* ([1939] 2012), and Plath occasionally employs Joycean techniques such as transcribing phrases acoustically, like the train conductor's call of 'Root Wan Twenny Ate!' ([1963] 1971: 109).

Wicomb, like Plath, employs similar techniques to James Joyce – from frank descriptions of bodily functions to vignettes told from the perspective of interrelated characters. There is certainly room for further investigation of references to Joyce in Wicomb's fiction. The short-story sequences of *You Can't Get Lost in Cape Town* and *The One That Got Away*, for instance, appear very similar to the structure of Joyce's *Dubliners* ([1914] 1956) and the 'Wandering Rocks' section of *Ulysses* ([1920] 1987). Wicomb also briefly mentions Leopold Bloom's breakfast in *David's Story* (35). The influence of the Irish writer further suggests her preoccupation with corporeal sensations like desire and disgust. Since Frieda is forced into multiple disturbing and uncomfortable situations – whether this is an abortion or a sexually coercive tryst – Wicomb is clearly experimenting with many definitions of deviance. In the titular chapter of the text, for instance, Wicomb displays an almost Joycean awareness of corporeality (for both writers frankly address traditionally taboo topics). However, while Joyce's interests are more scatological and ironic, Wicomb interrogates how the unpredictability of Frieda's desire – whether gastronomic or sexual – is mirrored by the excreting, bleeding female body, particularly when she undergoes an abortion. In this section, the definition of a 'good girl' – wealthy, white, married or chaste and childless – contrasts strongly with her identity as a working-class, coloured, unmarried and un/pregnant woman (Wicomb 1987: 80).

When Frieda is travelling to the abortionist's house, she eavesdrops as a housekeeper on the bus tells her friend that women who have premarital sex must be careful, because most men would not 'have what another has pushed to the side of his plate', like a 'bay leaf and a bone' (71). This metaphor calls to mind Carol J. Adams' landmark feminist-vegetarian monograph *The Sexual Politics of Meat*, which theorizes how patriarchal and carnist cultures intersect and perpetuate each other by positioning women as 'flesh' to be 'consumed' (Adams [1990] 2015: 72). The woman on the bus asserts that even privileged women are subject to objectification and degradation because of their sexual desires or identities. In the case of women of colour, who are likely to be fetishized or animalized, racial identity further intersects with the politics of desire. Yet the woman's friend retorts that purportedly promiscuous women may disgust men who compare them to leftover food like 'yesterday's bean soup, but we women mos know that food put aside and left to stand till tomorrow always has a better flavour' (Wicomb 1987: 71). In the light of Adams' synthesis of feminist theory with ethical vegetarianism, it is interesting that the second woman chooses to refer to a meat-free meal to imply that the sexist trope of leftovers is both inaccurate and indicative of such misogynists' sexual conservatism. Instead of playing into shameful associations of women's flesh and bones with consumption, the woman embraces desire through a metaphor of vegetal excess.

Plant-based foods further figure for thematic tussles between physical embodiment and metaphor as Frieda leaves the bus and walks to meet Michael before the abortion. One of the most important passages of the text uses craving as its point of departure, as she stands before a dried fruit shop and describes its wares:

> Rows of pineapple are the infinite divisions of the sun, the cores lost in the amber discs of mebos arranged in arcs. Prunes are the wrinkled backs of aged goggas beside the bloodshot eyes of cherries. Dark green figs sit pertly on their bottoms

peeping over trays. And I too am not myself, hoping for refuge in a metaphor that will contain it all. I buy the figs and mebos. Desire is a Tsafendas tapeworm in my belly that cannot be satisfied and as I pop the first fig into my mouth I feel the danger fountain with the jets of saliva. Will I stop at one death?

(77)

Gogga is an informal Afrikaans word, derived from the Nama language, which refers to insects or vermin (Kromhout [1952] 1992: 53). In imbuing the fruit with qualities of celestial, animal and human bodies, Wicomb creates a metaphorical hybrid. The above references to infinity and the uncontainable are immediately reflected by Wicomb's deft movement between a range of evocative imageries. All colours of the spectrum (contained in pure sunlight), and the vivid hues of dried fruits, are linked to gruesome images of tapeworms and saliva by a small but crucial clause: the protagonist's reflection on the 'refuge' of 'a metaphor that will contain it all'. This sentence serves as a semantic bridge between the animalized – and anthropomorphized – food and Frieda's return to dwelling on more human matters. Yet it also, importantly, foregrounds how the fruits should be read as both figurative and literal entities. Figs are a particularly interesting choice of symbol. Not only does the concept of the fruit have abstract connections to female sexual embodiment and desire in the Bible (again, one is reminded of Mr Shenton's evocation of the book of Genesis), but furthermore, the origins of *real* figs are equally complex and relevant to Frieda's anxieties about the abortion.

In cases where fig trees cannot self-pollinate, female fig wasps pollinate their inverted flowers. The wasp loses its wings and antennae when it enters the immature fig and dies shortly after laying eggs and pollinating the fruit. The fact that the fig-wasp is essentially ingested by the fruit, and that it dies before its offspring are hatched, is particularly interesting for our discussion of autopoiesis. One cannot but think here of Deleuze and Guattari's wasp–orchid rhizome ([1980] 1987: 11), a model of an interspecies assemblage that is famously discussed in *A Thousand Plateaus*, first translated into English the same year that *You Can't Get Lost in Cape Town* was published. Their model explains how the labellum of an orchid develops to resemble the form of a female wasp in order to be pollinated by a male. In this act, the wasp becomes part of the orchid's reproductive apparatus; yet, the plant-organization also becomes part-wasp. (Although the plant produces an enzyme which breaks down the body and exoskeleton of the insect, there are some who avoid eating figs for fear of ingesting animal content.) This is an expression that accounts for genesis and agency, exceeding dualistic notions of mimicry or representation. It is worth stressing again that neither cross-pollination nor self-pollination is an inherently autopoietic process, but they are often aided by individual living systems' intra-actions. Wicomb's developmental symbol thus holds theoretical resonance with materialist theories of becoming, as well as biological facts of growth.

Another significant association of the fig is the tree that forms its origins. The common name strangler fig refers to a number of species, including some endemic to South Africa, that germinate upon and grow around other trees: they differ from true epiphytes like orchids in that their roots eventually reach the ground. Although they are not actually parasitic organisms, strangler figs often kill the trees they are embedded upon due to accelerated growth and competition for resources. Wicomb is thus approaching the same theme of parasitism that Stockenström does, but with even more layers of nuance surrounding questions of origins and complicity. Frieda's question at the end of the paragraph – 'Will I stop at one death?' – resonates most ambiguously. Sue Marais reads this rhetorical query as evoking the metatextual 'deaths' of Frieda's parents, as she 'kills off' her mother in her earlier stories and then her father in the final section of the text (1995: 40). Yet I contend that the imagery of tantalizing fruit promotes even more forms of textual indeterminacy. It could be read as referring to the death of the wasps which pollinated the figs (food she craves, and is thus likely to overeat). Another alternative is that she is evoking the destructive symbiosis of the strangler fig, the not-quite epiphytic mirror of Deleuze and Guattari's rhizome. Finally, she may be asking whether her lack of discipline with food will lead to further, and more serious, moral transgressions. Thus even before terminating her pregnancy, the protagonist is preoccupied by speculating about ethics at the end or beginning of life; the symbiotic mutualism of fig trees and wasps (and, indeed, strangler figs and other trees) serves as both a metaphorical and literal reminder of consumption and sacrifice, of reproduction and death.

A further complication in this passage is that Frieda imagines her hunger to be driven by a parasite, a 'Tsafendas tapeworm'. Although his name may be unfamiliar to the contemporary reader, at the time of writing Dimitri Tsafendas was infamous, especially amongst South Africans: the parliamentary messenger assassinated apartheid Prime Minister Hendrik Verwoerd in 1966 by stabbing him in the House of Assembly, claiming he acted under the influence of a giant tapeworm that told him what to do. By evoking Tsafendas' name and his crime at several points in the text, Wicomb experiments with utilizing Hendrik Verwoerd's death as an extended metaphor for the ethics and politics surrounding termination. Sitting in the cafeteria, Frieda and Moira discuss the assassination:

> 'Well, do you?' I persist. 'Can you imagine being a member of his family or anyone close to him?
>
> 'No,' she says. 'Do you think there's something wrong with us? Morally deficient?'
>
> 'Dunno. My father would call it inhuman, unchristian. It seems to be as if common humanity is harped on precisely so that we don't have to consider the crucial question of whether we can imagine being a particular human being. Or deal with the implications of the answer. All I can tell of the human condition is that we can always surprise ourselves with thoughts and feelings we never thought we had.'
>
> (Wicomb 1987: 54)

That 'common humanity' is contingent upon the imagination is crucial, particularly because of the human mind's manifold possible responses to tragedy. Here Frieda observes that failure of the imagination may either be because one fails to sympathize (with the 'architect of apartheid', and his family) or because one can foster fellow-feeling (with a murderer, or others who are seen as immoral – as she later will be by anti-abortionists). This exchange between the two young women serves as an important precursor to later narrative developments, especially since Moira is the only person with whom Frieda will discuss the abortion. Tsafendas' may be a frustrated response to the mind that constructed an unthinkable political system, but it is still a horrific and violent act. Frieda's desire to abort the foetus may be read as immoral, but an unsupportable pregnancy would undoubtedly jeopardize her academic and creative careers. Here we are forced to contemplate how abortion may be labelled as murder when such situations are so clearly divorced from one another, and to question how Frieda, as a coloured woman, may be classified just as 'morally deficient' as Tsafendas under apartheid law. Yet at the same time, her suspicion of the rhetoric of choice becomes quite apparent when she imagines that she is 'persecuted by a body of words that performs regardless' of her own wishes, 'making its own choices' (98). The protagonist's fixation on the 'inhuman' and 'unchristian', and her arrival at such ideas through discussing an intellectual written response, is therefore a further extension of the text's concern with the development of dominant discourses surrounding women's bodily and creative autonomy. Even the hybrid-form of a sustained abortive metaphor, it appears, simply cannot 'contain it all'.

In equivocating the narrator's bodily cravings to an organism named after Tsafendas, Wicomb is obviously foregrounding the socio-political setting of 1960s apartheid South Africa and its formative influence upon Frieda. Yet she is also melding politics with the protagonist's personal life and ontological desire for freedom. One is reminded once again of Rosi Braidotti's shared interest in the term desire and its queer potential. The forward-looking trajectory of feminist desire may appear, on the surface, not to be dissimilar to any other narrative *Bildung*. Yet Braidotti's theorization is careful to stress how an understanding of autopoiesis as active and networked is central to this concept. In the case of Wicomb's novel, too, desire cannot be read with only one organism, or species, in mind. Frieda has a lifelong yearning for food, but the fig is a fruit of hybrid origins, an assemblage constitutive of multiple life-forces (to apply Braidotti's wording). After satisfying her craving she does not acknowledge the seed of doubt, or the imaginary tapeworm, until after the operation. Desire is thus an autopoietic force which kickstarts both the protagonist's and the narrative's formation. Wicomb experimentally inverts the deviance that Braidotti diagnoses as symptomatic of patriarchal control. As a man of mixed racial descent, Tsafendas was victimized for his dark skin tone, but nevertheless classified as white by apartheid officials. It is thought that his rejected application to be reclassified as 'coloured' may have provoked the assassination. It is of the utmost importance that the parasite is named after an ambiguously 'white' man: as she goes to meet Michael, it is the body of the oppressor which is coded as deviant. The tapeworm's is a destructive agency that carries death; simultaneously, and even though she is left with 'the kernel of shame' (Wicomb 1987: 86), Frieda recognizes the termination of the foetus has allowed for a different kind of life to emerge. What is inside the gestating body – both the foetus itself and shame that arises from disposing of it like a parasitic organism – is ultimately overridden by a desire to live and thrive.

In Wicomb's novel, men's desires are perpetually rendered just as taboo as the putatively immoral decision to have an abortion – if not more so. One of the first indicators of this fact is Mr Weedon's bizarre behaviour when he visits the village. He is so 'overcome' by 'the earth, baring her bosom of rosy gypsum' that he is 'forced to look away, at a cloud that raced across the sky with such apparent panting that in all decency he had to avert his eyes once again' (6). That the mounds of fertilizer are feminized (both by their pink colour and the comparison to breasts) is more than coincidental. Yet just after fetishizing the environment, Frieda perceives that Weedon sexualizes the male workers, too (7). Environmental systems, women and men are all debased by his racist, libidinal gaze. The man certainly lives up to the phonetics of his name. At best, Weedon is an intruder in the village who founds his success on the labour of others; at worst, it is implied, he is a sexual pest. What one defines as a weed is often dependent on the plant's origins: colloquial usages of the term show that any species that is out of place may be seen as undesirable. This is particularly true of plants that are perceived as reproducing aggressively, as my earlier discussion of strangler figs shows. In a sense, then, the white man's looming presence and desire serves as an important reminder about the sexual violence of colonial and nationalist expansion. Further, it signifies how coloured identity is rooted in histories of sexual coercion, uncertain birth origins and shame.

The pun on Weedon's name takes a further and scatological turn when Frieda recalls a childhood memory of playing house with another male figure: urinating upon her toys, a little boy desecrates a clay shrine she made from the earth (23). Here the protagonist's aesthetic sensibility and creative energies are negated by a perverse action. Even when Frieda grows into adulthood, she continues to view the male body as alien and fearful, particularly when Henry initiates sexual intercourse (123). The sex is not in any way a positive experience; Frieda's uncomfortableness with her own desire results in a confusing and uncommunicative encounter that borders on sexual abuse. There is a line break after this scene, followed by a change of setting: she comes home to her father stooping over a peach tree, and the offer of coffee with cream (124). It is important to note here that immediately after her first kiss with Henry, Frieda is fed canned peaches and cream by her father (116). The reappearance of both foods – one, uncomfortably, the product of the milk separator from her youth – signifies that the heterosexual encounter is not a signifier of personal development for the protagonist. By now it should be clear that there is a distinction to be made between the experimental deviance that Wicomb embraces and the abject actions of men in the text. This is made most apparent when such characters are, ironically, fixating on the supposedly grotesque female form. For example, in the penultimate section Moira's husband Desmond asserts that 'a good figure in your youth is no guarantee against childbearing. There are veins and sagging breasts and of course some women get horribly fat; that is if they don't grow thin and haggard' (147). Frieda is determined not to react to his sexism, choosing instead to focus on the beginnings of a sickening pimple on his chin. Her silent refusal to be objectified, and her reversal of his gaze, speaks of a desire to transform associations of both womanhood and manhood, or domesticity and domination.

Alone with Moira in the domestic environment of the kitchen, Frieda speaks freely with her friend for the first time about the abortion and her relationship with Michael. It is only when she is offered one of the children's bedrooms that she feels any sense of bodily shame: 'grotesque in the Lilliputian world of the child', Frieda cannot fit into a tiny chair and struggles to sleep in the 'chaste little bed', with her eyes following 'a mad moth circling the rabbit-shaped lamp by the side of the bed' (162). Once again the narrator is likened to Gulliver; yet, in this instance it is not in his diminutive form; she has grown since seeing Henry in the doctors' rooms. It is crucial that the shapeshifting moth reappears at this moment, but this time, it is together with an aesthetic object, shaped in the form of a rabbit. This symbol of irrepressible fecundity reinforces that neither her failed relationships with Michael nor Henry cause the narrator to discover herself. Rather, it is the fact that she is finally able to discuss creation and failure with another woman of colour. I develop this point further in the final section of this chapter, exploring the text's formal experimentations with autopoiesis and the female writer-narrator as a creative force.

Creative formations

Viewing its ten standalone segments from the outside (or the contents page), *You Can't Get Lost in Cape Town*'s very form is suggestive of autopoietic self-containment. Yet when one reviews each section's contents, sustained thematic preoccupations of the text quickly become apparent. This could cause one to receive it as if it is an allopoietic – or, as Dempster and Haraway would say, sympoietic – system which is organizationally open. A recent example of such a reading is Meg Samuelson's 'Oceanic Histories and Protean Poetics: The Surge of the Sea in Zoë Wicomb's Fiction'. Samuelson's fascinating study is, by necessity, a brief overview that analyses the titular section (2010: 544–6); it would be even more interesting to consider how the river-estuary's flow in 'Home Sweet Home' connects with, and possibly extends, this oceanic imagery. Nevertheless, extrapolating the text's overall meaning as merely allopoietic/ sympoietic would ironically adhere to a rather limited and closed understanding of self-referentiality. The failure of reproduction or allopoiesis in the narrative structure – from Frieda's abortion to her coercive separation from South Africa, and the subsequent decline of the apartheid regime – asks for a different reading to be performed. Developing an analogously literary approach from Braidotti's theorization that the whole of each living system holds as much moral worth as each of its parts, we can analyse formal elements which recur throughout the entire text, and explore how they interact with Wicomb's thematic formations – and negations – of desire. Creating a bodily *Bildung* from plant-based lifeforms to more developed living systems, the text presents a perverse and forward-looking understanding of intra-actions and separations. Once again, we are reminded of the parallel between the metaphorical tapeworm and the aborted foetus. Frieda's supposed deviance is actually indicative of development, but in an autopoietic, rather than allopoietic, sense.

In one of her aforementioned essays, Wicomb writes appreciatively of Toni Morrison's 'curious use of deixis. The discourse refuses to provide unambiguous referents for "I", "me", "you", "this", "now"' (1990: 151). Operating in the legacy of Morrison's experimentation, *You Can't Get Lost in Cape Town* features similarly obscure and subjective interpretations: an intertextual signifier of germinating identities. This is particularly apparent when the narrative switches between female referents in 'A Clearing in the Bush'. There is a sudden change to focalization through Tamieta (Wicomb 1987: 37), followed by first-person narration and then a return to 'she, Tamieta' analysing Frieda Shenton, 'the girl' who 'speaks English' (46). To make matters more confusing, the same narrative technique is utilized in the story of a character named Skitterboud's wife, which is embedded in his conversation with Frieda in 'A Fair Exchange' (136). These changes in perspective are only sometimes accompanied by a line break. Wicomb's disjointed narrative style is further displayed when the protagonist remembers unwelcome sexual advances from several men on two different continents in 'Behind the Bougainvillea' (122). Another instance of deixis is presented in 'Home Sweet Home' when an older Frieda converses with Oom Dawid, who talks about 'the white stones of our mother's grave on the koppie' (95). The man may not be her literal uncle (the Shentons' extended familial connections are rarely verbalized), but he is significantly older than her, which raises questions about who exactly 'our' mother may be, or why he chooses to use the collective pronoun. Paradoxes abound even in the very language of her home community. The Afrikaans phrase *ja-nee* literally means yes-no (94), but is used colloquially to signal agreement. It is repeated by both Oom Dawid and Frieda's own father: 'Father licks his bone conscientiously and says, "Ja-nee" with the sense of the equivocal born out of watching rainclouds gather over the arid earth and then disperse. "Ja-nee" he repeats' (83–4). This quotation is of interest for several reasons, not least of all its subtle reference to Bessie Head's *When Rain Clouds Gather* (1968). Merging Modernist literary techniques like repetition with language from the local community, Wicomb experiments with creating a modern South African woman's Bildungsroman. The split of this feminist *Bildung* is navigated in material(ist) terms, as the above actions evoke an earlier conversation between two female characters about the paradox of men treating desirable women as 'leftovers'. Modernism and its deictic legacy thus foreground the manner in which discourse develops and is maintained, and how this is central to understanding Frieda's creative formation through autopoiesis.

In addition to intertextual references to European Modernist novels (and Western Judeo-Christian scripts), there are also elements of semi-autobiography, and instances where South African historical events merge with the fictional narrative. One of the many changes in focalization reverts to Frieda thinking that her essay deadline has been extended by 'a pet abdominal tapeworm' that 'hissed persuasively into the ear of its Greek host, whose trembling hand grew still for a second to aim a fatal shot at the Prime Minister' (39). The assignment she is writing is on Hardy's *Tess of the D'Urbervilles* ([1891] 2003), a novel which evokes nothing but confusion in the narrator. Although she internalizes that 'Murder is a sin which should outrage all decent and civilised people' (42), she appears not to judge Tess – a character whose tragic fate is precipitated not by her own ambitions but by the failures of *others*. The timing and topic of the essay emphasize how Tsafendas's crime is a central key to understanding the supposed tragedies which Frieda either suffers or commits, depending on one's views on abortion. Tragedy, as a literary form, is discussed in further detail in my subsequent chapter on Yvonne Vera.

If the issues of language and metaphors mean it is unclear whether self-formation is achieved or not, then it is worth turning to one final manifestation of a creative form: that of the motherly figure, which reappears in the last section. Mrs Shenton is initially outraged by her daughter's stories, reading her absence – assumedly, the earlier sections of the text – as immoral and disrespectful (163). She is particularly offended by the mention of an abortion, implying that this, too, is quite literally mortifying: 'You've killed me over and over so it was quite unnecessary to invent my death' (172). Both the racial and sexual associations of shame intersect and are epitomized by the narrator's mother, and Frieda, in turn, internalizes these feelings. Yet while the narrative terminates without explicitly articulating her fate, it is important to stress that the concluding section does clarify that neither she nor Wicomb has written out the maternal figure. The appearance of various motherly women in later stages of the text suggests that Frieda finds self-acceptance through nurturing female relationships and non-reproductive parenting. Her sexual naïveté and bodily discomfort are first discussed when she reunites with Moira (155). Next, her Aunt Cissie joins her in the airport bathroom, leading to another almost Joycean exchange about beans and samp while both women urinate (167–8). Their discussion is also a reminder of similar vegetarian dishes in the text: *sousboontjies* (a stewed bean dish), *stamp-en-stoot* (beans and maize) and the bean soup that is mentioned in the conversation between two other female characters in the titular story. Given that beans are the *seeds* of leguminous plants, this recurrence appears more than coincidental.

The ultimate signifier of the protagonist's identity formation, however, is the manner in which she grows to care for her mother. Although Frieda writes Mrs Shenton back into the text after a conversation with Moira about how she would not be a good mother, it is significant that she is tending to the grieving maternal figure in the final scene. Her visit takes a crucial turn when she agrees to drive her mother to the Gifberge, a mountain range which her dead father always promised they would visit. When hiking up the mountain, she is no longer an insecure and anxious girl who desires to morph into a foetal form. One is reminded of the earlier inversion of patriarchal infantilization: here the parent is physically weak, while her child offers to drive and informs her of the correct colloquial names for flora (180). After the long disappearance of the maternal figure, the now-adult narrator discusses issues ranging from her ancestors to hair straightening with another woman of colour. This is not to say that the women hold identical beliefs. Frieda is hyperaware of discursive violence, viewing nationalist symbols with suspicion and confessing that she has 'no desire' to trespass on a farm for a better view of the valley (180). The fact that she and her mother do not agree on these issues is an important aspect of her self-formation – it suggests that conversations about women must be made between them, and that sometimes ethical solutions are not easily presentable. Yet she and her mother do reach something of an understanding as they see proteas growing on the fertile land and hum a folk song together that compares a young woman to South Africa's national flower (177). Immediately Frieda asserts that she is only singing ironically about this nationalist symbol, and she further mocks her mother for asking her to uproot a protea bush so she can take it home. Her mother is quick to retort that 'those who put their stamp on things may see in it their own histories and hopes. But a bush is a bush; it doesn't become what people think they inject into it' (181). Here her mother reminds her, surprisingly, that agency lies in materialist resistance. The protea represents the autopoietic process that the narrator undergoes: her development is not from reproducing with men, but from expressing care for her mother by taking her to an unnamed and untouched land. It is implied that while the refuge of a metaphor is a fabrication, women of colour may find autonomy by venturing forth into the material world and rejecting nationalists' purported power over the landscape.

Shortly before Frieda meets her mother in the final section, Aunt Cissie informs her relatives that 'it never rains but it pours; still, every cloud has a silver lining', and then concludes that 'these thoughts must sprout' in the ears of the young (169). In contrast to these clichéd homilies, Frieda's 'terrible stories' may seem deviant and bizarre (182). Yet the formation of her identity from a young girl into a feminist writer and her interactions with various women from her youth demonstrate the importance of language in creating and sustaining one's cultural identity. The final section of the text offers a transformative perspective on uprooting the seeds of various oppressions. Frieda continually alludes to hybrid forms: a mule, parasitic tapeworms, the wasp–fig assemblage or even animist fables interacting with Judeo-Christian symbolic systems (which are also concerned with personal development). Adopting a caregiving role as a childless adult, she too grows to embody a transgressive formation of literal and figurative miscegenation. Rather than an interlinked short story collection, her narrative operates as an experimental engagement with the Bildungsroman genre, full of ruptures and terminations. All ten sections are formations that undo the erasure of female and foetal forms in controlling and colonialist discourse. There is a cumulative effect of formal developments, causing the text to form an autopoietic system of self-sustaining references and images. Ironically, Frieda reaches the point of locating potential agency by voluntarily separating herself from the supposed Mother Country and choosing to discuss the naturalization of gender roles with women of colour. The mother is not dead; the narrator has come to confront her desires. If anything has been killed to achieve this formation, it is the violent rhetoric that simultaneously sexualizes and infantilizes women who opt out of reproductive parenthood.

Notes

1   This is not to say that the Bildungsroman form is necessarily masculinist. For several feminist studies of (predominantly white and Western) Bildungsromane, see *The Voyage In: Fictions of Female Development* edited by Elizabeth Abel, Marianne Hirsch, and Elizabeth Langland (1983).

2   For more on this philosophy, see Catherine Obianuju Acholonu (1995).

3 See Chapters 1 and 4 for further discussions of how gynaecological phenomena were associated with witchcraft.

4 For more on abortion and birth control in South African urban settings during the twentieth century, see Catherine Burns (2004).

5 The final chapter of Jean Rhys's *Voyage in the Dark* ([1934] 2000) concludes with an abortion scene, while Virginia Woolf's *Between the Acts* ([1941] 1992) refers to a 1938 newspaper article about Dr Alex Bourne, who was arrested for performing an abortion on a fourteen-year-old rape victim, as Stuart N. Clarke notes in a 1990 article in *Virginia Woolf Miscellany*. I discuss abortion and Olive Schreiner's *The Story of an African Farm* in Chapter 3.

6 British legal scholar William Blackstone notes that the quickening has historically been used to determine whether or not a terminated pregnancy constitutes murder, homicide or manslaughter ([1765] 1979: 388). Many – but not all – people still see this to be an important milestone in a foetus's development, although it does not affect contemporary laws such as the 1996 South African CTOP.

7 Hemingway's short story 'Hills Like White Elephants' (1927) is one of the most well-known and commonly taught examples of a fictional abortion narrative, as demonstrated by its presence on the reading list at the University Still Known as Rhodes that I discuss in my introduction.

8 For further discussion of this language and infantilization, see Chapter 1.

9 For an analysis of milk's metaphorical role in Wicomb's oeuvre – particularly *October* – see Caitlin E. Stobie (2018).

10 See Christina Hauck for a study of abortion and 'reproductive failure' in European and American Modernism (2003: 225).

3

Minerals

The in/organic tragedy of Yvonne Vera's *Butterfly Burning*

The previous chapter advances a transformative definition of development, equating it with autopoietic processes of formation rather than linear models of growth. Zimbabwean author Yvonne Vera further transforms associations of development and crossovers between literal and metaphorical birthings in her 1998 prize-winning novel, *Butterfly Burning*, which tells the story of a rural woman who self-induces an abortion. In her preface to *Opening Spaces: Contemporary African Women's Writing*, Vera recalls a scene from Haile Gerima's film *Sankofa* (1993) in which a pregnant woman's corpse mysteriously gives birth after she is whipped to death (1999: 1). At the conclusion of her commentary, she returns to the theme of fertility by proclaiming that the authors of the collected stories are 'witnesses, in that seemingly impossible birth' of African feminist fiction (Vera 1999: 5). Yet throughout *Opening Spaces* – and *Butterfly Burning* – it is the fear of childbirth which recurs for those living in rural and urban environments previously colonized by the British 'motherland'. Written after the 'birth' of postcolonial Zimbabwe in 1980, but set in colonial Rhodesia during the 1940s, Vera's novel utilizes natural elements to figure for reproductive anxieties in previously colonized locations.

This chapter argues that Vera foregrounds interconnected material systems similar to the ecological model of abortion stigma that I discuss in my introduction – creative forms which repeatedly manifest in her work include human, animal, vegetal, elemental or textual participants in ecosystems. After contextualizing my analysis with an overview of the discourse of tragedy that surrounds both literal and literary discussions of reproductive agency, I perform a close reading of the termination of pregnancy in *Butterfly Burning*, paying particular attention to the interplay of organic and inorganic forces. Next I analyse the second abortion scene, which is often completely overlooked by critics in favour of reading the protagonist's suicide as the text's ultimate tragedy. The final chapter of the novel, I argue, resonates with various earlier appearances of in/organic agencies throughout the text. Having scrutinized these crucial (and hitherto under-investigated) passages and themes, the chapter concludes by considering how postcolonial feminism in the broader social and geographical context of southern Africa transforms the text's aesthetics, and, by extension, its ethical impetus to exceed humanist discourse.

Set in the Makokoba township of Bulawayo during 1946, *Butterfly Burning* is a short novel about a young woman named Phephelaphi who develops a sexual relationship with an older man named Fumbatha. Over the course of the predominantly third-person narrative, it is revealed that the protagonist was raised by two sex workers: Zandile, her biological mother, abandons her in infancy, leaving her in the care of her friend Gertrude. The domestic drama of Phephelaphi's upbringing foregrounds reproductive health as a primary thematic concern, which is reinforced when an unsupportable pregnancy impedes upon her plans to train as a nurse, resulting in a self-induced abortion. The text is composed of twenty-one brief vignettes – the more lyrical of which, on the surface, may seem to have little or no impact upon what many have read as its 'tragic' central plot point (see Lunga 2002: 193; Primorac 2002: 107; Shaw 2002: 92). Yet despite such assessments of the abortion as a central conflict in the storyline, the literary event of the procedure remains relatively unexamined; Ranka Primorac's otherwise comprehensive analysis, for example, mentions in parentheses that the 'ritual' of abortion is 'superbly described in chapter 16' (2002: 106), but only engages very briefly with quotations from this chapter (which, at fourteen pages, is the longest of the novel). Instead, most studies of the novel to date have focused on elements such as musical imagery, urban space and repetitive time. There have been some discussions of materiality in *Butterfly Burning*, such as Sarah Nuttall's consideration of how material 'things' come to signify intersubjectivity between subjects and objects (2005: 186). I am less concerned with cities and assemblages, focusing instead on how human reproduction is represented through – and transformed by – materialist ecologies in the novel. Critics have failed to address the transformative ambiguities that surround the supposed tragedy of Phephelaphi's decision to terminate her second pregnancy by committing suicide. Performing a close reading of the first abortion scene – which unfolds over a strikingly large amount of discourse time – and the novel's final chapter, I argue that Vera anticipates and exceeds the work of several new materialists by resisting repronormative understandings of gender dynamics and social development. The two terminations of pregnancy in *Butterfly Burning* explore materialist elements of southern African feminisms, thereby foregrounding issues relating to reproductive agency as well as the philosophical ramifications of treating all entities as political agents. The novel aestheticizes animate and inanimate co-implications, but Vera's investment in centralizing women's agency means that the text ultimately formulates a feminist ethics while still bearing witness to ongoing and intersectional social struggles.

Transforming 'rock bottom'

Yvonne Vera died from AIDS-related meningitis in 2005. She was just forty years old but had published one short story collection and five novels – frustratingly for critics and readers alike, her sixth manuscript titled *Obedience* remained unfinished – and attracted significant international acclaim for using literature to thematize ethically charged issues like abortion, incest, infanticide and rape. The writer lived in her country of birth until 1987, when she chose to read for her BA, MA and PhD at York University in Toronto. Although she returned to Zimbabwe for a few years preceding her final trip to Canada, Vera's personal, professional and academic papers are currently housed at her alma mater; much of my argument in this chapter is informed by research from her recently re-catalogued fonds in the Clara Thomas Archives and Special Collections.

As Sarah Kastner notes, it may initially seem difficult to reconcile the 'silence-breaking' reputation of Vera's fiction with the fact that she chose not to disclose her HIV-positive status during her lifetime (2016: 213). The contrast between her public and private personas becomes more apparent when reviewing her records and letters: even in emails to close friends and family members, her health is often elided as a topic of conversation. Although HIV medicines were being developed in the early 2000s, the virus was declared as the leading cause of death in Africa by the WHO in 1999 and as the biggest killer in sub-Saharan Africa by UNAIDS in 2002, and social stigmas about homosexuality, racialized poverty or overgeneralized risk factors were still fairly widespread. Some may therefore be tempted to read the author's silence as an indication of the tragic disjuncture between literary ethics and lived realities during the AIDS epidemic. Yet I follow Kastner in resisting this urge. Could it be the case that Vera's decision not to discuss her diagnosis is actually indicative of agency, particularly a decision to prioritize her artwork and resist being read as a victim? Kastner argues convincingly that by 'assigning agency to the land that is not determined by human meaning', Vera's fiction 'claims an insurgent form of agency in her own silence' (2016: 224). Following Chapter 1's reflections on an ethics of attentive listening in *The Expedition to the Baobab Tree*, I am interested in further exploring how *Butterfly Burning*, another abortion narrative culminating in suicide, surpasses human (and humanist) meanings in aestheticizing silence, indeterminacy and agency.

Like Zoë Wicomb, whose literary debut was published eleven years prior to *Butterfly Burning*, Yvonne Vera's fiction thematizes ecological and reproductive agency in southern African environments. An earlier manuscript of *Nehanda* (1993) contains many moments of multispecies growth (fittingly, this version of the novel is titled *Bird of Bright Plumage*). A densely imaginative example examines ceremonies and rituals surrounding childbirth: old men borrow lives from the branches of trees, passing images to future selves through dreams, while women see new people birthing themselves and growing out of thin air (Vera n.d.: 161). Most notable here is the way the living and the unborn, the present and the future, are melded through transformative repetitions (Vera n.d.: 161). Related to this meshing of chronologies, it is worth noting Vera changes this passage – which remains otherwise almost exactly the same – to the present tense in the final version of *Nehanda* (1993). Waking from dreams of labour, women are imagined as toddlers when they rise and seemingly learn to walk again. Elderly men at the brink of death are also involved in this dreamlike conversation with those who are yet to be born. Yet the links between the villagers and nonhuman agencies exceed biological connotations of materialist interconnections. They are demonstrative of an understanding of personal development that is measured through intersecting continuums, rather than the teleological model which colonial chronologies proffer. Traditional associations of birth with festivity and death with tragedy are likewise called into question. This has radical implications for many rites of passage celebrating life stages, but the evocation of the so-called unborn foregrounds how abortion, too, is transformed when reading ideas of growth in this new light.

Tragedy is perhaps one of the most easily recognizable literary forms: tragedies often involve a hubristic tempting of fate leading to the protagonist hitting 'rock bottom', the death of one or more characters and, ultimately, an unhappy ending. Although tragedies often feature dramatic plots and many classic examples are plays (such as Greek tragedies or Shakespeare's dramas), it is important to note that tragedy, as a literary form, is not synonymous with theatrical work. In this study I dissociate tragedy from dramatization, favouring discussion of the novel form. Paul Hammond studies examples from classical, renaissance and neo-classical literature in *The Strangeness of Tragedy* to argue that tragic protagonists are estranged from their environments through the genre's transformation of language, space and time. The temporal is perhaps the most obvious dimension where this displacement is apparent; in contrast to comedy, Hammond notes, 'tragedy forces events to their conclusion, refusing time for reflection and repentance and recovery' (2009: 7). One should note that postcolonial literature is not included in his discussion. There are so many variations of tragedy – including works such as Wole Soyinka's Yoruba dramas that destabilize the genre's apparent Eurocentricism[1] – that it is worth pausing to consider to what extent Vera's thematic treatment of ethical dilemmas is participating in this literary tradition. Yet similarly to Hammond, postcolonial critic David Scott explicitly addresses the fact that tragedy is tied to circular understandings of time (Scott 2014: 801). Through an analysis of Orlando Patterson's novel *The Children of Sisyphus* ([1964] 2012), Scott argues that the tragic vision in the postcolonial text is 'in effect, a structure of anomic, Sisyphean repetition' (2014: 805), and that in 'such a world it is scarcely possible *not* to choose badly, no matter what the context of *choice*' (2014: 806; original emphasis). Scott's point is immediately reinforced by the reference to Greek mythology in Patterson's title.[2] From the shared concerns of Hammond and Scott, one can deduce that cyclical chronologies define the tragic form. Unavoidable recurrences appear in tragedies from classical literature to contemporary writing; in a sense, then, the very repetition *of repetition* as a technique and theme is the tragic genre's primary defining marker. Repetition figures as both a lack of choice on the part of the characters and the fact that the author is bound to certain literary conventions which have been rehearsed since antiquity.

The result of evoking repetition through a text's content and form is that agency – both of the human protagonist and of the forces who may or may not determine the future – is complicated, particularly as 'the boundaries of the human world, and of the human self, become permeable' (Hammond 2009: 12). In canonical tragedies, this often involves imbuing abstract concepts like Fate or Justice with agency. In the case of Vera's novel, I will argue, all matter is imbued with agency to complicate the nature of tragedy itself. Scott takes a Hegelian approach to the tragic and its destabilizing of human actions and agency, arguing that in contrast to melodrama's tendency to prioritize one actor in a conflict, postcolonial tragedies present both forces in a confrontation with equal legitimacy (2014: 801). His reading of such subjective indeterminacy has radical implications for the discursive treatment of ethics at the beginning and end of human life. The termination of pregnancy is, after all, often figured as tragedy in literary and public discourse (whether this is by those who vehemently oppose the procedure and catastrophize it as murder, or by those who support it but with the clause that it is a 'last resort' for desperate cases only).

Let us ignore for a moment the fact that abortion does not necessarily result in trauma. In fact, let us go further and accept the claim that abortion is tragic. If this is the case, and if tragedy involves the confrontation of two or more equally legitimate sets of interests, then what does this say about the comparative worth of the developing foetus and the pregnant person? One must conclude that both the foetus and woman are growing agencies, not that one life is more sacrosanct than the other. The rhetoric of tragedy thus ironically does not serve the purpose which anti-abortion activists would have it do – that is, privileging a foetus's 'rights' over the wellbeing of a woman. It seems, then, that there is a disjuncture between tragedy as literary event (traditionally associated with unavoidable disaster, the thwarting of one's agency) and form (a more indeterminate matter, encompassing moments of both death and development).

Scott argues that despite readings of supposedly unrelenting pessimism in *The Children of Sisyphus*, the novel is a generative site in which postcolonial themes like nationalism and political sovereignty and tragic themes such as conflicting actions and agencies are united for both ethical and political purposes (2014: 802). This ethical-political problematization of nationalism is rife in Vera's academic work, as I shall discuss in further detail shortly, and has also become something of a marker of her oeuvre in the academy. In an introduction to a special issue of *Research in African Literatures* on Vera's fiction, Liz Gunner and Neil Ten Kortenaar rightly assert that 'both Vera and [Dambudzo] Marachera re-vision history away from the impassioned cultural nationalism of the songs of liberation [...]. Both distance themselves from the nationalist romance genre of some postliberation Shona fiction' (Gunner and Ten Kortenaar 2007: 2). Yet, much like those critics whom Scott claims have overdetermined Patterson's cynicism, Gunner and Ten Kortenaar move from this fascinating point to declaring that Vera's fiction is largely marked by 'pessimism' (2007: 4). I would argue against the equation of ethically challenging material with moral pessimism. I also use the term termination of pregnancy in deliberate contrast to Gunner and Ten Kortenaar's 'pregnant mothers [who] abort' (2007: 3): the latter wording frames the pregnant person in the future tense, normalizing the desired outcome of fertilization as motherhood. Is Vera's narration of terminations of pregnancy really indicative of an 'absence of ordinariness' (Gunner and Ten Kortenaar 2007: 3–4), or are we erroneously assuming that abortion is not a regularly contemplated reality for women lacking access to reliable contraception in southern Africa? Echoing my earlier question about reading Vera's silence as a generative act, could it be that we are not listening to the transformative potential of tragedy as an aesthetic form?

Unprovoked, in an interview with literary scholar Ranka Primorac, Yvonne Vera announces how abortion is a most misunderstood theme in her fiction: 'It's an unspeakable theme and anyone who I've seen in Zimbabwe has omitted to mention that [*Butterfly Burning*] is about abortion' (Vera in Primorac 2004: 160). This seeming squeamishness on the press's part is proven by the author's archives. Of all her recorded correspondence with Zimbabwean and international journalists, the only mention of abortion is found in questions for an interview by Sebastiano Triulzi, who astutely moves from discussing medical ethics to asking whether the dialogic elements of Vera's fiction suggest a melding of Modernist and African literary traditions (2004–5: par. 7–9). Triulzi's notes were sent to Vera for publication in *l'Espresso*, the political and cultural magazine of the Italian newspaper *la Repubblica*: although she initially replied in February 2005 to say that 'circumstances' were preventing her timely response to the interview questions, the reality was that Vera's health was rapidly declining, and unfortunately she did not send her answers before her death in April of the same year. In contrast to Triulzi's fascinating line of enquiry, journalistic features for *Worldpress* and *The Sunday Mail: Zimbabwe News Online* discuss how Vera 'breaks the silence' by writing of rape, incest and infanticide (Soros 2002: par. 2), but abortion remains curiously unaddressed even when *Butterfly Burning* is mentioned by name.

This omission seems particularly bizarre when one considers how abortion informs not only the novel's plot, but the very origins of its author's life. *Petal Thoughts* is a biography of Yvonne Vera written by her mother, Ericah Gwetai, which opens with the striking confession that her daughter was the result of a so-called unwanted pregnancy ([2008] 2009: loc. 11).[3] Gwetai was impregnated by Jerry Vera at the age of seventeen. Faced with the shame of disclosing to her parents that she had fallen pregnant out of wedlock, Gwetai approached a friend who had previously had an abortion and asked her to terminate her pregnancy; when this proved unsuccessful, she visited a doctor who gave her a tonic, claiming it was an abortifacient ([2008] 2009: loc. 15). Despite her account that several strangers seemed unbothered by her teen pregnancy ([2008] 2009: loc. 12) – and her partner's support of her decision to abort the foetus – Gwetai surmised that the doctor's prescription of fake medicine was intentional ([2008] 2009: loc. 15). After this encounter, she chose not to terminate the pregnancy and was thus forced to abandon her studies in nursing. From this (auto)biographical story, we see several themes and events that recur throughout Vera's novel. We also are confronted by complex, conflicting attitudes towards extramarital sex, pregnancy and abortion in post/colonial Zimbabwe.

The origins of Zimbabwe's Termination of Pregnancy Act – first passed in 1977 and still operational in the present day – reveal it is one of the most restrictive laws regulating reproductive health in southern Africa. The Act was passed before the country gained independence in 1980, and is thus grounded in Roman-Dutch Common law, a product of the Rhodesian government's conservative, Christian ideology. Abortion is conditionally legal under Section 4 of the Act, which states that a pregnancy may only be terminated if there is risk that the foetus will be born with congenital, mental or physical defects or if the woman's life or physical health is endangered (Mbanje 2015: 3). The mental health of the pregnant person is not deemed worthy of consideration. Yet, with extramarital pregnancy often resulting in expulsion from school or employment (as exemplified in *Butterfly Burning*), it remains evident that illegal abortions will continue to be sought by women for reasons other than those detailed in the 1977 Act.[4] Supposedly advanced laws may therefore result in restrictive legal praxis, such as the regulation that at least two doctors' consent must be obtained before an abortion can be performed. The result is that many women in contemporary Zimbabwe seek illegal abortions at the risk of illness or death. Brooke R. Johnson et al. report that approximately a fifth of so-called maternal deaths in Zimbabwe from the late 1980s to early 1990s were as a result of complications from unsafe abortions (2002: 195); furthermore, nearly 5 per cent of the participants in their study on postabortion family planning intervention and education died (Johnson et al. 2002: 201).

With a history of missionary schools and imperialist outreach programmes, Zimbabwe remains a predominantly Christian nation. Furthermore, in repronormative traditions such as Shona culture, it is generally understood that a woman's predominant societal purpose is to have children. If both baby and mother face the risk of health complications after delivery, caretakers tend to prioritize stabilizing the former's health.[5] An additional dimension of traditional gendered roles and reproduction relates to the legacies of Zimbabwean liberation movements from the 1970s, as feminist historian Kate Law notes. Law observes that one of the most popular slogans of the Zimbabwe African National Liberation Army (ZANLA) was 'Forward with the Mothers! Forward with the Cooking Stick!' (2021: 252). Women were thus typically encouraged to contribute to the struggle by staying in rural areas and caring for children. Even after the country's liberation and associated sexual revolution of the 1980s, when many gained greater access to birth control, women were still discouraged from using contraception – leading to increased reports of child abandonment and infanticide, which were seen as direct threats to both normative femininity and Zimbabwe's new 'African' identity (Law 2021: 256–7). Much as in the case of post/apartheid South Africa, changes to legislation surrounding (and even access to) reproductive health did not necessarily change cultural norms about feminism and motherhood. These observations support the wariness that I detail in my introductory chapter about framing decolonization as a singular moment that precipitates nation-wide change. Considering colonial legacies of gestational violence, African nationalist movements that utilize maternalist metaphors, and traditional cultures which evaluate foetuses as more important than pregnant people, it remains unlikely that Zimbabwe's Termination of Pregnancy Act will be revised – or even revisited – in the near future.

There are some popular beliefs in southern Africa that ritual cleansing is necessary for improving a woman's fertility, either in the weeks following an abortion or when women are trying to conceive (Hodes 2016: 92). Yet, although the force of ritual is important in some of her work, Vera resists traditionalist tropes in her depiction of the physical procedure of abortion. Ritual seems somewhat ill-fitting when applied to abortion in particular, given the word's association with sequential rites that are often performed in religious and communal settings; although solemn and more commonplace than one might believe, abortions are hardly normalized as ceremonial cultural customs. Furthermore, it is vital to note that the emphasis in traditional rituals is to exacerbate a woman's fertility; abortion is not seen as a rite of passage so much as an undesirable event to be rectified or circumvented. Nancy Rose Hunt cites the example of women who were forced by both colonial authorities and Meru chiefs to perform their initiation ceremonies earlier than planned so as to avoid any unsupportable pregnancies and resulting abortions (2007: 301). As I discuss in my previous chapters (and particularly in the case of Wicomb's fiction), the residual association of terminations of pregnancy with shame and even witchcraft means that abortion is not a ritual per se. Vera conveys both fertility rites and abortion through the literary technique of repetition, but this one commonality is not sufficient evidence to label the latter as rituals, as Primorac does (2002: 206). Rather, these transformative repetitions reflect a broader experimentation with tragedy as literary event and form.

I have already expressed that most readings of the novel state Phephelaphi dies 'tragically' (Hunt 2007: 296); furthermore, Nancy Rose Hunt reads the protagonist's suicide as an 'alternative' to abortion, a point which my later literary analysis contests. Helen Cousins' reading of abortion, infanticide and

sterility in Vera's work, however, provides interesting insights that I wish to
develop further. She supplies a critical interrogation of Zimbabwean parenting
in *Butterfly Burning* (Cousins 2010: 37), arguing that Vera is making a cultural
point about constructions of motherhood in Africa and Zimbabwe (2010: 32).
Cousins' most original contribution is her focus on both motherhood and
fatherhood and 'how men can be integrated as responsible nurturers through
"mothering"' (2010: 38). Although her reading of gendered roles is not framed
through queer theory, I find it to be a most intriguing and productive starting-
point. While pursuing Cousins' line of inquiry, the emphases in my study are
somewhat different: my reading grapples with the land (both its aridity and
fecundity) and interrogates graphic biological imagery in both abortion scenes.
Furthermore, I am more concerned with reproductive agency than the issue of
parenting (be this maternity or paternity). My literary analysis focuses on literal
and figurative birthings: the latter includes 'birth of the nation' tropes as well as
gestational implications of the novel's colonial setting (Rhodesia). Both of these
figurative models of birth are rejected in the text, without clear alternatives
emerging in their place. In this sense, the novel is as sceptical of liberationist as
of paternalistic rhetoric, though perhaps most suspicious of the usurpation of
such discourse by nationalist interests.

Returning to her interview with Primorac, Vera continues to explain why
Butterfly Burning's narrator describes the full process of terminating her
pregnancy. She is careful to stress the material reality of how the abortion is
induced, tackling subject matter which many Zimbabweans view as unthinkable:

> How can I write about thorns and such things? But I wanted to. And I felt very
> much that I wanted to write a novel about my own city. About the people here.
> About the land. And this story when it developed, as I was writing it, I wanted
> to incorporate into the body of the story the land itself. Elements of it. You
> know, how [Phephelaphi, the novel's heroine] feels. In that chapter you can see
> that it opens with a wish, a feeling which heralds the emotion of what kind of
> vegetation she would like to experience, that would liberate, that would give her
> some freedom [...] and the land is implicated in the act.
>
> (Vera in Primorac 2004: 161)

From these words one can infer that the novel's organic and elemental imagery
serves a vital purpose in conveying emotional content with an ethical impetus.
I use the word vital in this description of Vera's feminist ethics to deliberately
evoke the queer vitality presented by Bessie Head's fictional corpus; it is
of no coincidence, I would argue, that the Zimbabwean author references

Head in both her Master's thesis (1991: 8) and her doctoral dissertation (1995: 279).[6] Phephelaphi's corporeal agency is not merely mirrored by the metaphorical state of the vegetal landscape. Rather, the environment comes to acquire its own agency which intermingles with, and even determines, her decision to abort the unsupportable foetus. The vegetation is not a source of nourishment or comfort. Its agency is far more duplicitous and even violent in some aspects, challenging repronormative views by exceeding humanist associations of reproductive health with rights. As the writer herself states, this novel's crucial contribution to society is to 'go into the moment of the abortion, and say it; and moment-by-moment of a woman's feeling of tenderness towards herself, and violence towards herself: both those things' (Vera in Primorac 2004: 166). Thus, while the novel does not didactically privilege a singular point of view, its duplicity clearly centralizes *women's* feelings about agency. In short, its experimentation with the ecological model of abortion stigma does not detract from feminist issues, but rather illustrates a richly intersectional and ethical approach to storytelling.

The new environment of an independent Zimbabwe is also at the forefront of these concerns about literary figurations of landscape and ecology. In her Master's thesis on images of women in Chinua Achebe's writing, Vera criticizes the Negritude movement as an exemplary ideology that attempts to positively reclaim African identities and origins through nationalistic myths of maternity – particularly the Mother Africa trope used by men to describe African women in idealistic poetry (1991: 2). The Mother Africa trope creates homogeneous portraits of both womanhood and the African continent.[7] Woman is figured as inherently nurturing, even before taking on a maternal role; national politics and particularities are overlooked in favour of an idealized and gendered origin of cultural roots.[8] Vera is thus clearly disillusioned by postcolonial theories and literatures that fail to address material reality or that create negative and/ or unrealistic representations of women. Analysing Achebe's novel *No Longer at Ease* ([1960] 2001), she argues that the character Clara's abortion thematizes a conflict between traditional and modern values (Vera 1991: 83), but there are several dissatisfying outcomes of merely turning from mythologized representations of maternity to an equally clichéd representation of modern womanhood as callous or unfeeling. One major concern is the predicament of those who cannot mother, who face emotional and social problems for something that is ultimately not their choice (Vera 1991: 94). But perhaps most crucial is the fact that Achebe does not narrate the abortion from Clara's point of view, choosing instead to focus on a male character's perceptions of the event

(Vera 1991: 83). Writing at least seven years before the publication of her own fictional abortion narrative, it is conceivable that this is a formative realization for Vera. For in *Butterfly Burning*, the event of abortion is repeatedly conveyed through densely material forms, not as an abstracted report. Abortion (and, implicitly, Phephelaphi's suicide) is not the only route to freedom available or the only way out. Rather, tragedy is rendered indeterminate and the reader is invited to consider a plethora of corporeal co-implications. Vera transforms the naturalization of abortion as tragic content through her repeated, achronological melding of ecological and elemental forms.

Theorizing the grammar of identity in transnational literature, Stephen Clingman draws on linguist Roman Jakobson's structuralist figuration of metaphor and metonymy along two axes, where the former serves the linguistic function of substitution and the latter involves combination or contiguity (2009: 13). In addition to these associations, Jakobson conjectures that the metaphorical bears resemblance to literary romanticism, whereas realism appears to rely on metonymy. From these sets of observations, Clingman concludes that metonymic prose tends to allow us to imagine interlocking combinations of possibilities rather than a plethora of similarities or dualisms; he states that metonymy 'guards against representation in specific senses, where the definition of identity claims to represent the sole and absolute possibilities of the self, whether our own or that of others' (Clingman 2009: 15). Rather than further complicating vexed ethical issues through abstraction, Clingman suggests, one can approach a realistic and nuanced sense of representation through the aesthetic technique of metonymy. Yet representation is a vital concept which calls to mind both the legal and moral associations of abortion advocacy, and the aesthetic issue of conveying reproductive agency through fiction. As Vera's academic theses repeatedly stress, African literature and literary criticism tend *not* to represent women, whether through metaphor or metonymy – this may be due to the fact that female characters are caricatured and rarely act as narrators, or because women writers face more hurdles in sharing nuanced stories. It seems remiss to create a grammar of transnational literary identity without acknowledging the extent to which sexual difference has been inscribed within supposed realistic literary representations. One should question whether literary experimentation with metaphor can truly be discounted due to a supposed complicity with dualistic models of difference. For if tragedy as a literary form is interested in advancing subjective indeterminacy, then creative, experimental and metaphorical approaches are undeniably important in creating a sense of textual duplicity.

Jacques Lacan writes, 'If the symptom is a metaphor, it is not a metaphor to say so, any more than to say that man's desire is a metonymy. For the symptom *is* a metaphor ... as desire is a metonymy' ([1977] 2001: 175; original emphasis). Following on from my theorization of desire as agency in the previous chapters, it seems apt to privilege metonymy in the following discussion of Vera's creative form. There are several reasons for this. Firstly, as I have already noted, most readings to date have tended to gloss over the matter of abortion, diagnosing it as nothing more than politicized metaphor. I take seriously the physical permeability of abortion ecologies in Vera's text and how this informs the extent to which Phephelaphi is a tragic protagonist. Another issue is the figure of the author herself, and her desires to aestheticize political and ethical issues through a form that does not adhere to literary realism. It must be stressed, however, that many of the instances of metonymy discussed below are deliberately rendered indeterminate through their interaction with more traditionally metaphorical literary techniques (often describing medical symptoms of pregnancy and/ or its termination). The two abortion scenes employ metonymy to transform understandings of the tragic: tragedy is not simply a linear event, but rather encompasses multiple subjectivities. Echoes of communal and interspecies interests here cause one to recall Greta Gaard's ecofeminist ethics of attentive listening, which I adapt in my analysis of Wilma Stockenström's *The Expedition to the Baobab Tree*. Importantly, Stockenström's is the only other abortion narrative in this study which terminates with the protagonist's desire to commit suicide. Although both texts culminate in what is commonly conceived as tragedy, the human characters remain hyperaware of environmental agencies, even during their dramatic performances of abortion and self-immolation. This opens up new associations for the genre: for tragedy involves not only the demise of personal development, but also collective desires.

Reproductive agency in two abortion scenes

Public discourse surrounding abortion often revolves around issues of personhood – specifically, establishing when an embryo (or foetal tissue) can be said to have gained personal agency. Rhetoric used by anti-abortion activists often draws attention away from the physical capabilities of the foetus in the present and focuses instead on its future potential as an autonomous human being. Simultaneously, discourse surrounding abortion highlights the agency – or lack thereof – of the person who is pregnant. In an article on the diversity of

African feminisms, Pontsho Pilane states that 'the root of feminism is choice' (2016: 12). Indeed, this very word has become emblematic for pro-choice activists who stress how a woman's reproductive decisions are personal. This section, however, is not concerned with persons – or rather, it does not adhere to the typical conflation of humanity with personhood that often leads to a stalemate between anti-abortion and pro-choice activists. Instead, it suggests that we should reconceive the very notion of agency. To best represent how new formulations of this concept are created, I analyse how Vera counter-intuitively prioritizes women's agency by transforming humanist (and typically anthropocentric) discourses of personhood. It is with this in mind that I perform a close reading of *Butterfly Burning* in conjunction with Stacy Alaimo's articulation of transcorporeality, which asserts that 'human bodies are not only imbricated with one another but also enmeshed with nonhuman creatures and landscapes' (2016: 67).

Chapter 16 of the novel begins a week after Phephelaphi learns that she is pregnant; in the previous section, she lies awake during Fumbatha's absence and wonders whether to bring the pregnancy to term. The chapter's opening sentence – a simple, declarative 'No' (Vera 1998: 113) – not only predicts her decision to abort the foetus, but also instils a sense of negation which is reinforced by descriptions of the earth as a 'bare and spare [...] stretching flat land' (114). At surface level, such images may appear to serve as metaphors for the protagonist's fear of sexual reproduction. According to this reading, her body becomes analogous with the landscape, which is figured earlier in the novel as 'swaying twin hills with a valley in between, grooved, wet with newborn things' (81–2). Choosing to pursue a professional career path instead of motherhood, Phephelaphi seemingly subverts Fumbatha's notion that she is the gendered 'land beneath his feet' (28–9). She thereby questions the metonymical links that connect the earth-mother trope to reified ideas of Mother Africa and African motherhood. However, while it is important to equip women with political agency and the power to choose their futures, such an understanding perpetuates gender essentialism by continuing to define womanhood and female sexual creativity in relation to nature. Replacing images of feminized fertility with sterility neither overcomes the nature-culture dichotomy nor dispels simplistic gender binaries. It is therefore worth pausing to closely consider the introductory passages of this chapter, which present a nuanced portrait of the earth as a 'flat expanse', where 'you can smell its absence of weight' (113–14). Here is one of few instances where the text deviates from third-person omniscient narration. This rare use of the second-person pronoun engages the reader as an active participant in the scenes to follow (a point to which I will return later in my analysis); the only other passage where readers are directly interpolated is in the first chapter, when the narrator describes 'Dying in your sleep' (7). Furthermore, a strange synaesthesia evoked here – the suggestion that lightness has a scent – shows that paradoxes and ambiguities inform Vera's understanding of reproductive agency. It is from this important understanding that I now turn to analysing how various duplicitous fertility symbols recur throughout the abortion scene.

As Phephelaphi performs the termination, her body is not compared to terrain, as female physiology is wont to be in masculinist, pastoral literary traditions. Rather, she is aligned with atypical natural elements: first described as a swimmer in water (116), and then as lightning and fire and finally as a phenomenon of lightwaves (117). While not living organisms, these last three natural forces hold certain agentive qualities which complicate traditional understandings of inorganic material as inert. Watery imagery, for instance, immediately evokes Neimanis' posthuman gestationality and Alaimo's aqueous posthumanism, particularly the latter's assertion that 'the human becomes more liquid, less solid' (Alaimo 2016: 123). Lightning is an unpredictable electrostatic discharge which can result in flames. Waves of light may bend or otherwise spread via diffraction when they pass through a barrier or substance. There are certainly metaphysical implications associated with such active natural imagery. In *Meeting the Universe Halfway*, Karen Barad uses the process of diffraction to visualize her methodological approach. While the process of reflection, she argues, is often concerned with the literal and metaphorical differences between 'who' and 'what' matters, 'diffraction is not merely about differences […], but about the entangled nature of differences that matter. Significantly, difference is tied up with responsibility' (2007: 36). That is, her methodology prioritizes how certain materials or organisms come to matter, in an ethical sense. For the moment, however, I want to consider how Vera's utilization of such terms is complicated by obscurity and ethical indeterminacy. As the protagonist attempts to clear all tissue from her uterus with a long thorn picked from a bush, she eventually feels the foetus wrench away: 'She clutches something as dead as a root', a 'dead substance which promises no anchor' (117). The combination of simile and metonymy here seems immediately jarring; roots typically ensure the stability and nourishment of plants, and are thus rarely associated with death. Yet in this instance, the foetal form – imagined as a decomposing plant – is granted less livelihood and agency than Phephelaphi, who is described as holding the strength of all elemental forces.

In an interview with Jane Bryce, Vera repeats explicitly that the abortion takes place in a forest (2002: 222–3), an area which is stereotypically lush – yet the duplicity of arid symbols continues as the protagonist lies bleeding. Through her pain Phephelaphi sees the thorn bush and observes that it appears to have spontaneously gone into bloom (Vera 1998: 117). Soon it is revealed that the red 'flowers' are actually the beaks of birds which fly out from the bush (118). Merging vegetal and animal life, the scrub's microcosmic ecosystem mirrors the spots of blood which begin to fall beneath Phephelaphi as she removes her clothing. The protagonist herself notices the similarity between these two images as she surveys her surroundings: 'The hills have disappeared and are gone. They have been flattened to the ground by the simple drop of her eyelids. In a mixture of laughter and tears she sees again the crimson beaks' (119). Here, it is vital to note that, once again, stereotypical associations of women's bodily curves with mountainous vistas have been called into question; in this instance, the smallest motion on Phephelaphi's part results in a transformation of the entire landscape. Agency is therefore rendered as a central concern even when the very matter of the aborted foetus is not drawn into focus. Another point worth stressing is the fact that she feels both relief *and* melancholy after inducing the miscarriage. Emotional ambivalence is perhaps one of the most important elements that is often ignored by the divisive framing of pro-life and pro-choice activists within a debate. In Vera's novel, however, Phephelaphi's mixed feelings are the first of many complications to arise following the procedure.

Another indeterminate element of the chapter is the description of the foetus, as compared with the pregnant woman. Firstly, foetal tissue is described as 'lukewarm warmth' thrice in one paragraph (115), and twice again later in the chapter. As this phrase is repeated, the foetus develops into a more tangible object: Phephelaphi observes that it 'becomes a solid', 'like handfuls of saliva' and then 'is no longer her own' (118; 121). Importantly, the very comparison to spittle creates a sense of inconsistency; within this simile, liquid is rendered as a solid, highlighting how shifting states of being are a central thematic concern. Furthermore, here the foetus comes into independence only once it has exited the protagonist's body, thereby suggesting that the woman holds more agency than the potential being inside her. This echoes the new materialists' blurring of external and internal phenomena – a formulation of intersecting agencies that we have already witnessed as manifesting earlier in the fiction of Stockenström and Wicomb. As Ann Furedi notes, those who are against abortion often make emotional appeals by speaking of a mother and baby, even when what is inside the uterus does not resemble a child (2016: loc. 776). *Butterfly Burning* explores differentiations between biological states of growth by framing the foetus as an indeterminate phenomenon. Firstly, Phephelaphi attempts to distract herself 'while the child pulls away from her' (Vera 1998: 119). Yet as it exits her body she observes that 'beneath her *the child, not yet*, is released' (120; emphasis added). Referred to with a definite article rather than a possessive pronoun, any sense of the foetus's potential personhood is undone in this moment. Such negation is reinforced later in the chapter by a description of 'the unborn child too small to be a child, just a mingling within the nylon, something viscous and impolite amid the lace' (122). Here, the words just and something show that while the foetal form is organic, the protagonist does not imbue it with the same sanctity of life as a fully developed human. There are many agencies at play in this scene, but the political issue of reproductive agency is never forgotten.

Concurrently, while the foetus is considered as both a potential person and a collection of cells, Phephelaphi's very personhood is called into question after inducing the abortion. A barrage of nullifying statements follows when she is described as swimming yet 'not being part of anything at all, not her body, not the sky above her, not the not-here tree which she imagines, not even the not-hereness with hills to be imagined, the emptiness and none being. Not here. Instead, a quiet stretch of time where she is not. Not being' (116–17). In this passage, her attempts to create meaning by (re)imagining natural imagery result in failure. She is not depicted as the typical strong-willed or self-assured woman whom pro-choice ideology enlists; both her biological creativity and the burden of responsibility are shifted as her body is reduced from an active subject to a negative space. Envisioned in a pool of liquid, the so-called mother-to-be is defined by what she is *not*. Yet certain complexities linger within this image. As I have already discussed, the figure of the developing foetus (contained in amniotic fluid) is often described by relying on comparative stages of growth. The above quotation similarly presents Phephelaphi in a pool of liquid, reducing her to a comparably aqueous state. Furthermore, she is likened to a homologue of the mammalian amniotic sac; 'she is a transparent membrane coating the inside shell of an egg' (120). Both of these images call to mind Karen Barad's argument that the 'foetus as a phenomenon "includes" the apparatuses of phenomena out of which it is constituted: in particular, it includes the pregnant woman [...] as well as her "surroundings"' (2007: 217). Although 'nothing has been born at all' (Vera 1998: 120), it is worth exploring how the novelist utilizes the gestator-foetus-phenomenon. For example, before all the foetal matter has been removed, Phephelaphi observes that 'It is herself', 'It is she' (116). To the undiscerning reader, this statement may appear to validate the foetus's moral status – yet it is worth noting that the child is only referred to through the gender of its mother. Similarly, after the termination she reassures herself, 'The heart beating is hers, her arms, and *she is she*' (124; emphasis added). The foetus is thus portrayed as one constitutive element of the broader gestational landscape; although it possesses a 'changing heart' (Colb and Dorf 2016: 5), it is only one transcorporeal element of the larger, and more ethically significant, figure's biology.

Time expands over the course of the chapter to further explore these nuances. Phephelaphi feels each moment as she is 'living it, living in it, part of it, and parting from it' (Vera 1998: 124). The part played by this repetitive wordplay is strikingly similar to neologisms used by Barad, who reinvents terms from the school of physics to interrogate how science informs how one views not only physical matter, but also the significance of discourse (2007: 3). Barad's feminist philosophy is principally concerned with how scientific discourse is often associated with rationalist ideology. This is not to say, however, that she (or, more broadly, the new materialism) views physics and related fields as inherently misogynistic and logocentric; instead, she uses linguistic inventiveness to simultaneously engage with practising scientists' belief-systems and trouble such dualistic stereotypes. The novel's merging of ruminations on posthuman gestationality and queer time makes Barad's inventive, immediate discourse of intra-actions seems particularly apt. Indeed, the present tense comes to figure for a form of ethical indeterminacy towards which all the contrasting images of decay and rejuvenation, or sterility and fertility, gesture. The narration implies, for instance, that natural elements hold an agency which is not benevolent, but rather indifferent: 'Is. Is. Is. This soil just is. It does not move. No kindness to it. [...] Water could not dissolve its rigid hold, its stiff will' (Vera 1998: 122). Instead of predetermining the earth as an anthropomorphized mother, or imbuing women with characteristics of the supposedly passive landscape, it is suggested that one should merely perceive them as what they are in the present. This is not to say, however, that the narrative positions people and natural elements as separate entities. On the contrary, according to Vera both shape each other's potential through a repetitive process of relationality. By the end of the chapter, Phephelaphi is no longer figured as the foetal phenomenon or uterine environment: she has 'emerged out of a cracked shell. There is a soothing emptiness in this canopy of sky. She has endured the willed loss of her child. Willed, not unexpected. Expected, not unwilled' (124). Her deliberate actions are certainly figured through ecological phenomena, whether this is the presence of a thorn bush or a flock of birds, but the duplicitous nature of such images shows that they determine neither her decisions nor her essence. One's will, according to Barad, is a process of becoming or a 'congealing of agency' (2007: 151). The foetus amounts to a 'liquid ferment' (Vera 1998: 123), a potentially important factor of Phephelaphi's future; but once it exits her uterus, it ceases to constitute a defining part of her identity.

The political implications of such views are manifold, especially for a Black woman in the colonized landscape of Rhodesia – a country whose very name is a literal reminder of Cecil John Rhodes's violent legacy, his imperialist desire to sire a new nation. The rhetoric of progeny and repronormativity is inescapable, it appears, as one cannot erase such a pervasive history of thwarted agencies. This much is made clear by what follows after the terminated pregnancy: devastated by his partner's decision and her refusal to discuss the matter with him, Fumbatha immediately loses interest and begins an affair with another woman. Phephelaphi is aware of his betrayal but chooses not to confront him, merely contrasting the 'strange woman's solid ground' with her own (135). The penultimate chapter of the novel is relayed through Phephelaphi's first-person narration (it is the only section to do so), revealing that she has fallen pregnant for a second time. Once again, words like 'nothing' and 'absence' are used to distinguish between her current emotional landscape and that of Fumbatha's lover, her former friend Deliwe (146). So-called pro-life activists often describe abortion as an act of denial. For example, the procedure has been described as 'the negation of [parental] love' (Carter 2011: 25) – thereby implying that terminating a pregnancy is both epistemologically and morally unsound. Yet in Vera's novel, the termination of pregnancy does not cohere with a moralistic binary of pro-life and pro-choice ideology. This is evidenced by Deliwe's betrayal of her friend's trust in committing adultery: before they begin their affair, Fumbatha describes Deliwe's allure in an unconventional manner; he looks upon her as 'the sort of woman to make a man crawl as though he had never walked on his own two legs' (Vera 1998: 64). The femme fatale is a familiar character type, but her sexuality is rarely if ever described in relation to maternal power. Thus, even here, Vera evokes fertility in order to deviate from socially acceptable dualisms. She further demonstrates the protagonist's perpetual suspicion of parental love and the maternal role that is sanctified by repronormative discourse in the final chapter, which suddenly reverts to third-person narration. The chapter opens with a longing for negation; a desire is expressed for 'the time before, in its not-knowing, its not-tragedy', 'what restores like a torn membrane the time before' (148). Yet as the transition from Rhodesia to Zimbabwe shows, there is no turning back; the only solution is in liberationist rhetoric, which is often similarly guilty of utilizing paternalistic tropes.

In her quest for resolution, Phephelaphi ironically chooses to enact what many interpret as the ultimate tragedy of the text: she soaks herself in a flammable 'soft liquid' (149), sets it alight and embraces Fumbatha as he arrives home. It is interesting to note that liquid is used here as a destructive element (as opposed to the earlier chapter, where it evokes hydration or nourishment from amniotic fluid). Phephelaphi's metamorphosis into the titular burning butterfly – a fully grown organism and the final embodiment of the insect's life-cycle – is certainly a tragic event in two senses; she not only terminates her second pregnancy – albeit indirectly – but also her own life. Yet as she burns, she assures Fumbatha that 'their unburied child, the one inside her body' is 'free and weightless like herself, now, safe, now' (150). The sanctity of liberty, one of the central tenets of human rights, is denied to Phephelaphi when her partner punishes her for exercising reproductive agency. Her second abortion is thus not only a removal of the foetal form, but also of her own body – Barad's foetus-mother-phenomenon – from the political landscape. Both her biological mother, Zandile, and her adoptive mother Gertrude (also referred to as Emelda) are recalled in the closing lines of the novel. Particularly, they are mocked for their 'foolishness' to have become mothers (151). In colonial Rhodesia, where women are the victims of both racial hatred and patriarchal hegemony, the protagonist believes that resisting this domestic role is the one political act that she can fulfil, even if it requires self-immolation and death, the ultimate antithesis of action. The notion of an ethics of refusal is advanced and expanded upon in Bessie Head's fiction, as I discuss in my subsequent chapter on queer vitality.

It would be overly reductive, though, to conclude that *Butterfly Burning* figures society as completely unchangeable or that it contains a condensable biological telos. The earlier sections of the novel recount the budding romantic relationship between Phephelaphi and Fumbatha, who initially meet at a river near the Makokoba township. Yet instead of exploring sexual reproduction solely through natural imagery – which is typically associated with female physiology – Vera challenges such stereotypes through poetic descriptions with dense connotations. The protagonist's indeterminate feelings about fertility and motherhood are mirrored by the inorganic environment, particularly inanimate objects like textiles and other manufactured products. For example, when handed a glass of water, she feels 'rescued' by its cool and smooth texture (103). Yet as Phephelaphi lies in bed, a passer-by shatters her window (110);

this disruption of her solitude reminds her of her pregnancy and marks her desire to terminate it. Furthermore, as she contemplates whether to abort the foetus, the red fibres of her blanket are likened to blood on her hands (107). Sewing, needlework and other crafts are typically associated with domestication and feminized servility. Yet the textile is likened here to an organic plasma which both transcends gender and emblematizes the protagonist's decision to forego motherhood. Aqueous texturing of the inanimate is also used to draw attention to narrative form. In one of the aforementioned sexual encounters, the lovers' words are described as 'laced, dipped in a fragrance soft like milk, words chiselled like stone' (50). While both milk and stone are inanimate, they hold contradictory symbolic associations: the former calls to mind nourishment and growth,[9] while the latter is unyielding and immovable. And yet the word chiselled implies artistic rendering, much as how the blanket which Phephelaphi lies underneath is a product of labour (considering patriarchal traditions in rural Zimbabwe, this labour would most likely be a woman's). Foregrounding the potential of creation, narration and the imagination – and evoking the discursive developments of autopoiesis demonstrated in *You Can't Get Lost in Cape Town* – these complex metaphors lend a metafictional element to the text. That is to say, they emphasize how Phephelaphi's fate is not only influenced by others' words, but also shaped by the reader's perceptions in the act of reading. In her emphasis on narration and retelling, Vera draws attention to the very physical nature of the textual form, and its capacity to influence the reader's life. Similar to a mixture of oil and water 'shining like new fabric', the text is implicitly both 'stagnant and breeding' (20): it may produce an ideological shift in society, but only if individuals are open to the transcorporeal relationships within it.

The novel opens with an image of workers singing as they cut grass: variations on the words 'the grass' recur ten times in quick succession (4), to the point that the prose itself takes on a lyrical quality. At surface level, the evocation of song in the *veld* appears to be an intertextual reference to Doris Lessing's *The Grass is Singing* ([1950] 2007), a novel which was written and set in colonial Rhodesia around the same time as Phephelaphi's and Fumbatha's story. Lessing's novel is focalized through Mary, a white settler who is most happy when she is single and situated in the metropolis. Her desire to remain unmarried in her thirties and wear 'little-girl frocks in pastel colours' seems to suggest a fear of the roles and responsibilities that a patriarchal society associates with womanhood (Lessing [1950] 2007: 38). When Mary marries and is forced to relocate to a farm, she grows isolated and mentally ill. The novel 'repeatedly stages the refusal of mothering' (Graham 2007: 62), both through Mary's fear of fertility and through the symbolic barrenness of the landscape surrounding her. While the farm yields less crops and becomes harder to live on, the protagonist grows increasingly insulated and uninterested in conversing with others. Her only meaningful attempts to connect with another human being (a Black farm worker named Moses) result in her death. Both novels clearly thematize fecundity and sterility in the southern African landscape. In this respect, they can be grouped with others which take an anti-pastoral approach to the South African landscape, such as Olive Schreiner's *The Story of an African Farm* ([1883] 2008), or J. M. Coetzee's *In the Heart of the Country* (1977). Both of these texts are focalized through independent women who resist the role of motherhood: in fact, Helen Bradford suggests that the feminist character Lyndall in *African Farm* rides a jolting ox cart to try and terminate her unsupportable pregnancy (1995: 640). In Schreiner's case, the focalization is only partial, but Samuel Cronwright's explanation that one of her earlier titles for the text was *Mirage: A Series of Abortions* is particularly fascinating, showing how the topic of termination figured on at least a metaphorical level for Schreiner when writing (Cronwright [1924] 2008: 307). Importantly, however, Vera's novel diverges from the others in that she focalizes the narrative through Black characters. Initially, these are the men who foreground the political potential of protest by singing through their work: a scene which unconventionally pairs men's labour with natural imagery and is ostensibly concerned with colonial nationalism's effects on masculinity. Soon, however, the narrative shifts its focalization to the domestic sphere; notwithstanding, and defying gendered expectations, the later segments are set in the township, which is far less natural than the opening passage.

The scene is set for Phephelaphi's final act during the beginning of a storm, constituted of soil, sand, lightning, air and leaves: together, they are described as 'particles of time' (147). There is a long history of such forces dramatizing tragic developments – as demonstrated in plays like *King Lear* and *Macbeth* – yet Vera's choice of elemental symbols is particularly apt for our discussion of development as *formation*. Earlier, I elucidated how lightning is an agentive inorganic force. This image not only highlights the importance of agency, but also mirrors an earlier instance of clouds and flames which occurs when an oil tank explodes, killing many working men. In a run-on sentence, children are described watching 'the acrid smoke which spreads sideways and upward like something living, with a will playful and bright unlike their own' (21). Once again, Vera uses the word will to foreground how political agents are situated within wider natural landscapes that also display agency. The man-made cloud evokes a sense of awe in the young witnesses of the event: 'This figure rising before them is more commanding, much more rare [*sic*] to their curiosity, than the tiny bodies which they had watched from a distance' (22). In the aftermath of the fire, questions are raised about the comparative worth of life – not with regard to foetal growth, but rather to racial politics. Those who were victims of the explosion were exposed to such risk because of their limited options for employment; in colonial Rhodesia, manual labourers would undoubtedly be Black. In this scene, paradoxically, Black children are centralized as observers who are granted the agency to discern whose lives come to matter. Similarly, in the wake of Phephelaphi's suicide, the reader is challenged to confront how sexist discourse alienates women who are also forced to make a living through dangerous means. Importantly, it is not only the woman and foetus who die, but also Fumbatha. *Butterfly Burning* thus does not merely anticipate, but rather exceeds, new materialist conceptions of the blastocyst (see Barad 2007: 217; Bennett 2009: 90) – imagining the foetus as a phenomenon constituting a zygote, woman and man who are victims of various discriminations.

The intersection of political oppressions is thus repeatedly explored throughout the novel, highlighting how all beings – adults, children and other organisms – shape each other's worth in the world. It is at this point that I want to return once more to the few moments when the third-person narration is broken, particularly by use of a first-person plural pronoun. The first instance occurs early in the narrative as it is stated that Kwela music conveys how 'we do it together. This and that – fight, escape, surrender. The distinction always unclear, the boundaries perpetually widening' (7). The tragic dimensions of the novel are explicitly communal, much like the associations of natal alienation and social death presented by the protagonist's suicide in *The Expedition to the Baobab Tree*. *Butterfly Burning*'s opening lyrical imagery suggests that the narrative is concerned with both material *and* metaphysical issues, a fact that is later confirmed when abortion and indeterminacy take the forefront of the text. Towards the end of the second chapter, the first-person plural recurs when the narrator asserts that 'there is nothing we can do to save the dead' (14–15). Here, again, the pronoun acts as a bridge: but this time it is not between physicality and abstraction, but rather between being and nothingness.

The third instance where this word takes precedence is in an earlier (and happier) moment of Fumbatha's relationship with Phephelaphi; engaging in sexual intercourse, they repeat the words 'We are here' (72). In this instance, deviation from third-person narration not only speaks to the connectedness of the two lovers, but also highlights how immediacy and presentness – both in space and time – are repeatedly considered as a solution to discourses that predetermine one's societal roles and identity formation. Finally, as the abortion scene reaches its climax, the reader is actively engaged in a didactic passage: 'The stars are all carried in our eyes, this is why we are alone. We are yet to be born. Some of us are never to be born. To be born is chance and good fortune, and to survive into tomorrow, sheer motive and interest. She was not interested' (119). This passage stands apart from the others in the sense that it is not concerned with merging two distinct concepts or entities (physics and metaphysics, life and death, or space and time). Rather, here the word we is only employed to emphasize one's existential isolation, a solipsism which is incommunicable and yet, paradoxically, shared with every other being on the planet. There is thus a social as well as planetary or cosmic scale to the use of the collective pronoun. Phephelaphi's decision to surrender to 'a death as intimate as birth' and a 'birth as certain as love' is not in order to reinforce supposedly separate phenomena such as self and other or birth and death (149). As I have illustrated, the novel is full of ironies and paradoxes, but such juxtapositions also call dichotomies into question. Vera's biological preoccupation in both abortion scenes theorizes the ecological model as materialist, but simultaneously anti-essentialist and postcolonial in its scope. Instead of positioning itself as either for or against abortion – as much contemporary rhetoric does – the narrative merely sets the scene for reproductive agency, and then presents multiple perspectives on intersecting issues which impact upon Black women's desires.

Literal and metaphorical heartbeats abound in the novel's more urbanized settings, whether these are eavesdropping neighbours' anxious breathing in the township (49), or pounding vibrations caused by an approaching train (55). The sound of the heartbeat – typically associated with bodily organs, or the lifeline of a developing foetus – thus exceeds the human corporeal dimension, pointing to the shared vulnerability of all beings in a setting where colonial hegemony is often propagated by 'naturalized' rhetoric and metaphor. In one of the earlier passages of the novel, the narrator meditates on the importance of audibility, asserting that Kwela music is crucial for 'embracing choices that are already decided. Deciding which circumstance has been omitted and which is set free, which one claimed, which one marked, branded, and owned' (6). Here, Vera melds musical imagery with the rhetoric of choice. The ekphrastic elements of the text are deliberately foregrounded to show how artistic creativity is an integral component of political action. The aesthetic form is a transformative tool: in thematizing the ethical matter of abortion, it inspires a more-than-humanist approach to reproductive agency. Vital commonalities between new materialist frameworks are manifest in Vera's novel, particularly in this scene that evokes Greta Gaard's critical ecofeminist ethics of attentive listening, which I discuss at length in Chapter 1. The circumstances of listeners – whether dancers in the narrative, or readers of the text – are thus rendered similarly to Barad's aforementioned notion of phenomena, which informs the work of Alaimo, Gaard and many other materialist feminists. An ethics of listening means that there is no easily discernible subject to centralize and privilege. The novel's listeners are not merely personified through metaphor, but also rendered as acquiring agentive potential through a metonymic, creative process.

Beating hearts or striking rocks

Only a decade after the year in which *Butterfly Burning* is set, a crowd led by the South African Federation of Women marched to the Union Buildings in Pretoria, South Africa. Although the federation discussed wide-ranging issues on 9 August 1956, such as equal pay and rights for all, their aim on this day was to protest the introduction of pass laws for Black women made in 1952 by the apartheid government. Marchers used both a petition and songs to reinforce their message; the event is often remembered alongside lyrics from 'Wathint' Abafazi, Wathint' Imbokodo', a feminist protest song. Yet the campaigners' and political dissidents' anxieties – about women's bodily vulnerability during police searches, or the blurred lines between childcare and paid work – speak to a broader set of intersecting concerns about reproductive agency in colonial southern Africa.

Early in *Butterfly Burning*, Yvonne Vera foregrounds how working-class men are affected by the control of autochthonous peoples, particularly in rural spaces. She provides historical context by describing how many Black husbands and fathers were hanged from trees for minor misdemeanours – crimes which, in some cases, it was dubious that they even committed. Fumbatha is born during the same year that his father is sentenced to death; in the wake of the hanging, his mother expects him to be 'a witness to dying, a pledge to life. She expects him to know his link with the past' (14). At this point it is worth pausing to reconsider Vera's description of African feminist fiction that I evoked at the start of this chapter, and its resonance with another of the author's comments. In her aforementioned interview with Jane Bryce, Vera says of the novel: 'I want you to be *there*, I don't want you to hear about it, I want you to be a witness, which means taking part in what is happening in each moment, as it happens' (2002: 222–3; original emphasis). From these three quotations – a literary passage, an excerpt from an editorial introduction and a passing comment during an interview – it becomes clear that Vera is perpetually preoccupied with the process of witnessing the present,[10] rather than projecting an agenda onto the past or the future. How, then, does she justify setting this novel retrospectively in Rhodesia during the mid-twentieth century – and opening a narrative about women's reproductive agency with what are ostensibly concerns about masculinity?

The answer to both questions can be found by analysing the formal nature of the text. Particularly, if one expands one's literary analysis of *Butterfly Burning* beyond the two abortion scenes, then it becomes clear why it is set not in contemporary Zimbabwe, but rather just two years before apartheid officially began, and a mere ten years prior to the South African Women's March. Vera is undoubtedly invested in discussing the wider socio-political context of southern African feminist and anti-racist movements in both her academic and fictional writing. Analysing Ruth First in her PhD, she argues that apartheid impacts upon women's conceptions of agency in the prison narrative (1995: 24). She notes that imprisonment has radically shifted intergenerational and familial relationships for African women, citing the 1960 Sharpeville Massacre and 1976 riots in South Africa as defining moments where it transpires that motherhood cannot be understood in relation to traditional beliefs (1995: 278). The novel constantly projects an association of aesthetics with ethics, of literary witnessing with presentness (in contrast with either strict retrospection or speculation). In her study of language, music and modernity in the novel, Lizzy Attree astutely identifies an intertextual reference to 'Strange Fruit', a protest song popularized by Billie Holiday which chronicles racist lynchings historically committed in the American South (2002: 75). I would argue that the description of murdered men and their mourning families provides commentary not just on musicality, but also on the duplicitous *presence* of textuality. The novel's ekphrastic and intertextual allusions specifically convey a recurring sense of immediacy. For example, Vera's unnamed narrator goes on to describe a transferable continuum of growth and death:

> The women keep the most vital details of their men buried in their mouths. They receive lightning from the sky with their bare hands and with it, they rename each of their children; the living and unborn. They find new names for the dead and utter them in daylight. Then everything changes; everything is new.
>
> (1998: 12)

The word vital connotes either necessity or livelihood. Here the latter could be conceived, in Jane Bennett's terms, as '*vital materiality*' (2009: vii; original emphasis) – something which Bennett argues we have the capacity to understand in childhood as we play with inanimate objects, but gradually lose as we grow older. Vitalism is discussed in further detail in the following chapter on Bessie Head, where I problematize the seeming lack of a political impetus in Bennett's framework and favour instead the concept of queer vital*ity*. Returning to the above quotation, it may initially be interpreted that by refusing to speak of the men's histories, the women are destroying their legacies. Yet Vera complicates this sense of negation and strict linear developments by insinuating that the men will be revived as a new generation is (re)named in their honour. In this passage, transcorporeality transcends mere biological exchanges. It begins, in other words, to adopt a temporal element of transference: the tradition of naming is identified as an important process for preserving cultural identity, and simultaneously creating the capacity for empathetic awareness. The inorganic force of lightning metonymically stimulates revival in society, as living children carry their forefathers' names. Importantly, however, this linguistic process does not affect the human community alone, but rather everything. Honouring the past through tradition therefore creates a sense of novelty by revisiting – and revising – transcorporeal relationships within the social environment. It is this sense of timeless imbrications which informs not only the novel's themes – Vera, after all, is daring to describe a taboo yet ancient medical procedure that has been repeated in secrecy rather than as ritual – but also its geographical situatedness. Setting the narrative retroactively causes one to pause and question the origins of prejudices which linger in the present.

It is imperative to note that the men who are brought to the foreground in the earlier chapters – workers in the outskirts of the township forced to take on menial tasks like cutting grass or transporting fuel – are frequently watched by groups of children who are always described in genderless terms. This element of non-gendered spectatorship causes the reader, in turn, to reflect upon the roles that young people are permitted to adopt in the township, and what implications these might have for the adults that they grow to become. There are essentialized synonyms for manhood which recur in many societies: these include physical strength, an exertion of power over nature or financial independence. In Vera's novel, it is true that men utilize natural resources in order to make a living, while children are more concerned with the countryside as a source of recreation. Yet racial oppression means that the former group are as excluded from the polity of colonial Rhodesia as the children who play in the wilderness surrounding them. That is to say, men are frequently denied access to the interior of the city and are forced to earn a pittance in the rural landscape. It hardly needs explaining that women's bodies have historically figured for natural ecology (or vice versa) in popular art, narratives and heteronormative social standards. Yet here, on the outskirts of Makokoba, men are rendered as women's allies; regardless of their gender identities, it is implied, all adults are infantilized and subjected to limitations which have been literally naturalized by the white metropolitan elite. It is easy to imagine how a woman in the township would struggle to access effective medical attention, particularly for reproductive health issues, during this historical period. Yet we are reminded that this is not all: gestating figures and foetuses are certainly susceptible to such risks, but the gendered domination of land creates an interlocking set of restrictions for the entire milieu. *Butterfly Burning* thus provides important insights about how men and women are subjected to similarly limiting roles by heteronormative patterns of discourse in both colonial Rhodesia and the nationalist country formed in its wake. Interconnections between adults and children in the novel queer linear models of development, much as in the fictions of Stockenström and Wicomb. In dissociating biological growth and sexual reproduction from development, Vera transforms personal and reproductive agencies in order to give them political implications. As an alternative to focusing on the future of a potential being, whether this the literal birth of a child, or the metaphorical creation of a new country, here it is implied that we should be more concerned with the quality of life of those who are living in the present, or 'the living' who 'are not dead' (Vera 1998: 12).

The novel strikes a fine balance between criticism of recurrence or idealized tradition, and a suspicion of new notions or terms. Shortly after witnessing a sublime rainbow and feeling assured of their immortality, members of the younger generation play games with urban waste like a broken record and a leather shoe, then hide inside an abandoned metal drum. Such barrels are ubiquitous in southern Africa, and mostly used to transport gallons of oil – the very substance which kills a group of men early in the novel after a tanker explodes. Empty drums, however, are frequently upcycled to be used as swings and/or tunnels on wealthy settlers' playgrounds, locally known as jungle gyms. Paired with a record which repeats itself, the echoing chamber thus serves a dual purpose: it is the literal site of the children's musical play, but also replicates oppositions of death and renewal, poverty and luxury, the manmade and the organic, or work and recreation. Curled in the foetal position, the children are 'coiled like caterpillars in this dark and temporary retreat, they touch every visiting belief with an anxious curiosity – and in their own unarticulated manner begin to question the whole notion of an innocent belonging. They are not free' (18). This passage epitomizes several of the novel's key themes. Firstly, by comparing the children to larvae (the second stage of the butterfly's life cycle, emerging after the egg but before the pupa and adult insect), Vera evokes the novel's title and anticipates Phephelaphi's duplicitous transformation in the final chapter. Termination typically denotes an end, but as she attempts to explain to Fumbatha when metamorphosing into the metaphorical butterfly, her desire to terminate the foetus and herself is not simply a tragic final act: instead birth, life and death are all rendered as transferable stages on a continuum. The model of a continuum is mirrored by the life cycle of the organism itself – and it implies that abortion, too, involves stages of growth and loss, or affirmation and refusal.

Further complicating this continuous experimentation with transformations in the above quotation, the term temporary is used to emphasize various levels of – and reasons for – transience; in colonial Rhodesia, children of the political minority are both physically weak and socially insignificant. To them, impermanence is not positive, as it is for many who anticipate the agency associated with adulthood, but rather a fearful state with associated risks. Despite the supposed innocence of youth, these children appear to be aware that appeals to a reified sense of freedom cannot assist them in achieving agency, even if they lack the vocabulary to articulate such suspicions. In my introductory chapter, I elucidate how the term reproductive freedom enshrines restrictive understandings of agency. One of the occasions when Vera gestures towards an attempt to reinvent such terminology is displayed when describing the outlying areas of Bulawayo; the words 'If not freedom then rhythm' articulate the township's vibrancy in more-than-humanist terms (8). In this instance Vera is once again utilizing negation, but with the aim of creating new understandings of liberty rather than prohibiting possibilities. Rhythm calls to mind the beating of a heart or a foetal lifeline. Yet here, being applied to the entire township's agency, it comes to evoke other forms of repetition, including the very cyclical nature of tragedy, itself. Even though such a radical narrative rethinking is characteristic of new materialism, here it is articulated in simple terms: in short, the sort of language that a child could understand.

While evoking the reader's sympathy for impoverished children, the text does not embody an unflinching devotion towards repronormativity. In light of Phephelaphi's decision(s) to abort, and her birth mother's similar rejection of motherhood (the narrator is adopted by another sex worker early in her childhood), it would be overly simplistic to argue that the novel conforms to the typically conservative stance that all life and childbirth is miraculous. Perhaps the most imperative indicator of this fact lies in a refrain about ideology and biology which is alluded to twice in Chapter 10 of the novel: 'The birth of a word is more significant than the birth of a child' (68). One may be surprised to learn that this position is focalized through Fumbatha, the 'witness to dying' who protests Phephelaphi's self-induced abortion (14). Yet his position and hypocrisy can be readily explained if one contextualizes this comment. He disregards human life only when it is presented in abstract terms: namely, when Phephelaphi announces her plans to study nursing. Consider the associations of this career. Nursing is typically envisioned as a predominantly female profession – not only because motherhood typically involves breastfeeding or nurturing a baby, but also because of the caregiving roles that women were forced to adopt during periods of war. In this sense, the protagonist could pursue a career while still adhering to the old-fashioned and pastoral ideals of femininity to which her partner prescribes. Yet Fumbatha fears that her financial independence would bring with it an affinity for the city, and thus a growing separation between the two lovers: 'A claim abandoned. A lover lost. It is the body addressed in its least of possible heights. A stone thrust' (7). This description of unrequited romantic affection is strikingly similar to language appearing in fake traditional healers' advertisements which can be found on street poles and litter bins in the streets of most South African urban centres. As I elucidate in my introduction, such posters claim to cure clients of bad luck, 'bring back lost lover[s]' (Jinga 2012: 82) or provide 'pain-free' and 'same-day' illegal abortions (Moore and Ellis 2013: 16). Therefore this quotation, which occurs early in the novel, simultaneously provides a social context for the following scenes and presents its first implicit clues of thematic undertones. Moreover, the small body which is addressed here may refer either to the foetus which will be aborted or to Phephelaphi's form as she lies in a weak and feverish state after the termination. Unaware of her pregnancy, however, Fumbatha is oblivious to any of the tragedies to come. Imagining his legacy as being reliant on the propagation of a family name is what causes him to claim that discourse always holds more power than a potential life – that is, until he learns that Phephelaphi has exercised reproductive agency by forgoing both her and his possibilities of parenthood.

Fumbatha's fixation on the future is thus what causes him to hold conservative views on reproductive agency. Elsewhere in the novel, though, fertility is normalized and constantly *present*, to the point of inanity. At a crowded train station, for example, it is observed that 'even here, a child is born' (Vera 1998: 55). Unlike the pastoral landscape, the station is a zone which resists gendered categorization. French anthropologist Marc Augé characterizes sites like airports and train stations as 'non-spaces' ([1992] 1995: 122): areas which foster a sense of anonymity and transience, because a multitude of humans are constantly moving through them. To those living in the township, however, the station holds more meaning; although many of its occupiers remain nameless, their intersubjective exchanges mean that it is not a mere placeholder devoid of significance. This is particularly true in the case of those who cannot afford to access or are not offered proper healthcare, and who must rely on others to help them navigate potential medical emergencies in public. The township's more urban and communal areas thus serve as sites of literal reproduction. Moreover, the lack of privacy is seen as a source of celebration rather than chagrin. As before, Vera renders this point through the eyes of the youngest members of the community, who 'possess nothing except an excited value placed on anything shared, and a glorious love of intimacy' (1998: 19). Their enthusiasm for common ground and identity is rendered even more tangible when a hungry crowd rips at bags of flour in a later scene, causing most of the product to be ground into the earth. Unexpectedly, even the adults 'embrace an entire loss', as 'at least there is sharing after the event, not gloating and pride on one triumphant side. [...] The loss is shared. There is joy to destroying a gift' (46). The useless expense of a rejuvenating substance is an image with obvious sexual associations, as colloquial connotations of words such as spent and seed show. However, it also symbolizes wider discursive issues. Crucially, the notion of loss permeates much discussion of unsupportable pregnancies: miscarriage is often rendered as a shared loss for both the gestating woman and her partner, while abortion is more insidiously described as a selfish refusal of the gift of life. Yet in the above quotations, such destruction is not only portrayed positively, but also viewed as a necessary step in uniting those who are *already living*. Furthermore, this scene serves as a metaphor which addresses the privileges that are conferred on some and denied to others, particularly in the uncritically nationalist climate of post-independence Zimbabwe. In short, the wasted product sparks a creative discussion of how nationalism transforms far more than simply political associations of agency. Much like a crowded station or a bustling square, the text is a shared space in which subjects' varying levels of agency are mirrored through transcorporeal relationships.

The aforementioned protest song against apartheid pass laws warns, 'Now you have touched the women you have struck a rock; you have dislodged a boulder; you will be crushed' (South African History Archive 1991: 11). Although utilizing an almost anaphoric sense of repetition, these words could not be more different from the maternalist lyrics of the ZANLA movement that I discussed earlier in this chapter. In 'Wathint' Abafazi, Wathint' Imbokodo', woman is simultaneously constructed as an individual entity and as a homogeneous ideological category: the figure's agency derives both from her inherent strength ('a rock') and from her shared struggle with others who identify as female ('the women'). There is a very similar sense of subjective indeterminacy at play in Vera's novel, particularly when the narrative focalizes multitudes of subjects. The description of a horde of hungry people, for example, appears directly alongside an image of 'a multitude of broken butterfly wings finely crushed' (Vera 1998: 46). I would argue that it is more than coincidental that this last word also appears in a song which advocates southern African women's political agency and mobility; it highlights the disjuncture between powerful and weak individuals by intimidating the addressee. Yet in this passage, the term serves a further and more multiperspectival purpose, because it is extended to contrast nonhuman animals' helplessness with the throng of human bodies in liminal colonial settings. Hence in both feminist struggles of the late twentieth century and Vera's novel, metonymy figures as a key narrative technique for foregrounding issues of power – a move towards agency which is less concerned with humanist or nationalist values, and more with the relationships between human and nonhuman desires. This materialist impulse is predicated by a desire to exceed humanist values by being held ethically accountable to all phenomena, without adopting a naïve or homogenizing notion that all beings are ever truly the same. It is open to differences, particularly those between organic and inorganic agencies, but also sensitive to postcolonial politics.

Invasive trees, imported by settlers, suck the water table dry. These species serve to visualize not only the process of colonization, but also that of growth and termination, particularly when 'dead leaves cling to their tinge of green, resisting their separation from the tree' (8). I have already elucidated how narratives of colonial domination often render the female form as land, or code environments as feminized entities. Yet the novel's constant engagement with multiperspectivalism and doubling means that there are more interesting metonyms at work, too – phrases that point to an uneasy, but indispensable, sense of politicized solidarity. When she begins to suspect that Fumbatha is committing adultery, Phephelaphi asks herself, 'Who was this other woman, and when?' (136). With its omission of an elaborative clause, this brief question renders the other woman not as a passive place, but as an embodiment of agency and simultaneously as a temporal setting. This relation of agency with an indeterminate, duplicitous understanding of time suggests that Phephelaphi does not view the affair as a tragic endpoint. Instead, Fumbatha's infidelity is one of many repeated instances of harm, rendering the exact moment of his betrayal into question.[11] Importantly, even after she learns the identity of his new lover, the protagonist desires to kill him, commit suicide and abort the second foetus: a solution which does not involve, or harm, Deliwe. While she is jealous of Fumbatha's desire for the other woman, Phephelaphi does not view their similar physiologies as a reason for exacting revenge. Rather, she negates the potential life inside her, in the hope that this will present another adult with a better chance of living independently. There is thus a sense of solidarity and transfer that informs not only southern African feminism's objective of a postcolonial political landscape, but also Vera's emphasis on the complex interconnectedness of in/organic agencies – whether these are countries, ecologies or fully developed human bodies. Solidarity is itself metonymic: it is forged through commonalities rather than identical views.

Emerging from the form and content of the text, then, is a plethora of alternatives to the outdated terminology that recurs in contemporary discussions of abortion (which, at the time of writing, continue over two decades after the first publication of *Butterfly Burning*). What would it mean, for instance, to act as present witnesses of a woman's struggles and desires, rather than as moralizing campaigners for or against a certain cause, the telos of which is inevitably projected into an uncertain future? Furthermore, how would the political landscape change if we were to speak of reproductive agency rather than rights? On the theme of ecology, in what way do the transcorporeal relationships of organic elements shape our understandings of womanhood and fertility? If there are answers to such questions, Vera suggests, they will be found by circumventing the rhetoric of liberation that has been appropriated by nationalist interests. Claims about rights often rely on an essentialist, default sense of authenticity which ironically fails to account for intricate differences between variant beings. A more viable alternative lies in an understanding situated between transcorporeality and postcolonial politics – a transformative ethics built by resisting tragic readings of feminist events and texts, and by focusing instead on how literary forms themselves may be illustrative of creative formations. Social realities are almost always more complex than any slogan or singular narrative can convey. If a text is true to its historical and geographical settings, however, then the creative discussions it provokes will always be predicated by a greater sense of reality: an ethics based on witnessing rather than overly convoluted metaphors.

The tangibility of metonymy forges a new and non-essentialist vocabulary for discussing abortion; it is sensitive to all beings, but simultaneously insistent that a person's worth simply exceeds that of any potential life inside them, from gametes to zygotes. In this way, we are reminded that men and children, too, embody creative agency; indeed, even a foetus holds some reproductive potential, as it develops its own set of sex cells. By focusing too heavily on a woman's choice, many play into the essentialist trope that the female sex is somehow more naturally astute at nurturing or creating new life. Paradoxically, it is only by accepting that women are not the sole creative forces that we can witness the comparative worth of life along a continuum. One can return to Vera's comment about the importance of presence, and Barad's theorization of emergence as a continual process, to further clarify this point. Both of these feminist thinkers point to how all beings are certainly worthy of ethical consideration, whether they are formed of organic or inorganic processes. Yet we are reminded that the situation of each agent within the context of Rhodesia – a literal creation of the male colonizer – means that some have been historically oppressed, while others are still incapable of exerting much agency (as far as the inevitably anthropocentric brain can conceive of such qualities). Doubling pregnancies and terminations, or fertility and negation, the novel troubles more traditional campaigns for freedom and agency without losing sight of feminist and anti-anthropocentric ideals. It limns a postcolonial position on a posthumanist ethics which is still coming into being.

Practising an awareness of presence – whether this is linguistic, corporeal or temporal – allows one to explore the interrelation of ecological issues which persist in southern Africa. These include, but are not limited to, environmental racism, exposure to health risks and a lack of access to sex education or reproductive agency. With her subversion of dualisms and coterminous associations, Vera stresses that these problems affect all members of a community. In the human sphere, and in the instance of abortion, this includes the foetus, gestating figure and her partner, as well as the surroundings they inhabit. Yet these agencies are not affected evenly or in equal ways: ecological models of egalitarianism do not necessarily lead to social equality.[12] Vera's materialist perspective on sexual and racial politics in a colonized landscape thus tempers the more idealistic and abstracted excesses of some new materialisms, and dares to venture beyond Barad's conception of the foetus-mother phenomenon.

Stacy Alaimo's emphasis on all organisms' shared origins, and on embracing rather than transcending the milieu, could emblematize several duplicitous twinnings that *Butterfly Burning*'s title evokes. Firstly, the titular butterfly may refer to an actual insect or to the figure of Phephelaphi. In both cases, the butterfly can be read in two ways: either as a subject possessing agency or as an object. A further layer of ambivalence is the word burning, which can be read as either a present participle (a verb, an action) or a noun (evoking Vera's aforementioned interests in ritual, tragedy and the act of repetition). Both of these dichotomies signify the stark difference between possibilities of agency and an apparent lack thereof, and yet the elemental evocation of fire concurrently calls this very binary into question. The act of burning evokes associations with death, much like the literary events of abortion and suicide which occur in the text. Yet, simultaneously, the protagonist metamorphoses through metonymy into a new form of agency through Vera's suggestive title. The transcorporeal human-butterfly that we encounter before beginning to read the novel – and again in its final pages – is thus indicative of an ever-changing and chronologically ambiguous transformation between birth, life and death. Although there are certainly tragic elements to the text, its constitutive duplicity signals that such terminations may not simply constitute an end. Instead, we are asked to imagine such instances of negation as no more than stages: through its continuous evocation of the present, both death and life are rendered as coterminous points on a continuum.

In my introductory chapter, I noted how there initially appears to be a slippage between the ambiguities and indeterminacies that tend to accompany a new materialist approach and the strategic acts of solidarity upon which postcolonial politics insist. Through its constant transference of transcorporeal desires and relationships in the present tense, however, *Butterfly Burning* illustrates that we must exceed humanist discourse if we are to articulate an alternative vocabulary for the supposed pro-life and pro-choice dichotomy: one which is elegant, yet accessible. At this point it is vital to stress again that posthumanist thought does not equate to an absolute rejection of all humanist ideals. This is especially true in the case of its postcolonial iterations, which must be careful to explicate how (and why) some lives have historically been privileged over others. There is no better way to embody such issues than through an abortion narrative, particularly one which is sensitive to recursions of unfair power relations in post/colonial settings. To date, many have read the novel as a tragic lament about abortion stigma in Rhodesia. The novel's aesthetic technique of metonymy is certainly feminist – and, in some senses, residually humanist – in that it stresses how a foetus simply does not hold the same political agency as a fully grown woman. Importantly, however, Vera chronicles two terminations of pregnancy. This suggests she is not interested in presenting a singular and didactic perspective on this ethical issue – a fact reinforced by her constant evocation of contradictions and the interplay of in/organic agencies. Thus, while the text presents a situated Zimbabwean perspective on abortion, a close analysis of its medical scenes reveals how this procedure also symbolizes how ecological, ethical and political interests all intersect in southern Africa. Evoking past traumas and yet witnessing the present, this points towards a notion of non-essentialist interconnectedness in the cultural sphere which can underlie both new materialist and postcolonial narratives about the comparative worth of all agencies.

Notes

1   For more on Soyinka's African drama, see Astrid van Weyenberg (2011).

2   Patterson's cultural history of slavery is integral to my analysis of Wilma Stockenström's abortion narrative *The Expedition to the Baobab Tree*; see Chapter 1 for my discussion of his theoretical work *Slavery and Social Death* (1982).

3   See my introduction for a discussion of the problematic elements of this commonly used phrase.

4   As Vera and the other authors in this study concentrate on terminations of pregnancy in their fiction, I focus solely on abortion rather than related reproductive health issues such as family planning and the insidious politics of population control. For a meticulous overview of the wider context of contraceptives in Zimbabwe, see Amy Kaler's *Running After Pills: Politics, Gender and Contraception in Colonial Zimbabwe* (2003).

5   Importantly, however, this phenomenon is not exclusive to southern African communities. A recent piece of investigative journalism from the United States found that an emphasis on neonatal care has resulted in exponential growth of the number of women's fatalities resulting from pregnancy and childbirth complications: see Nina Martin and Renee Montagne (2017).

6   See Chapter 4 for a detailed discussion of Head's influence on Vera, Wicomb and Stockenström.

7   For an extensive analysis of gendered national subjects and the 'Mother Africa' trope in the broader context of African literature, see Florence Stratton (1994).

8   For a full exploration of the distinction between origins and beginnings, see Chapter 1.

9   This is not to say that milk is always or even necessarily a nutritive substance, especially when considering the contemporary dairy industry. For a feminist and postcolonial material study of milk, see Greta Gaard (2013).

10 The sense of currentness inherent to this form of witnessing means that it differs from what is found in Mark Sanders's *Ambiguities of Witnessing: Law and Literature in the Time of a Truth Commission* (2007), a study reflecting upon literature and law in apartheid South Africa during the Truth and Reconciliation Commission.

11 This creative approach to chronology and time is taken to an even more explicit level of vital experimentation in Bessie Head's fiction, as I discuss in Chapter 4.

12 See, for example, Arne Naess's early conception of 'biospherical egalitarianism' (1973: 95).

4

Humans

Queer vitality and Bessie Head's fiction

I'm the New African who hasn't even started to exist in Africa. This is my
continent but I'm not a tribal man. I meet with no hostility just as long as I do
not impose my newness and strangeness.
  – Bessie Head to Pat and Wendy Cullinan, 28 September 1964

After three chronologically ordered analyses, this study deviates by ending at
the start: with South Africa's so-called first Black woman writer (Sam 1986: 55);
with a tale of natal origins and exilic beginnings. Academic and biographical
accounts of Bessie Head's life almost always begin by listing several formative
events, and this chapter follows in the tradition, if somewhat self-consciously:
born in the South African town of Pietermaritzburg in 1937, Head spent her
early years under the impression that she was the child of Nellie and George
Heathcote, a coloured couple. Then, when as a young teenager she moved to
an Anglican boarding school, authorities revealed that her biogenetic parents
were a white woman and a Black man. Her mother was a patient in a mental
hospital and her affluent parents were ashamed of both their daughter and
granddaughter, whom they saw as product and proof of an illicit relationship.
This traumatic revelation was one of many which Bessie Head would experience
while growing up in apartheid South Africa. After working for some years as
a teacher and journalist, she chose to exit the country on a one-way permit
and live as a refugee in Botswana. These are all facts that the writer is quick to
address in her own autobiographical writings (Head 1990: 3–5). When reading
her fiction, however, it is clear that the author was not as preoccupied with the
country of her birth as many believe. The plethora of historical recitations of
her early life convey the sense that the South African political climate should be
read as the primary thematic driver in her fiction: a strange situation, since Head
is simultaneously referred to as a *Botswanan* writer (nearly all of her fiction is

set in rural areas or villages like Serowe). Two text-book examples are Margaret Busby's (1992) and Margaret Lessing's (1994) edited collections on (South) African women and their writing, both of which introduce short summaries of Head's 'traumatic life' alongside excerpts from her fiction (Busby 1992: 482). In fact, reviewing secondary material on Head's work gives the distinct feeling that critics have overdetermined her supposedly tragic origins as a 'powerless' South African woman of colour, despite the fact that Head was extremely critical of nationalism and partisan identification.

In an interview on her identity as a southern African woman writer, Head comments that 'I tended to be born outside any box' (Head in Mackenzie and Clayton 1989: 17). Faced with a question about how she chooses to identify, she responds with seeming frustration: 'I am not torn by nationalistic arguments: "Are you South African?"; "Why have you settled here in the rural areas, and based all your books on Botswana rural life?" These arguments just don't matter to me – it's all props and things that I have found necessary' (Head in Mackenzie and Clayton 1989: 11). The writer has a strangely ambivalent, or even contradictory, attitude towards the role of inherited and acquired characteristics in shaping one's personal and artistic development. She insists she enjoys living outside of societally defined conventions or settings; yet, later she says that 'this particular environment' of Botswana has been vital to her art's formation (Head in Mackenzie and Clayton 1989: 18; 21). Seemingly counter-intuitively, in *A Woman Alone* she admits to being averse to liberation movements and the people who run them (Head 1990: 27), perhaps for the reason that 'nothing can take away the fact that I have never had a country; not in South Africa or in Botswana where I now live as a stateless person' (1990: 28). Head believes that an interest in politics is important, but she dislikes political parties and their often-polarized divisions between viewpoints (1990: 63). Examining her reactions closely, it transpires that the key here is not the name of any country, but rather the generative potential of the various environments in which her stories are set. Head notes, when asked about the importance of gardens in her novels, that 'I remember very well saying, because that was one of my attitudes, "Not the special "lily-white" artist, but somebody who touches the earth". I remember relating the writing of books to baking bread and peeling potatoes' (Head in Mackenzie and Clayton 1989: 24). Such vital labour with vegetal objects is genderless – the work of somebody, not some woman. Nevertheless, Head asserts that the work is performed in a mostly human, domestic sphere: 'No-one can abandon children, you just cannot abandon human life. If you haven't got your real mother concentrating on you, someone has to' (Head in Mackenzie and Clayton

1989: 29). While this definition of motherhood is rooted in the human realm, it nevertheless speaks to a form of gestationality that exceeds direct linear-genetic relationships, and which transcends any gendered definitions of maternity.

This chapter argues that Bessie Head's fictional writing queers materialism and its traditionally gender-dichotomous origins, presenting an understanding of development which exceeds temporal or national boundaries. Her treatment of human reproduction in both tangible and figurative terms disrupts teleological definitions of exile: separation and loss, rendered through abortions and related procedures, are seen as inherently vital processes for gaining agency in post/colonial southern Africa. My literary analysis explicitly concentrates on Head's biological imagery of growth and separation – whether this is coded through gardening, farming or literal human reproduction – and how this ruptures the sexist, racist and speciesist discourse underpinning colonial expansion in southern Africa. I refer to Head's ethical outlook as a critical form of humanism. My understanding of critical humanism differs from humanism proper in that it relies on queer associations[1]: both queerness as strangeness, as the epigraph to this chapter implies, and queerness as resistance to categorization (much like Head's critiques of essentialist national identities). Merging humanist affirmative stances with elements of queer posthumanism, Head's literary formulations of creativity and gestation – and the negation thereof – go on to inform later abortion narratives by southern African feminists.

The first southern African country to have gained independence from Britain, Botswana saw rapid economic and infrastructural growth from decolonization from 1966 onwards (Smith, 2013a: 44). With these developments came an apparent surge of popularity in liberal and feminist values. Published in 1977, Bessie Head's *The Collector of Treasures and Other Botswana Village Tales* presents a series of vignettes which investigate the relationship between physical and mental health, particularly in light of Botswanans' movements from rural to urban settings. Several of the stories allude to women's reproductive agency through adultery, infanticide and domestic abuse resulting in miscarriages. With such issues being brought to the fore of public discourse, one could optimistically believe that access to abortion would be relatively easy to obtain. Despite such artistic developments, however, the majority of Botswanans believed that abortion was immoral. The country continues to retain very basic laws relating to reproductive health. Up until 1991, its Ministry of Justice only allowed pregnancies to be terminated in extreme cases when the life of the woman was in jeopardy (Cook and Dickens 1983: 58); abortion is now legal under certain conditions, but only within the first sixteen weeks of pregnancy. Much as in the cases of Zimbabwe and South Africa, this means that poor, uneducated and/or Black women are most at risk for complications from unsafe terminations, while those who are more privileged find it easier to approach and pay specialists for their services.

Those who studied traditional attitudes towards abortion near the end of the twentieth century openly admitted that they were baffled by such conservative outlooks, considering that almost all cultures relied on abortifacients or surgically induced miscarriages long before the establishment of Western medical practices (Cook and Dickens 1983: 122). Rebecca J. Cook and Bernard M. Dickens observe that such hostility towards women's reproductive agency is at odds not only with international mandates like the Universal Declaration of Human Rights, but also with the 1981 African Charter which 'gives respect for life in Article 4 to "Every human being", and provides in Article 16.1 for the health of "Every individual", which does not clearly cover a child in utero' (1983: 63). Similarly, social anthropologist Stephanie S. Smith notes in her study of attitudes to abortion law that Botswana's Penal Code defines the murder of a child as only possible when it exists in a completely independent corporeal state from its mother (2013b: 30). There is thus clearly a disjuncture between Botswanan citizens' perceptions of foetal agency, national laws about abortion and the broader directives which most southern African states are purported to adhere to. While Smith's analyses contain some problematic stereotypes – such as the assumption that all modern democracies are necessarily beyond the influence of patriarchal ideology (2013b: 28), or the generalization that Botswanans have an 'informal attitude towards time' (2013a: 44) – she does generate some useful qualitative data about the average citizen's attitudes to reproductive health. Her research points towards the inextricable link between fertility and rites of passage in Tswana culture: not only is motherhood seen as synonymous with womanhood, but a Motswana woman is actually given a new name after the birth of her first child (2013b: 30). This tradition technically values both the gestating person and the foetus, but it is clear that the repronormative values of Tswana culture cause most to view abortion as irresponsible, thus giving preferential treatment to the potential life of the foetus. Furthermore, Smith reveals that the Setswana phrase for the medical procedure is '"go senya mpa", which translates as "to spoil/destroy the stomach"' (2013b: 50). The destructive denotation stands in direct contrast with the supposedly creative and nurturing traditional roles of women. Even if they may personally believe that they have the right to control their futures, this expression reveals how anti-abortion values may cause women to feel ambivalent or hostile towards voluntary terminations of pregnancy.

Abortion and reproductive health are most explicitly discussed in a chapter of Head's first novel, *When Rain Clouds Gather* (1968). Importantly, the section in question is published as a standalone story in her final (posthumous) collection, *Tales of Tenderness and Power* ([1989] 1990). Her fictional works published between these years – *Maru* ([1971] 2008), *A Question of Power* (1973) and *The Collector of Treasures and other Botswana Village Tales* ([1977] 1992) – are less direct, but no less important when it comes to discussing corporeality and the critical framework of new materialism. I am particularly struck by the term 'creative ferment', which appears in both *Maru* and *A Question of Power*,[2] and the concept of vitality, which recurs throughout all the texts in some shape or form. Vitality shares a root word with vitalism, the philosophical concept that states living organisms are distinct from inanimate objects because they are charged by an inexplicable life force. It must be stressed that Head does not use the latter term in her fiction and she also resists endorsing animist belief systems. Her views are more akin to the not-entirely materialist theory of Claire Colebrook, who writes of 'Queer Vitalism' in *Sex after Life: Essays on Extinction, Volume Two* (2014). In *Sex after Life* Colebrook attempts to recuperate vitalism from its spiritualist associations by queering the organic/inorganic dualism – but this new intervention remains myopic in its dismissal of agency as a political tool. Later in this chapter I engage with some specificities of Colebrook's argument, acknowledging the pivotal role of feminist contributions in this debate but further developing her work by forging a queer vita*lity* as seen in Head's fictional oeuvre. Vitality, according to my philosophical definition, is distinct from vitalism in that it has an ethical and political commitment to uncoupling growth from reproduction, and further disassociating both concepts from Western, materialist conceptions of development.

In two letters to the South African publisher A. D. Donker written during 1984, Bessie Head expresses that she desires for three of her earlier novels – *When Rain Clouds Gather*, *Maru* and *A Question of Power* – to be published as a trilogy titled 'Personal Choices'. While there is a broad sense of chronology here, the most important reason for gathering these texts is their *thematic* preoccupations, as reflected by the collective title which foregrounds choice (in opposition to power, a word that recurs in analyses of her work). The same letters state that a second trilogy would consist of *The Collector of Treasures*, *Serowe: Village of the Rain Wind* and *A Bewitched Crossroad*. She explains that these three texts are united by their interest in the Botswanan Chief Khama III and 'his care for women', his 'human grandeur' that allowed her to realize that 'an harmonious relationship existed between me and my environment'. Recalling Head's characterization of her creative output as cultivating a relationship between the human artist and the earth, and considering this comment alongside her environmentalist reflections provoked by Chief Khama III, it seems apt to begin my analysis with the first text from the second trilogy (neither of the collections, it must be noted, were published before Head's death).[3] I am particularly interested in the agentive in/action of negation that several characters undertake, which allows them to experiment with non-reproductive narrative chronologies.

After discussing the critical reception of Head's oeuvre, I move on to my cross-referential analysis of her aforementioned stories and novels and their communication with queer forms of vitality. My point of entry is *The Collector of Treasures*. The text overtly investigates violence displayed towards women, children and domesticated or farmed animals: nonhuman entities appear in this collection to address quite human concerns. My analysis draws predominantly on the titular story, in which conversations between female prisoners reveal that many of their pregnancies were terminated by their male partners' physical abuse, thereby complicating the rhetoric of choice which dominates much media coverage of abortion. Other short stories focus on adultery, infanticide and the gendered rural/urban divide; collectively, they thematize how restrictions in reproductive agency and gender roles impact upon both mental and physical health. This relationship between the tangible and intangible is broached in Head's other works. The second text to be analysed in detail is Head's first novel *When Rain Clouds Gather*, and particularly its engagement with growth and vitality. There are interesting parallels between the extended metaphor of termination that is employed when discussing Hendrik Verwoerd in Zoë Wicomb's *You Can't Get Lost in Cape Town* and Chief Matenge's resignation-by-suicide in Head's text. (As mentioned in Chapter 2, Verwoerd was assassinated in 1966, the same year that Botswana gained independence from Britain.) I argue that the material nature of her fiction highlights the intersections between patriarchal and nationalist anxieties about power in the 1970s. As discussed below, this text is notable for its frank treatment of abortion in a chapter which appears as a standalone story in Head's final collection, *Tales of Tenderness and Power*. For the sake of thematic cohesion, I move onto a discussion of the two remaining novels, *Maru* and *A Question of Power*, before briefly considering their continuities with *Tales of Tenderness and Power*. I conclude by considering how Head's queer chronologies present a new and materialist approach to southern African futures.

'Something or someone' and *The Collector of Treasures*

Gillian Stead Eilersen observes that Head wrote to her publisher that the order of stories in *The Collector of Treasures* was vital, as she viewed them as a unit wherein one segment flowed into another (1990: 11). While I would not argue against reading the text in a linear fashion, it is important to stress that this chapter will not be following a teleological model of progression, and that Head's definition of continuity clearly defies traditional understandings of chronology (Eilersen 1990: 11). Lee Edelman's queer critique of reproductive futurism has been indispensable here. As I briefly discuss in my introduction, he defines reproductive futurism as any heteronormative political discourse which limits the possibility of thinking through communal relations without revering linear familial ties (Edelman 2004: 2) – the most sacrosanct of these being the parent–child relationship. It is undeniable that even in supposedly progressive social spheres, veneration of traditional family models and values remains. As Edelman observes, 'Even proponents of abortion rights, while promoting the freedom of women to control their own bodies through reproductive choice, recurrently frame their political struggle, mirroring their anti-abortion foes, as a "fight for our children – for our daughters and our sons", and thus as a fight for the future' (2004: 3). Some may ask what harm there could be in framing abortion and reproductive agency as issues which will affect future generations. These are, after all, issues which involve both mother and child. Yet the semantics of reproductive futurism and repronormativity mean that woman and foetus are rarely granted equal ethical consideration or rights. The subtle grammar of Edelman's monograph insists that any younger figure is elevated to the status of the Child, while a parent's needs and worth are rendered as secondary concerns. (Rather problematically, Edelman seems pointedly uninterested in the gendered specificities of such erasure, a point to which I shall return shortly.) His proposed solution to this conundrum is an ethics of refusal: one which is averse to the binarized models of difference underpinning most political debates, and thus inherently opposed to its own oppositional logic (Edelman 2004: 4). His theory is somewhat esoteric in its paradoxical nature, but it nevertheless provides an important challenge to those who wish to support women's reproductive agency without eclipsing the importance of lateral (rather than linear) relationships. With this queer, unthinkable logic in mind, in this section I enquire how we may read abortion narratives so as to foreground women's embodied experiences, instead of privileging the incorporeal Child who may, or may not, come into existence.

Interpreting the issue of chronology on another, more metaphorical level, Head is also exploring tensions between the modern and the rural with references to folktale-inspired oral and written forms, and by referring to canonical anglophone writers. I am particularly interested in how she reads – or how her work has been read alongside – Modernist authors like Virginia Woolf. Head insists she is not in the same category as 'suicidal' writers such as Woolf or Sylvia Plath; she believes her writing is distinct from theirs because it approaches mental illness with a sense of humour (Head in Mackenzie and Clayton 1989: 26). While her thematic treatment of depression and suicide certainly differs from these writers, her work does hold some stylistic resonances with anglophone Modernism and the literatures which operate in its wake. In keeping with her rejection of the aforementioned women writers, most of her literary, philosophical and scientific influences operate in Western, masculinist traditions: Bertolt Brecht, Albert Camus, Charles Darwin and Friedrich Nietzsche are all referenced in her letters or non-fictional writings, overshadowing passing mention of less celebrated writers like Simone Weil, or southern African philosophical traditions (Head's suspicion of both feminism and tribalism appears to stem from her aforementioned fear of supposedly radical political identifications, resulting in an omission of movements like womanism from her literary corpus). It is worth mentioning that Jane Bennett's materialist vitalism is formed in a very similar manner: both women rely on the affirmative, absurdity-embracing power of the yes-man. Bennett's influential monograph *Vibrant Matter: A Political Ecology of Things* (2009) is composed of eight brief chapters with a plethora of references to secondary sources. The author draws on the affirmation of life – as seen in the philosophy of Friedrich Nietzsche, and the poetry of Walt Whitman – and the Actor-network Theory (ANT) of Bruno Latour. It is interesting that a supposedly feminist materialist follows such masculinist traditions, with only two mentions of Donna Haraway (and none of Rosi Braidotti). Yet of all the writers in this study, Bessie Head is least concerned with matters external to the human realm. Unlike Bennett, on the topic of materialism the author is decidedly ambivalent, a point which I develop in my literary analysis.

Adding another dimension to the issue of paradoxes, Head repeated in interviews and her non-fictional writings that she was not a feminist; she insisted that her fiction was not women's writing, that it was 'sexless' (1990: 95). I follow Elinor Rooks in considering Head's words not as anti-feminist, but rather as expressing dissatisfaction with white, cisgender, first- and second-wave feminisms which were popular at the time of writing (2017: par. 33). It is undeniable that Head seeks to unsettle the gender binary, as evidenced by her assertion that 'I'm not a feminist in the sense that I do not see women as separate from men' (Head in Eilersen 1995: 238). Her misgivings are therefore because she reads mainstream (white) feminism as unnecessarily divisive, and potentially alienating to Black men or other indispensable allies. It must be stressed that putting Head's work in conversation with feminism – and the legacies of philosophical vitalism – is not to disregard her suspicions about potential tensions that the political movement may cause. Rather, I wish to move past an apparent omission in recent scholarship, which has mostly tended to overlook how Head's fiction evokes and expands upon the same lexicon as supposedly new materialist theories. A notable exception is a recent article by Frances Hemsley on epigenetic imaginaries in *The Cardinals* (1995), a posthumously published novella that is thought to be the first piece of long-form fiction that Bessie Head wrote. Hemsley provides a convincing and astute analysis of environmental racism and heredity in the novella as Head experiments with distributive models of more-than-human agency (Hemsley 2021: 163–4).

Nevertheless, it is remarkable how many contemporary analyses of Head's work still focus exclusively on *A Question of Power*. Caroline Davis, for instance, provides an autobiographically informed reading of the text and Head's relationship with its publishers in a 2018 article. Two pieces written in the same year by Sayyed Rahim Moosavinia and Sayyede Maryam Hosseini, and Denae Dyck and Tim Heath, put the novel in dialogue with postcolonial theory – the works of Homi K. Bhabha and Njabulo S. Ndebele, respectively. The latter two articles both analyse the space of the garden but are more interested in metaphorizing this ground as a 'garden-variety' Third Space than in grappling with potential materialist implications of Head's textual environments (Dyck and Heath 2018: 53). One notable exception to this trend is Cajetan Iheka's *Naturalizing Africa: Ecological Violence, Agency, and Postcolonial Resistance in African Literature* (2017), which features an analysis of materialist-oriented distributed agencies in Head's *When Rain Clouds Gather*. Iheka's conceptualization of 'resistance from the ground' is less concerned with biological processes than with a broad schematization of potentially environmentalist ambiguities in the novel (2017: 127), and it is most refreshing for its conclusion that such narratives 'tell a story of nature's vitality and underscore the fact that human actions cannot be divorced from the effects on their environment and vice versa' (2017: 145).

While Hemsley's and Iheka's readings are in the minority, this is not to say, of course, that the author's fiction had never before been put in dialogue with materialist science studies. In a 2004 book chapter on the textual politics of Bessie Head, Desiree Lewis utilizes feminist retheorizations of standpoint epistemologies, briefly referencing how Donna Haraway and Patricia Hill Collins 'deal with the liberating consequences of "seeing from below" in terms of compound power relationships that shape multiple marginalities', thus leading 'beyond essentialist, fixed constructions of identity and cultural boundaries' (Lewis 2004: 123). Lewis is right to draw a parallel between the aims of intersectional feminism and feminist anti-anthropocentrism, particularly for their implicit investment in moving beyond essentialist markers of social belonging and meaning. Yet her analysis dwells more on spiritual matters than materialism proper. She distances Head's work from the poststructuralist turn against self-sufficiency by citing references to Eastern philosophy in her fiction, arguing that they are evidence of the author's 'tremendous faith in individuals' creative resources' (129). While it is true that the author did read and debate theology beyond the Abrahamic religions (mostly from Hinduism and Buddhism), it seems bizarre to privilege these often tangential references in her writing over a central theme and plot motif: marginalized southern Africans' (and, often, women's) attempts to attain agency through creative, playful subversions of power dynamics. The invocation of a universally liberating potential supposedly found in new iterations of standpoint epistemologies also ultimately reifies humanist ideals such as political power and rights, which Head undoubtedly desired but also critiqued, as the repeated and literal questioning of the word power in her titles suggests.

In a monograph published eight years prior to Lewis' study, Maria Olaussen analyses the roles of environmental setting and identity in *When Rain Clouds Gather*, *Maru* and *A Question of Power*. She also utilizes emerging theories by Donna Haraway, but goes further by citing Rosi Braidotti – as well as Martin Heidegger, Simone de Beauvoir, Frantz Fanon and other influential critical theorists – in a complex framework that she associates with 'post-colonial feminist theory' (Olaussen 1997: 14). Her reason for doing so, she explains, is because 'the contradictions in Head's vision of an identity which is at one and the same time both multifaceted and unitary, both sensitive to the precarious situation of women and highly sexist, both celebratory of the African village and Euro-centric in its evaluations, constitute a considerable theoretical and critical challenge' (Olaussen 1997: 14). Contradictoriness is crucial to remember when speaking of Bessie Head. Olaussen argues that the conflicts between the more contemporary theories and older (humanist) frameworks she uses are deliberate, helping to foreground the paradoxes in Head's own work (1997: 15). Her approach is inspirational, not least for asserting that the author was decidedly ahead of her time for redefining place and placelessness and the role that gender plays in shaping these concepts. It is a successful project in that it takes seriously matters which Head actively participated in and reflected upon in her non-fictional writing, such as housekeeping and gardening. Olaussen also reminds readers that Head's interest in religion was tempered by an equal fascination with Darwinian evolutionary theory (1997: 155). Where my approach differs from Olaussen's is that I am not concerned with the artist's construction of a 'positive female identity' so much as her interrogation of messier metaphors (1997: 16), and her foreshadowing of queer ecological theories.

Here I am referring particularly to Nicole Seymour's *Strange Natures: Futurity, Empathy, and Queer Ecological Imagination* (2013). Seymour is wary of Edelman's queer critique of futurism, not least since 'it is corporate and governmental *disregard* for the future that enables the (paradoxical) reproduction of capital [...]. These shortcomings are particularly troubling from both an anti-racist and environmental-justice standpoint' (2013: 7–8; original emphasis). I agree with this assessment and am also sceptical of the lack of consideration for the gestating (normatively female) figure in Edelman's critique. If one is to invoke materialist feminism as a critical framework, then one must commit to exploring entangled connections between textual and gestational environments. Furthermore, my analysis foregrounds multiple facets of women's reproductive agency and how they figure metaphorically for creativity. In Olaussen's last chapter, she concludes that 'Head's movement from a position of differences within to a place of dichotomous sexual difference is [...] not primarily a nomadic project' (1997: 289). I agree with her assessment that Braidotti's theory of nomadic subjects, which is heavily influenced by the work of Gilles Deleuze and Félix Guattari, is ultimately at odds with Head's words. This, however, leads me to identify a theory which may resonate with a large majority of the author's work. In short, Olaussen is open about the difficulties of applying theory to a contradictory author; my proposed solution is to utilize an equally paradoxical framework, such as Colebrook's and Seymour's. Drawing on the work of Michael Snediker, Seymour formulates a queer optimism wherein 'value is determined by the communal and empathetic process of valuing' (2013: 11) – a thought which is refreshing for its uncoupling of anti-repronormativity from failure and pessimism, but which nevertheless appears slightly tautological (it is unclear whether value precedes the empathic process or precipitates it).

As one of the most well-known authors originating from southern Africa, Bessie Head's fiction has been the subject of many interventions in postcolonial criticism; and, despite her misgivings about feminism, her identity as a *woman* writer means that her oeuvre has also been a source of interest to many gender studies scholars. The intersection of these academic interests is made strikingly apparent in *Motherlands: Black Women's Writing from Africa, the Caribbean and South Asia*, edited by Susheila Nasta. The collection of essays was published just five years after Head's death in 1986 and her presence is palpable throughout the text. *Motherlands* contains three comparative analyses that are most notable for their discussions of Bessie Head's life and work. In a sense, these responses serve as a barometer aggregating responses to Head in the academy. On one end of the continuum, Valerie Kibera examines instances of adoption in novels by Marjorie Macgoye and Bessie Head; her analysis epitomizes traditional approaches to Head's work which focus on the literal and metaphorical abandonment she felt after leaving South Africa in exile (1991: 315). One must stress that, despite involvement with unfortunate political events which precipitated her move, Head was not 'forced' out of the country (Kibera 1991: 315): she chose to leave. I take issue with terminology that portrays the author as ostensibly childlike in her helplessness – a characterization not unrelated to her precarious mental health, which is also regularly foregrounded in biographical and critical studies. Many argue that Head is a social commentator first and foremost (Kibera 1991: 326), and that any concerns with politics in her works are secondary to this fact. Yet in the case of gender justice – particularly issues involving reproductive healthcare – it is undeniable that the personal is political. By thematizing such sensitive material, Head is utilizing biological agency in the social microcosm to experiment with solutions to macrocosmic political problems.

Secondly, Jane Bryce-Okunlola compares the works of Flora Nwapa, Rebeka Njau and Bessie Head to explore how different representations of motherhood are utilized as metaphors for creativity in novels by African women. She draws on the work of Margaret Tucker, who describes Head's questioning of vegetal and human reproduction through female gardeners as a 'departure from linear time, [...] a sort of distorted prolepsis' (Tucker 1988: 174–5). In *A Question of Power*, the protagonist Elizabeth chooses to sell the fruit she grows in a panic instead of making jam, which Tucker argues means 'she appears to be in stasis; cut off from production for so long, she is not yet able to exert her own powers of reproduction' (1988: 175). This brief yet intriguing connection between material and metaphorical manifestations of gendered reproduction informs my later reading of *A Question of Power*. Bryce-Okunlola's analysis is interesting for its focus on feminine desire as a response to absence – this is particularly pertinent when considering the recurrence of desire as a critical concept in my earlier analysis of Zoë Wicomb's *You Can't Get Lost in Cape Town* – and artistic creativity as a fulfilling alternative to repronormative expectations (1991: 201). Once again, the emphasis here is predominantly on the social sphere. More accurately, it is argued that the predominant concern in Head's novels is the 'internal exile of motherlessness' and how this leads to a sense of alienation (Bryce-Okunlola 1991: 203). By all means, we are told, Head experiments with aesthetic production through her female characters, but this is only as a result of traumatic loss. According to these readings, abortion or adoption are not manifestations of desire but rather unfortunate narrative disruptions in normative social development. As I imply in my previous chapter on Yvonne Vera, however, it is highly infantilizing to regard childless or motherless protagonists as compensating artistically for a perceived lack. A more promising alternative would be for feminists to focus on developing an ethics of refusal – one which does not bemoan the social consequences of negation, but rather presents abortion as a process of desiring alternative forms of life.

This critical engagement with refusal, challenging the tendency for it to be associated with the tragedy of nothingness, is subtly posed by Caroline Rooney as she considers the poetics of survival in Ama Ata Aidoo's *Our Sister Killjoy* and Head's *A Question of Power*. Her analysis begins by reminding readers that the OED definition of motherland is native country:

> 'Mother' then functions as a substitute for 'native' and a trope for 'of origin'. It seems then that one could alternatively use the term 'fatherland' which is defined as: 'one's native land'. However, there is obviously asymmetry. *Fatherland is marked by ownership – one's – whereas motherland is, in comparison, 'no one's'.* 'Motherland' can also be placed next to 'mothercountry', defined as: 'country in relation to its colonies'. *'-land' therefore pertains to the native, while '-country' to the colonial relation,* which suggests that motherland/native country is only country in terms of terrain, whereas mothercountry, as country-country and not country-land, is a proper country, a territory.
>
> (Rooney 1991: 99; emphasis added)

Rooney's critical treatment of the terms through which her chapter – and the rest of the collection – emerges is crucial. Her etymological analysis speaks to concerns of natal alienation which preoccupied women living both inside and in exile from South Africa during the twentieth century, as my first chapter on Wilma Stockenström demonstrates. In *The Expedition to the Baobab Tree*, the author deliberately obfuscates the narrative setting: we only know the protagonist makes a journey inland from the 'native' country-land of her birth, since the mothercountry as 'country-country' is never identified by name. Throughout the novella, there is an explicit avowal of rejection and its transformative powers.

Certainly, Head's writing is more situated and explicit about geographical markers than Stockenström's. Yet both South African-born authors believed there was a clear linkage between colonial conquering, nationalism and heterosexual domestication, as seen in a letter from Bessie Head to Wendy Cullinan from 28 July 1964. She writes:

> We once had an Afrikaans teacher and he knew what it meant to love that country [South Africa]. He looked at its hills and its silence and made himself so much a part of it that he could not let anyone else love it. So jealous and possessive is he. [...] Afrikaners love that country possessively and its [*sic*] with a destructive kind of love that wants to crush and keep the loved thing all to itself. A land and a people can form that kind of affinity – just like a love between a man and a woman. [...] The whole world should not come to a full stop because someone loves something or someone!

Notwithstanding its reliance on generalizations (with which the Afrikaans native speaker would conceivably disagree), there are undeniable similarities between this passage and Stockenström's attitude to the concept of the motherland, and the possessiveness it enables. The animalized slave in *The Expedition to the Baobab Tree* attempts to queer the power dynamic between herself and her male owner/lover. When she loses her love interest, she chooses to withdraw from the world by escaping to the baobab tree, counting her remaining days with a string of beads and ultimately committing suicide. With a literally terminal 'Yes.' (Stockenström 1983: 111), she embraces negation as the only in/action which allows her to express agency. Likewise, Head utilizes punctuation in the above quotation to figure for the impossible logic of colonial domination and gendered control. Her description of Afrikaner nationalism is conveyed in grammatically sparse, lengthy sentences, until she finally disrupts the narrative with an exclamatory cry (rallying against a metaphorical full stop). It is particularly striking how she draws attention to the indeterminacies of subjectivity which such possessiveness enables. For example, if the object of veneration is a more-than-human construct like a country, it may be elevated to such an extent by the nationalist that it is seen as more important than a real human being, even someone who is a fellow patriot. Alternatively, the object of affection may be human (someone), but the intensity of possessiveness renders them as a literal object, as something. There are remarkable slippages here between human and nonhuman agencies because of colonialism, nationalism and patriarchal domination.

The negation implicit in 'no one's land', Rooney argues, can be reconfigured to denote different relationships with the environment: 'It could be a case of everyone's land; or, a case of being subject to the land or nature, and acknowledgment of a certain vital dependency' (1991: 100). Rooney seems to be gesturing towards materialism when she argues that spiritual figures and environmental actors in Head's fiction operate as more than mere metaphorical or metaphysical devices; she even creates an almost ecocritical term for the narrative's constant evocation of terminations and beginnings, namely a 'literary textual economy of recyclement' (Rooney 1991: 123). Yet she approaches this notion through psychoanalytic theory, and her text is more concerned by what is (or is not) an 'African' poetics of survival than the specificities in Head's writing that went on to influence anglophone writers like South African-born Zoë Wicomb and Zimbabwean-born Yvonne Vera. While acknowledging the uniqueness of Rooney's approach, I wish to focus on the critical humanism at play in Head's work, which uses images of growth, negation and separation to challenge both colonial and liberationist discourse.

Although something of a renegade in her national and religious values, Head was not immune to the moral alarmism characteristic of twentieth-century Botswana when regarding the sexual lives of young women. In her autobiographical writing, she likens pre- or extramarital reproduction to social crisis: 'a high rate of illegitimate births among the children [legal minors]' is a particular concern (Head 1990: 57). She insists that these are issues she wishes to address through her fiction (1990: 62), with her personal investment in ethics being particularly apparent in her earlier work (1990: 77). Yet there are moments in both her nonfiction and short stories that exceed didacticism and are imaginatively bizarre and transgressive. Marital sex-as-reproduction contrasts with traditional methods of abstinence like thigh sex, for example, a practice which renders sex as an unproductive and potentially queer act. And while she was concerned for young women's health, she appeared frustrated, or even bored, by discussions of their bodies. This was particularly true when she was the focus of such scandals. On 18 May 1970, she complains in a letter that Botswanan society fixates upon women's appearances (particularly their bellies) and how their bodies signify for reproductive responsibilities: 'I've had the longest pregnancy in history with no man in sight. And I have fantastic sex parts which have been thoroughly and widely discussed with no one really knowing what they are like' (Head 1991: 121). Her ironic interpretation of attitudes to her physical appearance may be intended as jocular, but it is also illuminating when considering the thematic preoccupations of her fiction. For here, as in Head's stories, a woman is subject to the dictates of sexist society: no matter if she is supposedly pregnant for longer than nine months, or if she denies having had sexual intercourse, she is still at risk of being called both a virgin and a whore.

Many of the women in *The Collector of Treasures and Other Botswana Village Tales* are pariahs: living both figuratively and literally on the outskirts, they have been abandoned – or at least disappointed – by men. On one level, this is obviously a sustained metaphor for how 'the choices made by individuals are linked to the choices made by the society in the ongoing struggle between the forces of tradition and modernity' (Johnson 2008: 156). Yet there is also another dimension to the insider/outsider dichotomy that Head evokes in this short story collection, especially when one considers that most of the controversial female characters are outcasts for transgressing repronormative values in their communities. With their condemnation comes a certain degree of moral scepticism. Gillian Stead Eilersen astutely notes that in stories involving murder or infanticide, the perpetrators are often portrayed as relatable, and village members are cognisant of how easily they could commit similar crimes (1995: 169–70).

Overall, Head's first published collection of short stories takes an unusual approach to narrative development. 'The Collector of Treasures' is the penultimate story in the collection and its form is disjointed. The first of its four segments opens with the focalizer, Dikeledi, gazing out of a police truck at the rural landscape as she is transported from her village to a prison in Gaborone: 'The everyday world of ploughed fields, grazing cattle, and vast expanses of bush and forest seemed indifferent to the hungry eyes of the prisoner who gazed out at them through the wire mesh grating of the back of the police truck' (Head [1977] 1992: 87). The mention of bovine animals here calls to mind how cows are transported in a similar way, immediately highlighting the linkage between colonial control and domestication of both women and farmed animals. For the crime Dikeledi has committed is the result of a domestic dispute: she killed her husband by cutting off his genitals with a knife (89). She learns from the prison warden that four other women have been imprisoned for the same offence. An inmate named Kebonye admits to having castrated her adulterous husband with a razor after she 'aborted with a child' when he kicked her between the legs (89); she takes the matter of others' contraception and safety into her own hands by killing him (90). The omniscient narrator explains, 'That kind of man lived near the animal level and behaved just the same. Like the dogs and bulls and donkeys, he also accepted no responsibility for the young he procreated and like the dogs and bulls and donkeys, he also made females abort' (91). Two things are notable here. Firstly, the earlier evocation of the 'dreaded comparison' of women's and animals' labour is subverted as this abusive man is repeatedly animalized (through reference to three species that have connotations of sexual exuberance in popular discourse). Head is undeniably relying on a traditionally humanist hierarchy of species, but her association of a man's poor behaviour with that of domesticated animals' is unusual. Secondly, it is notable that the word 'abort' is used here, and not 'miscarry'. Head's choice of word is doubtless deliberate, as in the same story she uses the latter word to refer to the loss of a pregnancy by a woman in a healthy relationship: 'Kenalape had a miscarriage and had to be admitted to hospital for a minor operation' (97). Abortion is normally seen as a women's issue – both by activists who are for or against the medical procedure – but in this instance, it is the result of a man's (or, when regarding the metaphorical rendering, a male animal's) actions. Indeterminacies of reproductive agency are thus foregrounded from Head's subtle engagement with anthropocentric diction and her inversion of species-based sexualization.

The second section of the titular story breaks into a meditation by the narrator about two types of men in modern southern Africa. Firstly, there is the sort of man whom Dikeledi married, a selfish and sexist character type who appears in several of Head's stories and novels. In an earlier story titled 'Life', for example, the story's namesake marries the controlling Lesego who cannot understand her sexual vitality and *joie de vivre* (it is not a coincidence that the spelling of her first name puns on a binarized contrast of 'Life' and 'death', personified (41)). The protagonist responds by initiating affairs with other men, and the impact of her behaviour is metaphorically foreshadowed by the death of new-born calves at Lesego's cattle-post (44): an interspecies variation on the theme of sterility and loss. He learns about the affairs and decides to use his slaughtering knife to kill Life (45). Some may argue that the similarity between Dikeledi's and Lesego's crimes is proof of Head's lack of a feminist agenda, and that her fiction is more interested in exploring the hypocrisies of the human condition than in gender-based violence. Yet it is crucial to note that Life never abuses her husband, and that he is made aware of her transgressive sexual proclivities long before they are married (when they first meet, she is a sex worker). Dikeledi, in contrast, is repeatedly emotionally and physically humiliated by her husband. Two further male characters who commit gendered crimes are the grandfather Mokgobja and his son Ramadi in 'Looking for a Rain God', who sacrifice Ramadi's two young daughters in the hopes that this will precipitate rainfall during a drought (59). Abuse, infanticide and murder are thus recurring themes throughout the collection, highlighting how common it is for the 'first type' of man to harm female-identifying persons – whether they have children or not, or even if they are children themselves.

Yet female characters in Head's oeuvre are far from helpless, as 'The Collector of Treasures' and other stories imply. In 'Snapshots of a Wedding', the third-person narrator suggests that women in rural Botswana may strategically plan when to present as pregnant (79). This display of agency complicates the traditionally tragic narrative of women being helpless subjects who must suffer due to the unpredictability of their excreting (either menstruating or childbearing) bodies.[4] A similar thought is expressed in the final story, 'Hunting', where a character assures herself that she will win a man's affections by feigning pregnancy: 'Agh, I'll tell him I'm expecting a child. I hate them all anyway' (107). In 'The Special One' (the only story in the collection that is narrated in the first person), a woman speaks frankly about female desire and sexuality, stating that the libido increases with age and especially after menopause (84). While the character's advice to other women is interesting, it is not necessarily helpful or true. For example, she adheres to the superstitious belief that period sex is dangerous (84), providing the bizarre justification that 'all primitive societies have their holy fear of a woman's menstrual cycle' (85). Ironically, while this is the only story to use first-person narration, it is also the only one to present such a distanced and anthropological perspective on African cultural practices – perhaps foregrounding tensions between the author's own indebtedness to traditional customs and modern Eurocentric attitudes. Here Head creates a memorable character who addresses an unspoken reality for many women: the fear of fertility, and the incongruence of biological realities (desire increasing with age) with societal narratives (of fertile young girls and desexualized older women). Working in tandem with these women's internal strength is their solidarity through sharing traumatic narratives.

One is reminded here of Edward Said's distinction between filiation and affiliation (1983: 23–4). According to Said, contemporary textual critics may form their opinions in one of two ways: either in response to unchosen genetic and early environmental factors like their nationalities or places of birth, or by actively forging new allegiances based on similar social and political values. In his recent work on transcultural adoption, John McLeod moves further beyond normative notions of literal or metaphorical family by envisioning identity formation not through a blood-line but as the 'life line' in the palm of a hand, a crease in the skin which is determined, up to a point, by biogenetic inheritance, yet shaped by the agency and actions of the individual (2015: 26). There are certainly differences between affiliation and 'adoptive being' (McLeod 2015: 23), but both Said's and McLeod's couching of this distinction in biological terms (between faithfulness to what one is descended from, and devotion to that which one is not related to) is particularly interesting. For Bessie Head – a writer whose work is informed by her own literal and figurative 'adoptive being' – women certainly gain agency through nonbiological linkages. This is even the case when they bond over shared stories of embodied processes like abortion, childbirth and domestic violence. In 'The Collector of Treasures', and many of the collection's other tales, women find kindred spirits beyond biogenetic kin.

Survival strategies may be necessary for women in some circumstances, but Head's vision of gender relations is not without hope. For there are two types of men, according to the author, and the second is far removed from the first. The narrator in 'The Collector of Treasures' reflects that 'there was another kind of man in the society with the power to *create himself anew*. He turned all his resources, *both emotional and material*, towards his family life and he went on and on with his own quiet rhythm, like a river. He was a poem of tenderness' (93; emphasis added). I am interested in the new, materialist potential embedded within this description of such a (hu)man and the echoes of Neimanis's posthuman gestationality and Alaimo's aqueous posthumanism as discussed in Chapters 1 and 3, respectively. Head is both using and subverting the gender binary: there are two types of people, implicitly (men and women), but it is clear that within these groupings there are further sub-categories. The second type of man is actually a queer amalgamation of both stereotypically masculine and feminine traits which flow like a river in their constant indeterminacy. In some instances, such a man appears to be more creative and (re)productive than women, as when Thato in 'Hunting' immerses herself in Tholo because of 'the barrenness of her own life' (96). This is also the case in 'The Collector of Treasures' when Dikeledi's neighbour Paul offers to care for her children and pay for their education as she is sent to prison (103). Unlike with the other male figure in her life, Paul's idea of delivering her from motherhood is not through an act of violence like enforced abortion, and he does not feel entitled to sexual rewards for his platonic kindness. Such masculine tenderness is also foregrounded from the very first story, 'The Deep River: A Story of Ancient Tribal Migration': as in both 'The Collector of Treasures' and 'Hunting', we are presented with a man (the chief's son, Sebembele) who is 'unmanly' (4).

There are echoes here of Virginia Woolf's assertion in *A Room of One's Own* that 'it is fatal to be a man or woman pure and simple; one must be woman-manly or man-womanly' ([1929] 2008: 136).[5] Woolf's blending of both male and female characteristics is particularly instructive when one considers that there are also powerful women in *The Collector of Treasures*. In other words, Head's classifications of 'men' refer to any human being. In the short story

'Witchcraft', for example, Mma-Mabele is given the nickname 'he-man' (Head [1977] 1992: 49). On the surface, this may appear a puzzling term: instead of the more commonly known insult, she-man, these words do not include any marker of female sex. Genital biology is not rendered as indeterminate so much as irrelevant: the nickname has less to do with brute strength than her social standing. She is thus not something to be mocked, but rather someone to be respected. The incongruence of gender and sex is prominent in this collection, and they merge with moments of vitalist continuities between the human and nonhuman. Despite charges of anti-feminism or gender-essentialism, Head's situated understanding of multiple genders within rural Botswanan society works against the Mother Africa trope found in many nationalist writings and sentiments of the time. The manly woman and womanly man are found in Woolf's Modernist works, certainly, but Head is equally invested in showing that flexible gender identities existed in premodern southern Africa and may be revived in the postcolonial present. Experiments with chronology in her earlier works show how male tenderness and female power are encoded with the queer and vital potential of self-formation.

Creative ferment in the *Personal Choices* trilogy

Claire Colebrook has recently grappled with vitalism's queer potentiality. Colebrook distinguishes between 'active' and 'passive' vitalism (2014: 100); while queer theory can be built on either, she argues that the former invests too heavily in the social construct of the self through familial relations (2014: 100–1). Considering the above discussion of af/filiation and adoptive being, it would appear that such a distinction would be useful for analysing an oeuvre like Bessie Head's, with all its references to abortion, adoption and other disruptions of repronormative teleology. Yet I take issue with Colebrook's dismissal of agency or activity in favour of passivity. In a 2014 article on creative becoming and patiency which explains and expands upon Colebrook's theory, philosopher Patrice Haynes criticizes how some theories informed by Colebrook's work associate masculinity 'with vibrant, creative productivity', while 'woman is aligned with less favoured qualities such as passivity, reproduction and inertia' (Haynes 2014: 132). This is a fair criticism of new materialisms, particularly those iterations which are dedicated solely to considering Western theorizing of agentive activity. However, I have already demonstrated by work done in previous chapters that reproduction is not passive; regardless of outcome (parenthood or childlessness), reproductive agency allows for multiple forms of vital potential to emerge. Just like Edelman, Haynes (and, by extension, Colebrook) relies here on the very dualistic nature of difference that she criticizes, by distinguishing one strain of vitalism from another and suggesting that only one holds feminist or queer potential. I do share their suspicion of materialist feminists' focus upon the agentive potential of matter, as a grown woman undoubtedly holds more intentional clout than foetal tissue (even if both possess agency in the recalcitrant and disruptive sense that the new materialists suggest humanist accounts exclude). That said, Colebrook's evocation of 'passive vitalism' tends too much to the side of political inertia, and her chapter in *Sex after Life* feels half-developed as it closes by quoting Deleuze and Guattari rather than formulating what her own queer vitalism entails. Furthermore, I am not inclined to invoke theology as a corrective to materialist theory's shortcomings (as Haynes does), and I have already illustrated that Head remains agnostic by evoking a range of religious images alongside distinctly Darwinist theories.

Yet it would be foolish to pose Colebrook's intricate philosophical construction as a strawperson argument. Her theory is notable, particularly when concerning this study, for its focus upon queer desire as a curative solution to vitalisms which focus too heavily upon biological reproduction as a normative marker of social development. She argues that queer vitalism is less involved with majoritarian modes of identity politics than with celebrating the potentiality of difference as a positive force that makes one queer to others and the multiple individuals within oneself. Wearing her poststructuralist influences firmly on her sleeve, she argues for considering 'life beyond the concept of the person' (Colebrook 2014: 166): using the example of a gay couple who want to have a child, she suggests moral arbiters should consider how both revolutionary and normative desires may constitute such a wish. The lack of political impetus in both Bennett's and Colebrook's work leaves more to be desired, but my earlier textual analysis of *You Can't Get Lost in Cape Town* shows that the concept of desire is itself a source of affirmative potential when employed in conjunction with postcolonial theory. The limits of deconstructionist theory, which informs most new materialist thought, may thus be overcome by utilizing more intentional conceptions of agency and vital potential. The analysis that follows adapts Colebrook's lexicon of queer vitalism and desire in conjunction with southern African feminisms; Head's *Personal Choices* trilogy, I argue, looks towards a fully formed and political mode of vitalism, a queer vitality (Stobie 2021: 2).

Head's first published novel, *When Rain Clouds Gather*, narrates the story of a South African refugee in Botswana named Makhaya who joins forces with a British-born farmer to try and help their adoptive village through a drought. Unsurprisingly, there is a recurrence of dust in the rural setting (Head 1968: 8), and the 'arid land' and 'barren earth' form a literally sterile environment (116). It simultaneously figures for the stifling sense of fear and social seclusion in southern Africa during the twentieth century: the narrator's observation that 'few black men in their sane mind envied or cared to penetrate the barrier of icy no-man's-land which was the white man and his world' could easily refer to any country with a history of racism and colonial control (125). Land, as a metaphorical device, also relates to tribalism (a word Head often invokes in her earlier works), particularly the issue of tribal land tenure (38). To the present day, land ownership remains a heated topic in southern Africa, since the governments of post-independence South Africa and Botswana did not compensate people whose ancestors were dispossessed of their properties under colonial rule. (Post-apartheid South Africa's fifth President, Cyril Ramaphosa, started initiating land reform in 2018, much to the chagrin of white minority landowners and then US President Donald Trump, who tweeted that he was concerned about 'the large scale killing of farmers'.)

Yet the text also presents various surprising moments of literal and metaphorical growth. There are disruptive images and passages where life emerges amidst barrenness, such as the fragile grass which grows and spreads as an allegory for development as a creative and agentive process (37). Makhaya reinforces experimental associations of identity formation when he invites the women of the village to help with farming and gardening: 'Perhaps', he thinks, 'all change in the long run would depend on the women of the country and perhaps they too could provide a number of solutions to problems he had not yet thought of' (43). His view of women as catalysts of social change is a somewhat unconventional attitude in the traditionally patriarchal setting of a rural village. Shortly after this scene, the narrator reinforces this sense of development by observing that 'things were changing rapidly [...] and the change was not so much a part of the fashionable political ideologies of the new Africa as the outcome of the natural growth of a people' (45). Here, Head is quite literally naturalizing an alternative narrative to those that render postcolonial southern Africa as dangerous and degenerating. The people of the village have not been influenced by new, imported materialist theories. Rather, they negotiate between themselves in order to best arrive at practical solutions to political or environmental crises. The repeated greeting used by the villagers, 'branch-of-my-tree' (76), is one illustrative instance of such interconnected vitality.

I have already elucidated that Botswana is a comparatively conservative country, especially when considering the issue of reproductive agency. Counter to this fact, the scene which addresses abortion in *When Rain Clouds Gather* marks a moment of development for the rural community. The fourth chapter of this novel opens with a detailed description of Chief Sekoto, a jovial man whose brother Matenge is the primary antagonist (later in the novel, he usurps Sekoto's role as chief of the village). Sekoto rules over court cases, and one day he is asked to make a particularly difficult verdict: a traditional healer named Mma-Baloi is suspected of killing children to use their body parts for witchcraft and accused of murdering a young woman who visited her house to seek medical treatment. Sekoto is aware of public opinion but turns to the local doctor, who reveals that the children's deaths were a result of pneumonia and the young woman 'died of a septic womb due to having procured an abortion with a hooked and unsterilized instrument. He would say that the septic condition of the womb had been of three months' duration' (53). Hearing this information, the chief rules that the people of Bodibeng are misguided and that they 'falsely accuse' the old woman 'of a most serious crime which carries the death sentence' (54). Importantly, the crime he is referring to is the practice of witchcraft; the traditional healer's attempts to cure a supposedly wayward woman of sepsis carry no consequences.

The chief rules that each family in the village must donate an animal as payment for their prejudice. His kindness towards the old woman is revealed to have personal motivations when he confesses that he is 'tired of the penicillin injections' that he is given at the hospital for 'an ailment', and he hints that 'perhaps your good herbs may serve to cure me of my troubles' (54). Penicillin is commonly used to treat sexually transmitted infections, and this vulnerable but humorous monologue from Sekoto reinforces a later offhand remark that 'the Chiefs all had syphilis' (65). Nevertheless, whether through Western science or traditional remedies, his decisions are motivated by medical facts. They are also in keeping with sentiments expressed earlier in the novel by Makhaya that 'witch doctors were human, and nothing, however odd and perverse, need be feared if it was human' (11). This humanizing impulse relies on a critical humanism, which renders supposedly bizarre or incomprehensible methods of healing as interconnected with normative (Western) understandings of human health and wellbeing. Anti-abortion or repronormative rhetoric may similarly be challenged by emphasizing the importance of agency in post/colonial contexts.

Chief Sekoto's benevolent attitude aligns him with the second type of wo/man which Head describes in *The Collector of Treasures*, s/he who is comfortable displaying both power and tenderness. In this way he is the antithesis of his brother

Matenge, whose personality the narrator summarizes as such: 'People were not people to him but things he kicked about, pawns to be used by him, to break, banish, and destroy for his entertainment' (176). Matenge's utilitarian approach to politics is reflective of Head's earlier concerns about Afrikaner nationalism's lack of distinction between someone and something, and it is particularly interesting to note that the violent act of kicking (which was linked to involuntary abortion in *The Collector of Treasures*) recurs to figure for patriarchal control. In this description, the writer displays a certain wariness of southern African tribalism, warning that it can be just as problematic as the masculinist rule of colonial powers. This becomes apparent to the villagers, too, after Matenge victimizes a bereaved mother whose child dies of tuberculosis while staying at a cattle outpost during the drought. Through 'a strange gathering-together of all their wills' (182), the community marches to the chief's house, where he locks himself inside and decides to commit suicide instead of facing justice. Not for the first time, Head's words have a distinctly Nietzschean ring to them, as the villagers display a collective will to power. Like the sustained metaphorization of Hendrik Verwoerd's assassination as abortion in *You Can't Get Lost in Cape Town*, there is an extended termination here, as a corrupt political figure is removed – in this case, by public pressure – from a position of power. After the chief commits suicide, rain starts to fall (184): a literal reminder of the potentialities of social formations, which Wicomb attaches to political agency in her novel. The last lines of *When Rain Clouds Gather* speculate that it was 'as if everything was uncertain, new and strange and beginning from scratch' (188). The rebirth of society in Head's novel is precipitated by a single mother's mourning, but it is achieved through collective agency, which, in turn, is informed by creative local leaders and the fresh views of outsiders like Makhaya.

Power and tenderness are uncoupled from gendered associations in scenes involving Makhaya and Chief Sekoto, two prominent male figures who express their authority playfully, appearing open to transgressive potentialities. Makhaya is a mysterious figure – he is referred to by himself and others as both Black Dog and 'mad dog' (130) – yet he makes people feel at ease. When a female character suggests that this is because 'he takes away the feeling in us that he is a man' (113), she appears to be referring not so much to his gender as to his transgressive anthropomorphizing of the elements, and his queering of human power through nonhuman agencies. As Makhaya builds a fire (a traditionally feminized activity in southern Africa), we are told that in contrast to the other villagers, he 'treated each stick as a separate living entity' (140). Earlier in the novel he reflects upon 'this mass of suffering mankind of which he was a part, but he also saw himself as a separate particle', and later he begins 'to stress his own separateness, taking this as a guide that would lead him to clarity of thought in all the confusion' (81). Through the inorganic agentive forces of particles – related to tinder and fire – Makhaya fixates not upon an inherent interconnectedness of all beings, but rather upon the agency that emerges from their distinctness. Returning to the earlier discussion of Colebrook's perspective on desire and difference, ecology is coded with queer vitality here in the sense that all these elements are individuals in a broader, political landscape. This transgressive developmental continuity is conceptualized even further in *Maru*.

The second text in Head's *Personal Choices* trilogy is also concerned with issues of literal and figurative re/creation – or anxieties about a lack thereof. As has been observed in several analyses of the text and in Stephen Gray's introduction to the Heinemann edition, the book's title (taken from one of its central protagonists), *Maru*, means the elements in Tswana (Gray 2008: ii). The metaphorical treatment of ecological sterility in the novel extends beyond the earth; as Joyce Johnson notes in her study of the novel, 'the contrast between the sun with its boundless and uncontrolled energy and the fretful and abortive rain clouds […] highlights difference in the personalities of Moleka and Maru' (2008: 97). The titular character is one of several Totems or chiefs in the village of Dilepe; Moleka is his friend, another chief who is more stereotypically masculine and ostensibly powerful in the rural community. Both men fall in love with Margaret Cadmore, a Masarwa teacher and artist who is discriminated against because of her San heritage. Margaret's biogenetic mother died the day she was born, and she was adopted by a white woman of the same name who treated her relatively generously but also viewed her as something of a test subject, with 'one of her favourite, sweeping theories being: environment everything; heredity nothing' (Head [1971] 2008: 9). Head places herself at a remove from such a deterministic position, opting instead to treat Margaret's identity formation ambivalently as the young woman negotiates the men's affections and her own growing feelings for Moleka.

Head's contestation of the so-called nature/nurture debate and affirmative rhetoric surrounding Westernized biological discourse begins early in the narrative with mention of blood: it is a pivotal substance in the narrative, particularly when establishing connections between characters. Maru imagines that other villagers are trying to conceal their thoughts from him, but reveals that 'he could see and hear everything, even their bloodstreams and the beating of their hearts' (2). The phrase 'They did not greet one another. Their bloodstreams were one' is repeated almost verbatim in reference to Maru's relationships with both his sister Dikeledi and his friend Ranko whom he employs as a spy (43). Here the filiative and affiliative are indeterminate, again, as characters' hearts and bloodstreams grow – in a manner not dissimilar to the transcorporeal repetitions in Vera's *Butterfly Burning* – to signify an interconnected vitality. The rural community's vital continuities are best epitomized through Margaret, an outsider who assimilates quickly in the village and who is described in strikingly similar terms to the 'New African' in Head's letters and the 'new and strange' societal rebirth at the close of *When Rain Clouds Gather*. The narrator explains of Margaret's nature, 'It was hardly African or anything but something new and universal, a type of personality that would be unable to fit into a definition of something as narrow as tribe or race or nation' (10). Margaret exceeds the definition and limitations of her Masarwa heritage, particularly as she goes on to destabilize the power dynamic between two traditionally authoritative men.

Moleka is described early in the novel as a stereotypically masculine figure: alongside his physical and sexual prowess as a womanizer, his voice is so commanding that it appears to cause rooms to vibrate (19). Vibration is symbolic shorthand for power here, much as it is for Jane Bennett in *Vibrant Matter*. Yet there are important differences between the two authors' definitions of authority: Head's philosophizing is distinctly southern African, and feminist, as the autochthonous figure Margaret grows more and more important in both the narrative and her community. The young woman desires 'a whole life of vibrating happiness' (13), and this vitality makes her romantically attractive to the infamously noncommittal chief. Yet, at the same time, Margaret also shares characteristics with Moleka's foil, Maru. The latter man is more artistically minded: 'Creative imagination he had in over-abundance. Moleka had none of that ferment, only an over-abundance of power' (45). Like bacterial cultures found growing in petri dishes or barrels of traditional beer, creativity and ferment appear synonymous to Head (and both, in this sentence, are at a remove from conventional definitions of political authority). In fact, the phrase 'creative ferment' recurs in a later description of Maru (54). Margaret is also creative-minded; her artistic 'skill for rapid reproduction of life, on the spot' draws the admiration of both Dikeledi and Maru (69). The lines between artistic and sexual recreation are blurred not only by this intense admiration, but also by the fact that the subject matter of her drawings is later described as 'What she was trying to give birth to' (87). In contrast to Dikeledi, who marries Moleka after being impregnated by him, Margaret remains childless throughout the narrative, even in the opening segment of the text, a vignette looking forward to her married life with Maru. In a sense, then, the potential ferment of an unsatisfying marriage is tempered by Margaret's artistic agency, the one arena in which she can express and act upon her true desires.

Margaret chooses to thematize ordinary village scenes in her work for the reason that they 'were the best expression of her own vitality' (87), noting that 'there was this striking vitality and vigour in her work and yet, for who knew how long, people like her had lived faceless, voiceless, almost nameless in the country. That they had a life or soul to project had never been considered' (88). Tackling Botswana rural life as subject matter is clearly an issue of representation to the Masarwa-born woman. Her artistic projects prove an underlying vitality connecting all those in the community, despite their various genetic or national roots. But it must be stressed that this worldview still treats the villagers as individuals: hers is not the homogenizing impulse of her adoptive mother, the white woman Margaret who would have liked for all human beings to be equal in a supposedly colour-blind epistemology that completely disregards genetic heritability. The young Margaret, in contrast, upholds the queer potential of vitality by refusing to take an all-or-nothing approach to philosophies of personal development. The New African is an artist who is attuned to the potential of both biology and environment, creation and fermentation; she is not a Nietzschean yes-man, but a maybe-woman. By this I do not mean that Head lacks a developed political agenda of her own; rather, there is a multifaceted and processual nature to her affirmative stance. Her seemingly paradoxical formulation of creative ferment accommodates negation to allow for an ethics of refusal. For at the end of the text, in scenes which chronologically precede its proleptic opening, Margaret loses her vitality. Learning of Moleka's marriage to Dikeledi, she falls into a 'living death' (101): 'A few vital threads of her life had snapped behind her neck and it felt as though she were shrivelling to death, from head to toe' (96). This catatonic state renders her vulnerable to Maru's marriage proposal, aborting her artistic capabilities and the agency they afford her. Both her creativity and her sexual desires are overridden by patriarchal domination and pressure for a heterosexist *telos*. In a sense, then, there are actually three Margarets in the text: the social-determinist adoptive mother, the docile wife whom we encounter at the nonlinear beginning of the novel, and the creative virgin whose aborted vitality courses through the rest of the text, charging much of its narrative development and the shifting philosophical and political outlooks of the village's previously prejudiced characters.

The most widely debated of all Head's novels is undoubtedly *A Question of Power*. Written two years after *Maru*, this text also thematizes a clear aversion to sexual reproduction in favour of other creative endeavours, as Margaret

Tucker notes in an instructive article (1988: 175). Reception of *A Question of Power* is particularly interesting for its association of Head with potential artistic influences: Desiree Lewis compares vacillating reception of Bessie Head to critical responses to Sylvia Plath (2004: 121); Joyce Johnson likens the novel to James Joyce's *Finnegans Wake* because of the use of myth and human 'types' throughout history (2008: 109); and Maria Olaussen notes that Head identified with elements of Olive Schreiner's work (1997: 155). Crucially, all three of these authors – Plath, Joyce and Schreiner – thematize women's reproductive agency in their fiction. Here I am referring, in particular, to the protagonist's vaginal bleeding in *The Bell Jar* (as elucidated in my chapter on Zoë Wicomb); Gerty MacDowell's 'female pills' or abortifacients in *Ulysses* (a text that is referenced in Coetzee's translation of *The Expedition to the Baobab Tree*); and Lyndall's potentially self-induced miscarriage in *The Story of an African Farm* (I briefly discuss abortion and the latter novel in Chapter 3). As Olaussen's words illustrate, these authors may prove to be fruitful comparative partners to Head for highlighting her continuous interest in tensions between the universal and the local, or the modern and the rural, and how these conflicts code for gendered power struggles.

I would go further by highlighting echoes in *A Question of Power* of another literary influence who is concerned with reproductive autonomy and societal pressures: Thomas Hardy. Like the appearance in *Jude the Obscure* of Little Father Time, who hangs himself and his two siblings with the suicide note 'Done because we are too menny' (Hardy [1895] 1999: 264), Head's novel features a strangely named boy who is unusually preoccupied with suffering for a young child. The protagonist Elizabeth has a son nicknamed Shorty whose morbid anxieties are frequently paired with misspellings or incorrect grammar; this is particularly apparent when he describes 'a dog what died' (Head 1973: 179), and, soon after, he writes in a letter to his mentally ill and hospitalized parent, 'Dare Mother, when are you coming home?' (182). Hardy's text is notable for its complex treatment of female sexuality through Sue Bridehead, a character who avoids engaging in sexual intercourse for most of the narrative and who miscarries one of the children she later conceives with her first cousin, the titular Jude. There is a clear fixation here on heredity and genetic anxieties, which is similarly extended in Head's novel through Elizabeth's dreamlike (or, more often, nightmarish) encounters with two imaginary figures named Sello and Dan. Her spiritual twin Sello is sceptical of Africanism, an ideology that the narrator raises when critiquing a term which is often used to rally sympathy in political causes in southern Africa, 'my people': 'When someone says "my people" with a specific stress on the blackness of those people, they are after kingdoms and permanently *child-like slaves*. "The people" are never going to rise above the status of "the people". They are going to be told what is good for them by the "mother" and the "father"' (63; emphasis added). Suspicion of sexual reproduction and filiation takes on a political impetus here. Head's critical humanism seeks to move past the condescendingly racist (and controllingly nationalist) undertones of the possessive pronoun 'my' – if not the very repronormative and heterosexist logic underpinning supposedly progressive identity politics. Yet Elizabeth is still susceptible to feelings of shame about her political positionality as an ostensibly coloured woman in southern Africa. When Dan mocks her indeterminate genetic origins, she imagines that 'he was African, she was mixed breed. What a plague that was! Perhaps in their past incarnations as lovers they had mercifully been of the same race and could peacefully join their souls together "at the roots"?' (147). Elizabeth's anxieties about genetic and metaphorical 'roots' are strikingly similar to those expressed in Zoë Wicomb's fiction, particularly by the protagonist in *You Can't Get Lost in Cape Town*. Another interesting comparative note is that both authors reference *Gulliver's Travels* by Jonathan Swift ([1726] 1982) when exploring discomfort with corporeality and embodiment (Head 1973: 146).[6] Through the rhetorical register of breeding, infection and biogenetic origins, Elizabeth renders her fears of an ultimately intangible figure – and his loyalty to an idealized and homogenized Africa – in clinical, scientific terms.

While it is illuminating to consider the literary roots of Head's thematic preoccupations as well as the cross-pollination of reproductive anxieties in both Euro-American and southern African anglophone aesthetics, it must be noted that *A Question of Power* is not as bleak in its outlook as Hardy's fiction. As Jane Bryce-Okunlola points out (1991: 215), Elizabeth plans to kill herself and Shorty but he stops her by showing he trusts her (Head 1973: 174), and when she plans suicide again later her son distracts her by asking for a football (193). Instead of terminating their struggles, she resolves to let them continue. This sense of cyclical inevitability is reinforced by Elizabeth's growing resolution to accept the nurturing role of motherhood. Initially focusing upon her own origins as an orphan whose biogenetic family pay a woman to care for her, like Phephelaphi's adoptive mother in *Butterfly Burning*, Elizabeth remembers with reverence her maternal grandmother, who visited her every weekend during her childhood in South Africa: 'It was such a beautiful story, the story of the grandmother, her defiance, her insistence on filial ties in a country where people were not people at all' (17). Yet in Botswana, the protagonist later prioritizes her own potential as a carer and exceeds received definitions of filiation. A striking illustration of this point is how she calls the American expatriate Tom her son (183), even after he asserts he left the United States and his biogenetic family because he does not need mothers (121). Her relationship with the foreigner grows into a 'life line'; when she suffers a mental breakdown, for instance, Tom is the only villager who visits her in hospital and he correctly predicts that she will recover. The thought of her biogenetic and adoptive sons living in a future without her is what keeps Elizabeth fighting against her spiritual visions, eventually leading Sello to reveal that he used her as a pawn in conquering Dan (whom he also discloses is Satan).

Elizabeth's mental rebirth is precipitated, rather fittingly, with the sustained description of a 'long thread-like filament like an umbilical cord' (117): 'Attached to its other end was Sello. [...] As she looked at it, it parted in the middle, shrivelled and died. The huge satanic image of Sello opened its swollen, depraved mouth in one long scream' (140). I say this is fitting and not ironic because the protagonist's identity formation is contingent upon her own agency rather than the actions of her supposed soulmate (whom, it is crucial to note, appears just as demonic as the devil himself). With the withering of the umbilical cord, and Sello's metaphorical abortion, both he and Dan begin to lose their hold on her mental health. Shortly after this scene we are introduced to a character called The Womb who acts as a sexual surrogate for Elizabeth with Dan (146–7). The Womb is pivotal to the text's denouement: entering the narrative at the exact moment that the spiritual twin loses his power, she provides Elizabeth with a new perspective on female sexuality – from the creatively embodied position of female reproductivity. At this highly symbolic point in the text, homosexuality is also raised as an ethical concern. Elizabeth reacts to queer desire (which Dan brands a universal phenomenon) with shock, thinking of both Dan and Sello as perverts for engaging in homosexual intercourse (138). Yet there are contradictions here in her attitude, not least because the two figures engage in heterosexual acts that she finds equally abhorrent. A standout moment illustrating potentially internalized homophobia is when Elizabeth 'gaily' says to her female friend Kenosi, 'If I were a man I'd surely marry you' (Head 1973: 90).[7] Her fear of carnality takes a quite literal turn when she says of Dan, 'He's a homosexual, but he also sleeps with cows and anything on earth' (148).[8] Yet she grows to disregard the coupled men and their taunting, becoming more concerned instead by the figure of The Womb, who steals one of her floral dresses which has a pattern 'symbolic of appeal, creativity and vitality' (165). Elizabeth thus embarks on a quest to reclaim the agency she has lost, which involves reconciling herself to the fact that she herself contains a strange amalgamation of embodied desire and queer vitality. Sello reinforces her similarity to The Womb when he confesses at the narrative's conclusion, 'It wasn't power that was my doom. It was women; in particular a special woman who formed a creative complement to me, much like the relationship you and I have had for some time' (199). Considering his words, it is clear the figurative abortion scene advances not an ending, but rather a new beginning: Elizabeth's male twin is replaced by his creative complement, the overtly sexualized Womb, who causes the protagonist to reflect upon her positionality as a mother and woman of colour in Botswana. In looking forward to a future without Dan and Sello, but with her two children, she chooses to embrace the fact that the 'creative ferment' of desire is integral to her identity (57).

A Question of Power is divided into two sections (named after Sello and Dan, respectively), and while discussing terminations, it is worth considering the literal endings of each part of the text. The first section closes with Elizabeth vowing to herself, 'Oh God [...] May I never contribute to creating dead worlds, only new worlds' (100). This emphasis on multiplicities implies that there are several creative forces at play in the society and the protagonist is one of several agencies who may decide to either help or hinder potential new ways of living. The final section of the text also concludes with the protagonist speaking to herself; as she announces, 'There is only one God and his name is Man. And Elizabeth is his prophet' (206). Head is constantly experimenting with the idea of a hybrid prophet in this trilogy. In *When Rain Clouds Gather* it is a 'mad' man-dog, but in *A Question of Power* it is a female prophet, specifically the woman who embraces negation for opening up alternative futures and lives. The Womb epitomizes creative ferment and encourages Elizabeth to accept the messy indeterminacies of embodiment, to divorce herself from her mental demons by grounding herself in material reality and desires. This is made particularly apparent by the closing words of the novel: 'As she fell asleep, she placed one soft hand over her land. It was a gesture of belonging' (206). These final lines advance a solution to the eponymous question: power lies in a sense of environmental situatedness and interconnected vitality. The protagonist's gentle reverence of the land appears to quell her earlier anxieties about how to belong in southern Africa as a woman of indeterminate genetic origins.

Aesthetically naturalizing agency throughout the *Personal Choices* trilogy, Head explores how individuals' actions and desires are all interlinked by a strange and persistent vitality: one which manifests itself in nonhuman and human forms. The trilogy both parallels and challenges contemporary understandings of intersubjective connectivity by conceiving of political power as contingent upon ecological forces, years before materialist and vitalist theories took their recent turn away from stereotypically white, male, heterosexual and cisgender figures of authority. Head's philosophy is distinct from the work of Jane Bennett and Claire Colebrook in that she is actively invested in foregrounding the figure and spirit of the fully formed human – even when utilizing elemental and environmental imagery and metaphors. Her vitality quite literally seeks to breathe life into old and new outlooks: she is against the nostalgic logic of colonial expansion as much as she is critical of emerging African nationalisms, since a repetitive and uncritically humanist hierarchy of power appears to underlie these disparate political causes. Abortion figures symbolically in her fiction for this tussle between established and developing regimes. Furthermore, scenes featuring discussions of actual abortions, adoptions and related processes display a surprisingly progressive attitude to reproductive agency; they present readers with an imagined alternative to dominant discourse on women's sexual health and rights.

Bessie Head's distinctly African perspective tempers the more apolitical aspects of new materialism. Her very texts are symbolic of life lines: setting her fiction almost exclusively in Botswana, but thematizing works by geographically distant writers who also fixate upon sexual reproduction and terminations, she foregrounds how identity is predicated by genetic material, environmental factors and individual desires. This has enormous political implications, particularly in postcolonial contexts, where the agency of autochthonous people (and their literary-theoretical treatment) has historically been ignored. Throughout Head's fictional corpus readers are confronted with images of bodies at all stages of life: foetal forms, stillbirths, abandoned children, virgins, sex workers, newlyweds, biogenetic and adoptive mothers, dying leaders and more. Her characters adopt multiple identities and her narratives alternate between varying perspectives and rebirths, complicating the linear continuum along which such markers of development supposedly fall. The result is that creativity and fermentation function synonymously in her fiction. Furthermore, her writing promises that a southern African feminism may emerge by cutting ties with colonial and repronormative tropes like Mother Africa and the motherland, focusing instead on queer desires. Queer, here, is both sexual and strange: it alludes to shared vulnerabilities between all organisms, but also instructs individuals to be open to difference and to recognize that one is constantly becoming a stranger to oneself, irrespective of whether one reproduces or not. Queer vitality questions the apparent continuity between parenthood and personal or social development. It also interrogates normative markers of development which are popular in Western cultural and literary canons. There is transgressive potentiality in subverting traditional chronologies through narrative form and content, not least for challenging capitalist and colonial excesses. Playful inversions of power dynamics affirm the potentiality of the New African, the embodiment of creative ferment. The most apt illustration of this figure is one who defies repronormativity: she who believes abortion is not the denial of a future, but rather an affirmation of agency.

Coda: New African time

By the time *Tales of Tenderness and Power* was published in 1989, Wilma Stockenström's and Zoë Wicomb's novels had already been released to critical acclaim. Yet narrative continuity between the abortion scene in *When Rain Clouds Gather* and the story 'Chief Sekoto' in Head's posthumous collection suggests that her earlier work had a marked impact on the southern African literary scene, particularly for authors interested in feminist issues like embodiment and agency. Much as in her first collection *The Collector of Treasures*, stories in *Tales of Tenderness and Power* repeatedly foreground reproductive health as a plot point or thematic concern. For example, a character in 'Village People' expresses her fears of having an illegitimate child but also of the baby dying (Head [1989] 1990: 45). In 'Property' there is also mention of an unexpected pregnancy (67), although it remains unclear whether the woman in question desires to have an abortion or bring the pregnancy to term. 'The Lovers' is another story that expresses anxieties about sexual reproduction, this time concerning infertility as an 'endless' story (88). Women are instructed to take precautions 'during times of menstruation, childbirth and accidental miscarriages', because 'failure to observe the taboos could bring harm to animal life, crops and the community' (93). Two things are notable in this quotation. Firstly, as in her earlier stories, Head still delineates between unintentional and intentional miscarriages, proving once again that abortion is not simply a women's issue. Secondly, the taboos are interesting for suggesting there is temporal and situational connectedness between human, plant and animal life (in contrast to new materialists' feminism, and Head's more ambiguous theorizations, interconnection is utilized in this case of Botswanan folklore to control women's bodies and actions). 'Dreamer and Storyteller' is an autobiographical reflection on the author's life as a so-called Botswana writer. Commenting on her process of reflecting on society, she notes, 'I seemed to be living too, all the time, with animals' eyes' (141), and she later restates that it is 'impossible to translate' some of the scenes she has witnessed 'into human language' because 'human beings, *when* they are human, dare not conduct themselves in such [contemptuous] ways' (142; emphasis added). There is always this multi-layered, conditional sense of the human in Head's work. The shifts between tense in these excerpts illustrate how her fiction repeatedly interrogates ethically fraught moments when people may be said to lose their humanity. Despite her ultimate loyalty to critical humanism, her narratives unsettle anthropocentric models of development, particularly if they appear to harm women and others who are most vulnerable in previously colonized environments.

This feminist and materialist challenging of linear chronologies is undoubtedly what goes on to influence future narrative forms in southern Africa. Analysing the closing pages of *A Question of Power*, Margaret Tucker argues that 'by exposing hierarchies of power and, in particular, the objectification of women as the foundation of patriarchy, Elizabeth jumps out of Dan's and Sello's "big picture" to form another time, exemplified by the Motabeng Farm Project. Elizabeth's new "time" is empowered by the community, not by some authoritative abstraction of History' (1988: 181). Viewing Elizabeth's personal triumph as just one instance of subversive development in the broader trilogy, and taking Tucker's words to signify a thematic subversion of narrative temporality in the fictional corpus, I would argue that the author's new time is decidedly queer in its scope.[9] Head's and Stockenström's narratives are more concerned with biological forms than ecological processes – the former writer's preoccupations mostly register at the human scale, while the latter is open to discussing nonhuman agencies – but both are notable for queering the figure of the human within nonhuman environments. Stockenström's narrative form negates internalized prejudices through an interspecies ethics of listening; Wicomb's protagonist desires to experiment with an autopoietic and environmental sense of formation; and Vera's literary work metaphorizes more non-subjective ecologies and repeatedly stresses transcorporeality's transformative potential. Head predates all these authors; yet, her investment in the New African is, paradoxically, what inspires them to move beyond the human realm in their forward-looking narratives. In a sense, then, her paradoxical melding of various dichotomies – rural and urban life, human and nonhuman forms, Anglo-European and indigenous aesthetics – creates space for a new lineage of southern African women writers.

As the circular form of this book has shown, materialist representations of feminism emerge and reappear continually throughout Botswana, South Africa and Zimbabwe in periods preceding, during and following colonial rule. The order of my chapters is crucial – not because Head is superior to the other authors but rather because she thematizes the very terminations and beginnings that recur in the others' works. Focusing on embodied entanglements, fictional abortion narratives by southern African women appear to hold more intersectional potential than the purportedly new theories on reproductive health and sexuality established by Western philosophers in recent years. Postcolonial fiction from the late twentieth century is thus not so much an ageing corpus as a living body of work which provides insight into ethical and political dilemmas still actively occupying feminists. Head's openness to paradoxes should be equally instructive to new materialists and postcolonial scholars; perhaps it is possible to temper utopian, apolitical theories of agency and rigidly anthropocentric perspectives on personhood, power and rights. Vitalizing feminist interconnections involves acknowledging that all individuals in an environment are constantly shaping each other's formation, without denying important differences (intraspecies and interspecies, organic and inorganic subjects). Becoming vies with being, it is an ethical duty not to forget that. But for the sake of collective wellbeing, we must acknowledge how political agency has historically been denied to many beings in favour of an incorporeal Mother Country, an abstract Father Time or a reified Child. Feminists from southern Africa have been mindful of the insidious links between nationalism, racism, sexism, speciesism and repronormativity for many years. Materialists of the future will do well to remember these linkages. As for the matter of abortion: reproductive agencies will have the last word by creating, first.

Notes

1   See my introduction for a discussion of Halliwell and Mousley's coinage of the term, and how my understanding differs from theirs.

2   As in the earlier chapters of this book, creative forms feature most prominently in my analysis. For this reason, I have decided not to engage with Head's historical novels, *Serowe: Village of the Rain Wind* (1981) and *A Bewitched Crossroad: An African Saga* (1984). I will cross-reference some concepts mentioned in her letters (1963–77; 1965–79; 1984), but these will not be my primary focus.

3   *When Rain Clouds Gather* and *Maru* are available in a duology by Hachette Digital, first published in 2010.

4   For a more detailed discussion of how the concept of tragedy figures in discourse surrounding abortion, see Chapter 3.

5   For a convincing and comprehensive materialist analysis of this famous phrase, see Derek Ryan (2013).

6   For a full analysis of the functionality of Swift's writing in Wicomb's novel, see Chapter 2.

7   Elinor Rooks intimates the potential queer undertones in Head's writings in a 2017 article titled 'Picking Up the Pieces: Embodied Theory in Bessie Head's *A Question of Power*'.

8   One is reminded here of Greta Gaard's exploration of ecosexuality in her recent work on critical ecofeminism (2017). For an analysis of this trope in abortion narratives, see my discussion of Gaard and Stockenström in Chapter 2.

9   Here I am indebted to the earlier work of Jack Halberstam, whose assertion that queer time 'creates a new emphasis on the here, the present, the now, and while the threat of *no future* hovers overhead like a storm cloud' goes on to inspire the title of Lee Edelman's monograph (Halberstam 2005: 2; emphasis added).

Conclusion

Questioning power, transforming futures

The previous chapter discusses how Bessie Head's fiction both questions and queers traditional associations of power, expressing an experimental and creative sense of agency. In part, this conclusion's title is a reference to what is arguably her most famous work. Yet it also returns us to the first literary analysis of the slave's quest and riddling questions in Wilma Stockenström's novella. One of the most crucial points throughout this study has been that the primary authors are, each in their own ways, questioning heterosexist understandings of political power and human rights. My modification of Head's title further speaks to the transformative potential of her creative corpus and the fictions that follow in its wake, engendering a queer vitality through the New African: a lively figure who transcends national borders without losing sight of political matters, particularly how literal and metaphorical reproduction is idealized to control gestational environments. The twinned issues of repronormativity and nationalism are challenged when a woman seeks an abortion. This latter point has been central to the concept of reproductive agency which I associate with individual and collective desires in my introduction, as initiated with respect to the legacies of Karen Barad and Edward Said.

The close reading technique of this study has been guided by theoretical dialogues initiated with reference to both postcolonial studies and work by new materialists. While the topic of temporality is included in all four sections, I wish momentarily to highlight the discussions of southern African futures emerging particularly in Chapters 3 and 4. In their introduction to the edited collection *African Futures: Essays on Crisis, Emergence, and Possibility*, Brian Goldstone and Juan Obarrio assert that 'to speak of "Africa" is not, inexorably, to advance some new (or not so new) reductionist argument' (2016: 3), contending instead that speaking of '"futures" in the plural' may help to prevent a teleological globalization of diverse histories (2016: 12). Their argument for pluralization signals a growing trend in postcolonial literary studies. In a special issue of the *Journal of the African Literature Association* co-edited with Nadja Ofuatey-Alazard, Susan Arndt associates the 'agencies of futureS' with what she views as the twinned concepts of hopes and dreams, yoked together by the concept of desire (2017: 5; original emphasis). As the previous chapters have shown, I also centralize both individual and collective desires for the sake of creating an intersectional and situated sense of agency. Much like several of the new materialist frameworks discussed in this book, however, Arndt is somewhat hasty in relying on a range of neologisms, including both the capitalized plural above and the term 'dream*hopes'. Initially she argues that the latter are not identical to agency, yet centrally to her argument,

> agency is born out of memory, nourishing dream*hopes for self-determined futureS in the process. Analogously, this agency is born out of (the longing for) dream*hopes, nourishing them just as much as a productive memory in the process. This very cycle of nourishing the nourishment, of dream*hoping memory into dream*hopes and remembering dream*hopes into memories, symbolizes [...] highly promising futureS pregnant with dream*hopes.
>
> (Arndt 2017: 10)

Following the repeated critique of metaphorical figurations of gestation and nourishment throughout my literary analyses, this statement seems an idealistic reading of 'African' futures. It could be argued that the tautology in Arndt's argument risks eclipsing its political impetus. In contrast, my readings are not so interested in memory; they connect agency with political and *material* desires. While the above refashioning of hopes and dreams relies on similarly discursive repetition as seen in some idealistic new materialism, my aim throughout this study has been to counterbalance such rhetorical embellishments with a grounded approach by discussing concrete realities of reproductive agency or its denial, and, further, by arguing that the primary texts emblematize a present, living and ever-relevant corpus rather than a record of hopes, dreams or memories.

My analyses have been organized with the aim of providing material insights into how the nexus between abortion narratives, postcolonial perspectives and queer ecocriticism can transform collective agency in southern Africa. This brings us to the second part of this section's title: transforming futures. Importantly, in the primary texts the concept of transformation holds true for both 'African' futures and new materialist ontologies. Yvonne Vera's *Butterfly Burning*, for example, proves how southern African feminist fiction surpasses

Barad's conception of the foetus-mother phenomenon by presenting a transcorporeal and gender-inclusive perspective on gestationality. In this novel the trope of tragedy – evoked earlier by Stockenström in her own narrative of abortion and suicide – is made and remade as literary form and event. Repetition and political witnessing in the present transforms the future. Ecological elements are considered alongside situated transformations in post/colonial society, such as Zimbabwe's transition from the literal and metaphorical progeny of Rhodes to a purportedly independent state. At the same time, *Butterfly Burning* is critical of some forms of novelty. Fumbatha is both obsessed with the future – a foetal form, a family name – and terrified of the new feminist ideals that his lover comes to embody. Through differences between Fumbatha and its protagonist, Vera's text cleverly draws out the contrast between idealistic dreams/hopes and material desires. While the narrative is undoubtedly feminist, its experimentation with chronological ambiguity demonstrates that we must remember colonial pasts and the present when transforming materialist theories on agency and desire. The other short texts in this study demonstrate similarly conflicted attitudes towards agency, narrative time and African futures. In *You Can't Get Lost in Cape Town*, for example, Frieda's memories of halcyon childhood play seem at odds with descriptions of how her terrified younger self lay coiled in the foetal position. The more that the narrator of *Expedition* asserts that she is a human being, repeatedly comparing herself to animals surrounding her, the less she speaks – until the only sound she can emit is a beastly bellow. The *Personal Choices* trilogy is also consumed with the problem of human agency, as illustrated through the new African: a figure whom characters such as Margaret try and fail to embody. Yet the combination of decidedly political settings with materialist metaphors means that the texts ultimately project reproductive agency as a continuum of ethical presentness.

The textual readings in this book have examined how metaphors and metonyms of reproduction are utilized by colonial and liberationist forces, both for the purpose of nationalist expansion. Birthing and mothering tropes are particularly pervasive, but in southern African fiction such metaphors are destabilized when development is conflated with materialist processes like autopoiesis, resulting in understandings of development as individual and collective formation. The forms of the texts themselves are cyclical; yet, their abrupt nature challenges associations of circularity with supposedly feminine rhythms. Watery ecologies in all four authors' works position gestationality as inherently queer, as a process involving but also exceeding the human female reprosexual body. Ecological metaphors for termination also intersect with

literally naturalized abortion practices in each of the texts. Head's fiction outlines
the distinction between accidental and intentional terminations of pregnancy
through animalistic imagery in abortion and miscarriage scenes. Stockenström
and Vera both employ vegetation to terminate their protagonists' pregnancies –
a root of a violet-tree, a thorn from a bush – thereby evoking methods by
indigenous, poor and/or Black women whose abortion practices have historically
been ignored in favour of discussing wealthy/white elites. Inorganic substances
are also used to terminate pregnancies whether through surgical operations,
as in Wicomb, or medically prescribed drugs. My claim throughout each of
my literary analyses has been that – in the right environments, and within an
ecological framework – abortion is an ethical expression of agency. Although
written during the height of reproductive and political restrictions, these textual
abortion ecologies are rooted in considering women's desires, widening the
possibilities of how we conceive of abortion now and in the future.

Achille Mbembe argues that if one is to think or write from Africa, then
the question of temporality and temporariness is the ultimate opening line of
enquiry since post/colonial chronologies are 'thoroughly entangled with the
vicissitudes of the affective, with the subjective play of desire and uncertainty'
(2016: 221–2). Once again I am struck by the prescience of desire as a critical
concept, and how it is now recurring in many contemporary theoretical
formulations of futures in African contexts. Yet, when commenting on the
implications of China's and India's economic ascents for the future of African
theory, Mbembe argues that 'it forces us to reflect anew on the multiple ways
to grow the wealth of a nation', since prior to capitalism, 'Africa may not have
known models of growth based on labor-intensive forms of production and
husbandry of natural resources' (2016: 229–30). He concludes that Africa
might try 'to formulate a place for herself in a world where the power of the
West has begun to decline' (Mbembe 2016: 230). Here there are strikingly
gendered abstractions about the 'labor' required in order to 'grow the wealth of
a nation', and a worryingly uncritical advocation for 'husbandry' between new
modes of power and production and the naturalized form of Africa 'herself'.
Such repronormative rhetoric contrasts distinctly with the sensitivities shown
by all the imaginative approaches to abortion and agency in this book. My
analyses have been organized with the aim of questioning the naturalization of
benevolent biogenetic relationships and their associations with nourishment
– as extensive discussions of parasitism and invasive species, and even queer
ecocritical readings of substances such as milk, have shown. Read together,
Arndt's and Mbembe's comments are illustrative of how postcolonial theory

would benefit from listening to queer, and particularly anti-repronormative, conceptions of time as presented in southern African feminist fiction.

This is not to say that postcolonial approaches have not played a vital role in this study. One of my aims throughout has been to show how unsettling anthropocentric models of development ultimately assists women and others whose reproductive agency has historically been aligned with the colonized environment. As I discussed in Chapter 1, narratives that queer the human form are crucial for questioning hierarchical structures of power, but only if they are open to discussing political histories of interspecies and intraspecies violence. Beastly riddles in *The Expedition to the Baobab Tree* certainly draw parallels between human and nonhuman gestationality, but the narrative situation never loses sight of slavery and its violation of biogenetic origins. Recent postcolonial analyses of adoption and other disruptions of repronormative discourse, such as McLeod's figuration of life-lines, develop and transform Said's work on beginnings and origins, and these exciting developments of the very concepts of personal development and origins are equally manifest in the fictions of Stockenström, Wicomb, Vera and Head. The readings in this book have not merely demonstrated an ethics of listening (in the interruptions and tragedies of Stockenström and Vera), but also staged an ethics of refusal by embracing phenomena such as disgust and negation (as illustrated by Wicomb and Head). Furthermore, they display how artistic desires – the desire, for example, to question metaphorical births and deaths as well as literal figurations of them – lead to political change, whether this is before, during or after periods of colonial control. Southern African fiction from the late twentieth century is therefore a living body of work which provides insight into present conversations between postcolonial and materialist theories of agency.

Returning finally to the general level of theoretical analysis, this book has consistently shown how aesthetic representations of abortion signal an important intervention for both new materialism and postcolonial studies. In an interview discussing the future of the African continent, Achille Mbembe asserts:

> There are a whole set of areas where Africa's contribution to the world of ideas and praxis can be highlighted for the benefit for the world with implications for all sorts of things: theories of exchange, theories of democracy, theories of human rights, and the rights of other species, including natural species, in this age of ecological crisis. It is work that has not been done, but it is time that we are doing it.
>
> (Mbembe in Blaser 2013: 16)

It is high time that theorists began to invest more heavily in southern African approaches to aesthetics and ethics; yet, this book has repeatedly demonstrated that fiction written by Botswanan, South African and Zimbabwean feminists has already been performing this work from the 1970s to the 1990s and onwards. Their experimentation with exile as a metaphorical state, and with reproduction as representing nationalist values, is crucial to understanding contemporary discussions of biocolonial and capitalist developments, as my earlier critique of Mbembe's own discourse shows.

Postcolonial feminisms are communal; they advocate for a collective sense of agency. This is something they share with materialist feminisms, but a marked difference is that the former still usually root their understandings of agency within co-opted forms of masculinist and humanist power. Simultaneously, in declining to discuss class and race as vectors of oppression, some new materialists risk promoting a depoliticized understanding of collective identity, thereby deemphasizing the importance of human agency and experience. Feminist materialisms, object-oriented ontologies and more should be interested in the material state we are in. This includes the interplay of physical bodies and the larger nation-state. As the triangulations of postcolonial texts with queer and materialist feminisms in this book have demonstrated, all fields are suspicious of linear teleologies, and all use agency as an imaginative force for discussing alternative futures. The usefulness of merging postcolonial and new materialist perspectives lies in developing a distinctly southern African theory of reproductive agency that is non-anthropocentric yet political. In other words, the trick is to query power while never forgetting that some inevitably hold more agency than others.

Animal, plant, mineral and human embodiments identified in this book position abortion as a formation of desire. This process involves both affirmation and refusal, with birth, death and desire developing along a continuum rather than merely a linear process of growth. Honesty about supposedly deviant desires is perhaps the most crucial contribution and ethical manifestation of materiality demonstrated by all the primary texts in this study. For if abortion is not (just) an ending, then many of the binarized dichotomies surrounding terminations of pregnancy in popular discourse are immediately called into question. Furthermore, metaphors of birth in previously colonized environments take on increasingly insidious undertones, particularly when one realizes how they continue to be replicated in theory and criticism of the postcolonial present. Cultural formations of abortion provide an important and compelling counterpoint to repronormative myths of origins and development, queering traditional gendered roles while remaining sceptical of imported and supposedly new theories of embodiment. The fictions in this study transform power – the power that underlies both colonial forces and African nationalisms – into a continuum of agencies. As Bessie Head's body of work shows, abortion narratives are crucial for forming a future-oriented sense of ethical presentness. What seems 'new' in postcolonial studies and materialist theory is reliant on southern African feminist literature and its ethics of listening, refusal and, above all, presentness. Such fiction envisions a future where the ecological model of abortion does not span concentric stigmas, but continuums of agency.

References

Abel, Elizabeth, Marinne Hirsch and Elizabeth Langland (1983), *The Voyage In: Fictions of Female Development*, Lebanon: Dartmouth College Press.

Achebe, Chinua ([1960] 2001), *No Longer at Ease*, New York: Bantam Doubleday Bell.

Acholonu, Catherine Obianuju (1995), *Motherism: The Afrocentric Alternative to Feminism*, Owerri: Afa.

Adams, Carol J. ([1990] 2015), *The Sexual Politics of Meat: A Feminist-Vegetarian Critical Theory*, London: Bloomsbury.

Ahmed, Sara (2008), 'Open Forum Imaginary Prohibitions: Some Preliminary Remarks on the Founding Gestures of the "New Materialism"', *European Journal of Women's Studies* 15 (1): 23–39.

Alaimo, Stacy (2016), *Exposed: Environmental Politics and Pleasures in Posthuman Times*, Minneapolis: University of Minnesota Press.

Amnesty International (2017), *Briefing: Barriers to Safe and Legal Abortion in South Africa*, London: Amnesty International.

Arndt, Susan (2017), 'Dreamhoping Memory into Futures: Reading Resistant Narratives about Maafa by Employing Futures as a Category of Analysis', *Journal of the African Literature Association* 11 (1): 3–27.

Attree, Lizzy (2002), 'Language, Kwela Music and Modernity in *Butterfly Burning*', in Robert Muponde and Mandi Taruvinga (eds), *Sign and Taboo: Perspectives on the Poetic Fiction of Yvonne Vera*, 63–80, Harare: Weaver.

Attridge, Derek (2004), *J.M. Coetzee and the Ethics of Reading: Literature in the Event*, Chicago: University of Chicago Press.

Attwell, David (2005), *Rewriting Modernity: Studies in Black South African Literary History*, Athens: Ohio University Press.

Augé, Marc ([1992] 1995), *Non-places: An Introduction to Anthropology of Supermodernity*, trans. John Howe, London: Verso.

Austen, Ralph (2015), 'Struggling with the African Bildungsroman', *Research in African Literatures* 46 (3): 214–31.

Barad, Karen (2007), *Meeting the Universe Halfway: Quantum Physics and the Entanglement of Matter and Meaning*, Durham: Duke University Press.

Barker, Clare (2011), *Postcolonial Fiction and Disability: Exceptional Children, Metaphor and Materiality*, London: Palgrave Macmillan.

Barker, Clare and Stuart Murray (2013), 'Disabling Postcolonialism: Global Disability Cultures and Democratic Criticism', in Lennard J. Davis (ed.), *The Disability Studies Reader* (4th edn), 61–73, New York: Routledge.

Benatar, David (2006), *Better Never to Have Been: The Harm of Coming into Existence*, Oxford: Oxford University Press.

Bennett, Jane (2009), *Vibrant Matter: A Political Ecology of Things*, Durham: Duke University Press.

Bigman, Fran (2016), 'Abortion Meets Literature', *Times Literary Supplement* 11 November: 28–9.

Bignall, Simone (2010), *Postcolonial Agency: Critique and Constructivism*, Edinburgh: Edinburgh University Press.

Biko, Steve ([1978] 1987), *I Write What I Like*, London: Bowerdean Press.

Blackstone, William ([1765] 1979), 'Amendment IX, Document 1', Stanley N. Katz (ed.), *Commentaries on the Laws of England*, 388, Chicago: University of Chicago Press.

Blaser, Thomas M. (2013), 'Africa and the Future: An Interview with Achille Mbembe', *Africa is a Country*, November: 16 pars. Available online: https://africasacountry. com/2013/11/africa-and-the-future-an-interview-with-achille-mbembe/ (accessed 18 August 2021).

Bloomer, Fiona, Claire Pierson and Sylvia Estrada Claudio (2019), *Reimagining Global Abortion Politics: A Social Justice Perspective*, Bristol: Policy Press.

Boehmer, Elleke, Chris Desmond, Alude Mahali and Hillary Musarurwa (2021), 'Storying Ourselves: Black Consciousness Thought and Adolescent Agency in 21st-century Africa', *Journal of Postcolonial Writing*. Available online: https://www. tandfonline.com/doi/full/10.1080/17449855.2021.1954542 (accessed 17 September 2021).

Bradford, Helen (1991), 'Herbs, Knives and Plastic: 150 Years of Abortion in South Africa', in Teresa Meade and Mark Walker (eds), *Science, Medicine and Cultural Imperialism*, 120–47, London: Palgrave Macmillan.

Bradford, Helen (1995), 'Olive Schreiner's Hidden Agony: Fact, Fiction and Teenage Abortion', *Journal of Southern African Studies* 21: 623–41.

Braidotti, Rosi ([1994] 2011), *Nomadic Subjects: Embodiment and Sexual Difference in Contemporary Feminist Theory*, New York: Columbia University Press.

Braidotti, Rosi (2010), 'The Politics of "Life Itself" and New Ways of Dying', in Diana Coole and Samantha Frost (eds), *New Materialisms: Ontology, Agency, and Politics*, 201–20, Durham: Duke University Press.

Braidotti, Rosi (2017), 'Posthuman Critical Theory: A Materialist Politics for Troubled Times', *Environmental Humanities and New Materialisms: The Ethics of Decolonizing Nature and Culture*, 8 June, UNESCO Headquarters, Paris. Keynote address.

Brown, Barbara B. (1987), 'Facing the "Black Peril": The Politics of Population Control in South Africa', *Journal of Southern African Studies* 13 (2): 256–73.

Bryce, Jane (2002), 'Interview with Yvonne Vera, 1 August 2000, Bulawayo, Zimbabwe: "Survival is in the Mouth"', in Robert Muponde and Mandi Taruvinga (eds), *Sign and Taboo: Perspectives on the Poetic Fiction of Yvonne Vera*, 217–26, Harare: Weaver.

Bryce-Okunlola, Jane (1991), 'Motherhood as a Metaphor for Creativity in Three African Women's Novels: Flora Nwapa, Rebeka Njau and Bessie Head', in Susheila

Nasta (ed.), *Motherlands: Black Women's Writing from Africa, the Caribbean and South Asia*, 200–18, London: Women's Press.

Burns, Catherine (2004), 'Controlling Birth: Johannesburg, 1920–1960', *South African Historical Journal* 50 (1): 170–98.

Busby, Margaret, ed. (1992), *Daughters of Africa: An International Anthology of Words and Writings by Women of African Descent from the Ancient Egyptian to the Present*, London: Jonathan Cape.

Butler, Judith (2009), *Frames of War: When Is Life Grievable?*, London: Verso.

Butler, Judith ([2020] 2021), *The Force of Nonviolence*, London: Verso.

Carroll, Robert P. and Stephen Prickett (eds), ([1997] 2008), *The Bible: Authorized King James Version*, Oxford: Oxford University Press.

Carter, Joe (2011), 'Abortion and the Negation of Love', *First Things*, 13 April: 25 pars. Available online: https://www.firstthings.com/web-exclusives/2011/04/abortion-and-the-negation-of-love (accessed 18 August 2021).

Chadwick, Rachelle (2018), *Bodies That Birth: Vitalising Birth Politics*, Abingdon: Routledge.

Chen, Mel Y. (2012), *Animacies: Biopolitics, Racial Mattering, and Queer Affect*, Durham: Duke University Press.

Chiweshe, Malvern and Catriona Ida Macleod (2018), 'Cultural De-colonization versus Liberal Approaches to Abortion in Africa: The Politics of Representation and Voice', *African Journal of Reproductive Health* 22 (2): 49–59.

Chiweshe, Malvern, Jabulile Mavuso and Catriona Macleod (2017), 'Reproductive Justice in Context: South African and Zimbabwean Women's Narratives of their Abortion Decision', *Feminism & Psychology* 27 (2): 203–24.

Cilano, Cara and Elizabeth DeLoughrey (2007), 'Against Authenticity: Global Knowledges and Postcolonial Ecocriticism', *ISLE: Interdisciplinary Studies of Literature and the Environment* 14 (1): 71–88.

Clark, Timothy (2016), '"But the real problem is ….": The Chameleonic Insidiousness of "Overpopulation" in the Environmental Humanities', *Oxford Literary Review* 38 (1): 7–26.

Clarke, Bruce (2011), 'Systems Theory', in Bruce Clarke and Manuela Rossini (eds), *The Routledge Companion to Literature and Science*, 214–25, Abingdon: Routledge.

Clarke, Stuart N. (1990), 'The Horse with A Green Tail', *Virginia Woolf Miscellany*, 34: 3–4.

Clingman, Stephen (2009), *The Grammar of Identity: Transnational Fiction and the Nature of the Boundary*, Oxford: Oxford University Press.

Coetzee, J. M. (1977), *In the Heart of the Country*, New York: Harper & Row.

Coetzee, J. M. (1986), *Foe*, Toronto: Stoddart.

Coetzee, J. M. (1990), *White Writing: On the Culture of Letters in South Africa*, New Haven: Yale University Press.

Coetzee, J. M. ([1999] 2000), *Disgrace*, London: Vintage.

Coetzee, J. M., ed. and trans. ([2004] 2016), *Landscape with Rowers: Poetry from the Netherlands*, Princeton: Princeton University Press.

Colb, Sherry F. and Michael C. Dorf (2016), *Beating Hearts: Abortion and Animal Rights*, New York: Columbia University Press.

Colebrook, Claire (2014), *Sex after Life: Essays on Extinction, Vol. 2*, Ann Arbor: Open Humanities.

Colebrook, Claire (2019), 'Humanist Posthumanism: Becoming-Woman and the Powers of the "Faux"', *Academia.edu*, 17 April. Available online: https://www. academia.edu/30806048/Humanist_Posthumanism_Becoming-Woman_and_the_ Powers_of_the_Faux (accessed 18 August 2021).

Cook, Rebecca J. and Bernard M. Dickens (1981), 'Abortion Laws in African Commonwealth Countries', *Journal of African Law* 25 (2): 60–79.

Cook, Rebecca J. and Bernard M. Dickens (1983), *Emerging Issues in Commonwealth Abortion Laws, 1982*, London: Commonwealth Secretariat.

Cousins, Helen (2010), 'Nothing Like Motherhood: Barrenness, Abortion, and Infanticide in Yvonne Vera's Fiction', in Pauline Dodgson-Katiyo and Gina Wisker (eds), *Rites of Passage in Postcolonial Women's Writing*, 21–40, New York: Rodopi.

Crenshaw, Kimberlé (1989), 'Demarginalizing the Intersection of Race and Sex: A Black Feminist Critique of Antidiscrimination Doctrine, Feminist Theory and Antiracist Politics', *The University of Chicago Legal Forum* 140: 139–67.

Cronwright, Samuel ([1924] 2008), 'Afterword', in Olive Schreiner (ed.), *The Story of an African Farm*, 305–10, Cape Town: Penguin.

Crous, Marius (2013), 'To Map across from One Language to Another: J. M. Coetzee's Translation of *Die Kremetartekspedisie*', *Literator* 34 (1): 1–9.

Dangarembga, Tsitsi (1988), *Nervous Conditions*, London: Women's Press.

Davis, Caroline (2018), 'A Question of Power: Bessie Head and Her Publishers', *Journal of Southern African Studies* 44 (3): 491–506.

De Beauvoir, Simone ([1949] 1956), *The Second Sex*, trans. H. M. Parshley, London: Jonathan Cape.

De Cervantes Saavedra, Miguel ([1605] 2003), *The Ingenious Hidalgo Don Quixote de la Mancha*, trans. John Rutherford, London: Penguin.

De Man, Paul (1979), *Allegories of Reading: Figural Language in Rosseau, Nietzsche, Rilke, and Proust*, New Haven: Yale University Press.

Deleuze, Gilles and Félix Guattari ([1980] 1987), *A Thousand Plateaus: Capitalism and Schizophrenia*, trans. Brian Massumi, Minneapolis: University of Minnesota Press.

Dempster, M. Beth (2000), 'Sympoietic and Autopoietic Systems: A New Distinction for Self-organizing Systems', in J. K. Allen and J. Wilby (eds), *Proceedings of the World Congress of the Systems Sciences and ISSS 2000*, 1–15, Toronto. Available online: https://citeseerx.ist.psu.edu/viewdoc/download?doi=10.1.1.582.1177&rep=rep1&typ e=pdf (accessed 18 August 2021).

Derrida, Jacques (2009), *The Beast and the Sovereign: Vol. 1*, eds Michel Lisse, Marie-Louise Mallet and Ginette Michaud, trans. Geoffrey Bennington, Chicago: University of Chicago Press.

Diabate, Naminata (2020), *Naked Agency: Genital Cursing and Biopolitics in Africa*, Durham: Duke University Press.

Di Silvio, Lorenzo (2011), 'Correcting Corrective Rape: *Carmichele* and Developing South Africa's Affirmative Obligations to Prevent Violence against Women', *Georgetown Law Journal* 99 (5): 1469–515.

Dolphijn, Rick and Iris van der Tuin (2012a), 'Interview with Karen Barad', in Rick Dolphijn and Iris van der Tuin (eds), *New Materialism: Interviews and Cartographies*, 48–70, Ann Arbor: Open Humanities.

Dolphijn, Rick and Iris van der Tuin (2012b), 'Interview with Rosi Braidotti', in Rick Dolphijn and Iris van der Tuin (eds), *New Materialism: Interviews and Cartographies*, 19–37, Ann Arbor: Open Humanities.

Douglass, Frederick ([1845] 2014), *Narrative of the Life of Frederick Douglass, an American Slave*, Minneapolis: First Avenue Classics.

Doyle, Jennifer (2009), 'Blind Spots and Failed Performance: Abortion, Feminism, and Queer Theory', *Qui Parle: Critical Humanities and Social Sciences* 18 (1): 25–52.

Du Plessis, Michael (1988), 'Bodies and Signs: Inscriptions of Femininity in John Coetzee and Wilma Stockenström', *Journal of Literary Studies* 4 (1): 118–28.

Durrant, Sam (2018), 'Creaturely Mimesis: Life after Necropolitics in Chris Abani's *Song for Night*', *Research in African Literatures* 49 (3): 178–206.

Dyck, Denae and Tim Heath (2018), 'Garden-Variety Holiness: Bessie Head's "Reverence for Ordinary People" in *A Question of Power*', *ARIEL: A Review of International English Literature* 49 (1): 53–77.

Edelman, Lee (2004), *No Future: Queer Theory and the Death Drive*, Durham: Duke University Press.

Eilersen, Gillian Stead (1990), 'Introduction', in Bessie Head (ed.), *Tales of Tenderness and Power*, 7–15, Portsmouth: Heinemann.

Eilersen, Gillian Stead (1995), *Bessie Head: Thunder behind Her Ears: Her Life and Writing*, Portsmouth: Heinemann.

Eliot, T. S. ([1963] 2002), *Collected Poems: 1909–1962*, London: Faber & Faber.

Emants, Marcellus ([1894] 2011), *A Posthumous Confession*, trans. J. M. Coetzee, New York: New York Review of Books.

Equiano, Olaudah ([1789] 2020), *The Interesting Narrative*, ed. Brycchan Carey, Oxford: Oxford University Press.

Esty, Jed (2012), *Unseasonable Youth: Modernism, Colonialism, and the Fiction of Development*, New York: Oxford University Press.

Federici, Silvia ([1998] 2004), *Caliban and the Witch: Women, the Body, and Primitive Accumulation*, New York: Autonomedia.

Fister, Barbara (1995), *Third World Women's Literatures: A Dictionary and Guide to Materials in English*, Westport: Greenwood.

Fleischner, Jennifer (1996), *Mastering Slavery: Memory, Family, and Identity in Women's Slave Narratives*, New York: New York University Press.

Foreman, Dave (2012), 'The Great Backtrack', in Philip Cafaro and Eileen Crist (eds), *Life on the Brink: Environmentalists Confront Overpopulation*, 56–73, Athens: University of Georgia Press.

Franke, Katherine M. (2001), 'Theorizing Yes: An Essay on Feminism, Law, and Desire', *Columbia Law Review* 101 (1): 181–208.

Furedi, Ann (2016), *The Moral Case for Abortion* (Kindle edn), London: Palgrave Macmillan.

Gaard, Greta (2010), 'Reproductive Technology, or Reproductive Justice?: An Ecofeminist, Environmental Justice Perspective on the Rhetoric of Choice', *Ethics and the Environment* 15 (2): 103–29.

Gaard, Greta (2013), 'Toward a Feminist Postcolonial Milk Studies', *American Quarterly* 65 (3): 595–618.

Gaard, Greta (2017), *Critical Ecofeminism*, London: Lexington.

Garuba, Harry (2003), 'Explorations in Animist Materialism: Notes on Reading/Writing African Literature, Culture, and Society', *Public Culture* 15 (2): 261–85.

Garuba, Harry (2013), 'On Animism, Modernity/colonialism and the African Order of Knowledge: Provisional Reflections', in Lesley Green (ed.), *Contested Ecologies: Dialogues in the South on Nature and Knowledge*, 42–51, Cape Town: HSRC.

Gaylard, Rob (1996), 'Exile and Homecoming: Identity in Zoë Wicomb's "You Can't Get Lost in Cape Town"', *ARIEL: A Review of International English Literature* 27 (1): 177–89.

Goldstone, Brian and Juan Obarrio (2016), 'Introduction: Untimely Africa?', in Brian Goldstone and Juan Obarrio (eds), *African Futures: Essays on Crisis, Emergence, and Possibility*, 1–22, Chicago: University of Chicago Press.

Graham, James (2007), 'An Abject Land? Remembering Women Differently in Doris Lessing's *The Grass is Singing* and Chenjerai Hove's *Bones*', *English Studies in Africa*, 50 (1): 57–74.

Gray, Stephen (1991), 'Some Notes on Further Readings of Wilma Stockenström's Slave Narrative, *The Expedition to the Baobab Tree*', *Literator* 12 (1): 51–9.

Gray, Stephen (2008), 'Introduction', in Bessie Head (ed.), *Maru*, i–viii, Harlow: Heinemann.

Gunner, Liz and Neil Ten Kortenaar (2007), 'Introduction: Yvonne Vera's Fictions and the Voice of the Possible', *Research in African Literatures* 38 (2): 1–8.

Gurnah, Abdulrazak (2011), 'The Urge to Nowhere: Wicomb and Cosmopolitanism', *Safundi* 12 (3–4): 261–75.

Gwetai, Ericah ([2008] 2009), *Petal Thoughts: Yvonne Vera, a Biography* (Kindle edn), Gweru: Mambo Press.

Halberstam, Jack (2005), *In a Queer Time and Place: Transgender Bodies, Subcultural Lives*, New York: New York University Press.

Hall, Lesley (2019), 'Literary Abortion', *lesleyahall.net*. Available online: https://www.lesleyahall.net/abortion.htm (accessed 18 August 2021).

Halliwell, Martin and Andrew Mousley (2003), *Critical Humanisms: Humanist/Anti-humanist Dialogues*, Edinburgh: Edinburgh University Press.

Hammond, Paul (2009), *The Strangeness of Tragedy*, Oxford: Oxford University Press.

Hantel, Max (2018), 'What Is It Like to Be a Human? Sylvia Wynter on Autopoiesis', *philoSOPHIA* 8 (1): 61–79.

Haraway, Donna J. (2008), *When Species Meet*, Minneapolis: University of Minnesota Press.

Haraway, Donna J. (2016), *Staying with the Trouble: Making Kin in the Chthulucene*, London: Duke University Press.

Haraway, Donna and Adele Clark, eds (2018), *Making Kin Not Population*, Boulder: Paradigm, 2018.

Hardy, Thomas ([1891] 2003), *Tess of the d'Urbervilles*, New York: Penguin.

Hardy, Thomas ([1895] 1999), *Jude the Obscure*, New York: W. W. Norton.

Harries, Jane (2010), *Abortion Services in South Africa: Challenges and Barriers to Safe Abortion Care: Health Care Providers' Perspectives*, Cape Town: UCT.

Hauck, Christina (2003), 'Abortion and the Individual Talent', *ELH*, 70 (1): 223–66.

Haynes, Patrice (2014), 'Creative Becoming and the Patiency of Matter', *Angelaki: Journal of the Theoretical Humanities* 19 (1): 129–50.

Head, Bessie (1968), *When Rain Clouds Gather*, London: Gollancz.

Head, Bessie ([1971] 2008), *Maru*, Essex: Heinemann.

Head, Bessie (1973), *A Question of Power*, New York: Pantheon.

Head, Bessie ([1977] 1992), *The Collector of Treasures and other Botswana Village Tales*, London: Heinemann.

Head, Bessie ([1989] 1990), *Tales of Tenderness and Power*, Portsmouth: Heinemann.

Head, Bessie (1990), *A Woman Alone: Autobiographical Writings*, Portsmouth: Heinemann.

Head, Bessie (1991), *A Gesture of Belonging: Letters from Bessie Head, 1965–1979*, ed. Randolph Vigne, Portsmouth: Heinemann.

Head, Bessie (1995), *The Cardinals, with Meditations and Other Stories*, Portsmouth: Heinemann.

Head, Bessie (2010), *When Rain Clouds Gather and Maru*, London: Hachette Digital.

Hemingway, Ernest (1927), *Men without Women*, New York: Charles Scribner's Sons.

Hemsley, Frances (2021), 'Reading Heredity in Racist Environments: Epigenetic Imaginaries in Bessie Head's *The Cardinals*', *BMJ Medical Humanities* 47: 156–66.

Hinton, Peta, Tara Mehrabi and Josef Barla (2015), '"New materialisms/New colonialisms" (position paper)', Turku: Åbo Akademi University, 2015. Available online: https://newmaterialism.eu/content/5-working-groups/2-working-group-2/position-papers/subgroup-position-paper-_-new-materialisms_new-colonialisms.pdf (accessed 18 August 2021).

Hodes, Rebecca (2013), 'The Medical History of Abortion in South Africa, c.1970–2000', *Journal of Southern African Studies* 39 (3): 527–42.

Hodes, Rebecca (2016), 'The Culture of Illegal Abortion in South Africa', *Journal of Southern African Studies* 42 (1): 79–93.

Huggan, Graham (2008), *Interdisciplinary Measures: Literature and the Future of Postcolonial Studies*, Liverpool: Liverpool University Press.

Hunt, Nancy Rose (2007), 'Between Fiction and History: Modes of Writing Abortion in Africa', *Cahiers d'Études Africaines* 47 (186): 277–312.

Iheka, Cajetan (2017), *Naturalizing Africa: Ecological Violence, Agency, and Postcolonial Resistance in African Literature*, Cambridge: Cambridge University Press.

Jackson, Zakiyyah Iman (2020), *Becoming Human: Matter and Meaning in an Antiblack World*, New York: New York University Press.

Jewkes, Rachel K., Tebogo Gumede, Margaret S. Westaway, Kim Dickson, Heather Brown and Helen Rees (2005), 'Why Are Women Still Aborting Outside Designated Facilities in Metropolitan South Africa?', *BJOG: An International Journal of Obstetrics and Gynaecology* 112: 1236–42.

Jinga, Tavuya (2012), *One Foreigner's Ordeal*, Bloomington: Authorhouse.

Johnson, Barbara (1986), 'Apostrophe, Animation, and Abortion', *Diacritics* 16 (1): 28–47.

Johnson, Brooke R., Singatsho Ndhlovu, Sherry L. Farr and Tsungai Chipato (2002), 'Reducing Unplanned Pregnancy and Abortion in Zimbabwe through Postabortion Contraception', *Studies in Family Planning* 33 (2): 195–202.

Johnson, Joyce (2008), *Bessie Head: The Road of Peace of Mind: A Critical Appreciation*, Plainsboro: Associated University Presses.

Johnstone, Cory (2014), 'A Review of *The Expedition to the Baobab Tree* by Wilma Stockenström', *The Literary Review: An International Journal of Contemporary Writing*, 18 December, 9 pars. Available online: http://www.theliteraryreview. org/book-review/a-review-of-the-expedition-to-the-baobab-tree-by-wilma-stockenstrom/ (accessed 18 August 2021).

Jones, Angela (2013), *A Critical Inquiry into Queer Utopias*, New York: Palgrave Macmillan.

Jones, Rachel K., Lawrence B. Finer and Susheela Singh (2010), 'Characteristics of U.S. Abortion Patients, 2008', *Guttmacher Institute*, May: 1–26. Available online: https:// www.guttmacher.org/report/characteristics-us-abortion-patients-2008 (accessed 18 August 2021).

Joyce, James ([1914] 1956), *Dubliners*, London: Penguin.

Joyce, James ([1916] 1993), *A Portrait of the Artist as a Young Man*, New York: Vintage.

Joyce, James ([1920] 1987), *Ulysses*, Ware: Wordsworth.

Joyce, James ([1939] 2012), *Finnegans Wake*, Ware: Wordsworth.

Kaler, Amy (2003), *Running after Pills: Politics, Gender, and Contraception in Colonial Zimbabwe*, Portsmouth: Heinemann.

Kastner, Sarah (2016), '"Only Words Can Bury Us, Not Silence": Reading Yvonne Vera's Difficult Silences', *Safundi: The Journal of South African and American Studies* 17 (2): 213–30.

Kibera, Valerie (1991), 'Adopted Motherlands: The Novels of Marjorie Macgoye and Bessie Head', in Susheila Nasta (ed.), *Motherlands: Black Women's Writing from Africa, the Caribbean and South Asia*, 310–29, London: Women's Press.

Klausen, Susanne M. (2015), *Abortion under Apartheid: Nationalism, Sexuality, and Women's Reproductive Rights in South Africa*, Oxford: Oxford University Press.

Kromhout, Jan ([1952] 1992), *Klein Woordeboek*, Cape Town: Pharos.

Lacan, Jacques ([1977] 2001), *Écrits: A Selection*, trans. Alan Sheridan, London: Routledge.

Laue, Kharys (2017), 'Reclaiming the Status of Human: Gender and Protest in Zoë Wicomb's Short Stories', *Scrutiny2* 22 (2): 18–32.

Law, Kate (2021), '"We Wanted to be Free as a Nation, and We Wanted to be Free as Women": Decolonisation, Nationalism and Women's Liberation in Zimbabwe, 1979–85', *Gender & History* 33 (1): 249–68.

Lessing, Doris ([1950] 2007), *The Grass Is Singing*, London: Harper Perennial.

Lessing, Margaret, ed. (1994), *South African Women Today*, Cape Town: Maskew Miller Longman.

LeTourneau, Kati (2016), *Abortion Stigma around the World: A Synthesis of the Qualitative Literature*, Chapel Hill: inroads. Available online: https://www.safeabortionwomensright.org/wp-content/uploads/2016/05/AbortionStigmaAroundtheWorld-HR-2.pdf (accessed 24 September 2021).

Letter from Bessie Head to A. D. Donker (1 July 1984), Amazwi South African Museum of Literature, Bessie Head Fonds, B11, Box 2007.12.1, Folder 12.9.

Letter from Bessie Head to A. D. Donker (20 July 1984), Amazwi South African Museum of Literature, Bessie Head Fonds, B11, Box 2007.12.1, Folder 12.10.

Letter from Bessie Head to Pat and Wendy Cullinan (28 September 1964), Amazwi South African Museum of Literature, Bessie Head Fonds, B11, Box 2015.176, Folder 1.4.

Letter from Bessie Head to Wendy Cullinan (28 July 1964), Amazwi South African Museum of Literature, Bessie Head Fonds, B11, Box 2015.176, Folder 1.3.

Lewis, Desiree (2004), 'Power, Representation, and the Textual Politics of Bessie Head', in Huma Ibrahim (ed.), *Emerging Perspectives on Bessie Head*, 121–42, Trenton: Africa World.

Lewis, Sophie (2019), *Full Surrogacy Now: Feminism against Family*, London: Verso.

Lopez, Patricia J. and Kathryn A. Gillespie, eds (2015), *Economies of Death: Economic Logics of Killable Life and Grievable Death*, London: Routledge.

Ludlow, Jeannie (2008), 'The Things We Cannot Say: Witnessing the Traumatization of Abortion in the United States', *Women's Studies Quarterly* 36 (1–2): 28–41.

Lunga, Violet Bridget (2002), 'Between the Pause and the Waiting: The Struggle against Time in Yvonne Vera's *Butterfly Burning*', in Robert Muponde and Mandi Turavinga (eds), *Sign and Taboo: Perspectives on the Poetic Fiction of Yvonne Vera*, 191–202, Harare: Weaver.

Mackenzie, Craig and Cherry Clayton (1989), *Between the Lines: Interviews with Bessie Head, Sheila Roberts, Ellen Kuzwayo, Miriam Tlali*, Grahamstown: NELM.

Macleod, Catriona Ida (2019), 'Expanding Reproductive Justice through a Supportability Reparative Justice Framework: The Case of Abortion in South Africa', *Culture, Health & Sexuality* 21 (1): 46–62.

Marais, Sue (1995), 'Getting Lost in Cape Town: Spatial and Temporal Dislocation in the South African Short Fiction Cycle', *English in Africa* 22 (2): 29–43.

Martin, Nina and Renee Montagne (2017), 'Focus on Infants during Childbirth Leaves
    U.S. Moms in Danger', *NPR News*, 12 May: 128 pars. Available online: http://www.
    npr.org/2017/05/12/527806002/focus-on-infants-during-childbirth-leaves-u-s-
    moms-in-danger (accessed 18 August 2021).

Maturana, Humbert R. (1980), 'Introduction', in Humbert R. Maturana and Francisco
    J. Varela (eds), *Autopoiesis and Cognition: The Realisation of the Living*, xi–xxx,
    Dordrecht: D. Reidel.

Maturana, Humbert R. and Francisco J. Varela (1980), *Autopoiesis and Cognition: The
    Realisation of the Living*, Dordrecht: D. Reidel.

Mavuso, Jabulile Mary-Jane Jace (2021), 'Understanding the Violation of Directive Anti-
    abortion Counselling [and Cisnormativity]: Obstruction to Access or Reproductive
    Violence?', *Agenda*. Available online: https://www.tandfonline.com/doi/full/10.1080/
    10130950.2021.1949692 (accessed 28 September 2021).

Mbanje, Phyllis (2015), 'Zimbabwe: "Legalise Abortion to Reduce Maternal Deaths"',
    The Standard, 22 February, 23 pars. Available online: http://allafrica.com/
    stories/201502220504.html (accessed 18 August 2021).

Mbembe, Achille (2001), *On the Postcolony*, Berkeley: University of California Press.

Mbembe, Achille (2003), 'Necropolitics', trans. Libby Meintjes, *Public Culture* 15 (1):
    11–40.

Mbembe, Achille (2016), 'Africa in Theory', in Brian Goldstone and Juan Obarrio
    (eds), *African Futures: Essays on Crisis, Emergence, and Possibility*, 211–30, Chicago:
    University of Chicago Press.

McLeod, John (2015), *Life Lines: Writing Transcultural Adoption*, London: Bloomsbury.

Meintjes, Godfrey (1996), 'Environmental Communication: Notes on the
    Relationship(s) between Ecology and Literature', *Communicatio* 22 (2): 57–62.

Meyer, Susan (2013), 'All That Is Left Is the Self: Sojourn in the Hollow of a Tree in
    Wilma Stockenström's *The Expedition to the Baobab Tree*', *LitNet Akademies* 10 (1):
    310–40.

Midgley, Mary ([1978] 1995), *Beast and Man: The Roots of Human Nature*, London:
    Routledge.

Mignolo, Walter (2011), *The Darker Side of Western Modernity: Global Futures,
    Decolonial Options*, Durham: Duke University Press.

Moore, Francesca P. L. (2010), 'Tales from the Archive: Methodological and Ethical
    Issues in Historical Geography Research', *Area* 42 (3): 262–70.

Moore, Jina and Estelle Ellis (2013), 'In South Africa, a Liberal Abortion Law Doesn't
    Guarantee Access', *Pulitzer Centre*, 3 January, 28 pars. Available online: http://
    pulitzercenter.org/reporting/south-africa-liberal-abortion-law-doesnt-guarantee-
    access (accessed 18 August 2021).

Moosavinia, Sayyed Rahim and Sayyede Maryam Hosseini (2018), 'Liminality, Hybridity
    and "Third Space": Bessie Head's *A Question of Power*', *Neohelicon* 45 (1): 333–49.

Moretti, Franco (2000), *The Way of the World: The* Bildungsroman *in European Culture*,
    trans. Albert Sbragia, London: Verso.

Morrison, Toni ([1992] 2001), *Jazz*, London: Vintage.

Mukherjee, Pablo (2010), *Postcolonial Environments: Nature, Culture and the Contemporary Indian Novel in English*, Basingstoke: Palgrave Macmillan, 2010.

Naess, Arne (1973), 'The Shallow and the Deep, Long-range Ecology Movement: A Summary', *Inquiry* 16: 95–100.

Neimanis, Astrida (2017), *Bodies of Water: Posthuman Feminist Phenomenology*, London: Bloomsbury Academic.

Nuttall, Sarah (2005), 'Inside the City: Reassembling the Township in Yvonne Vera's Fiction', in Robert Muponde and Ranka Primorac (eds), *Versions of Zimbabwe: New Approaches to Literature and Culture*, 177–92, Harare: Weaver.

Olaussen, Maria (1997), *Forceful Creation in Harsh Terrain: Place and Identity in Three Novels by Bessie Head*, New York: Peter Lang.

Olivier, Gerrit (2012), 'The Dertigers and the *Plaasroman*', in David Attwell and Derek Attridge (eds), *The Cambridge History of South African Literature*, 308–24, Cambridge: Cambridge University Press.

Palgrave, Keith Coates (1984), *Trees of Southern Africa*, Cape Town: Struik.

Palmer, Tim (2012), 'Beyond Futility', in Philip Cafaro and Eileen Crist (eds), *Life on the Brink: Environmentalists Confront Overpopulation*, 98–107, Athens: University of Georgia Press.

Patterson, Orlando ([1964] 2012), *The Children of Sisyphus*, Leeds: Peepal Tree Press.

Patterson, Orlando (1982), *Slavery and Social Death: A Comparative Study*, Cambridge: Harvard University Press.

Pick, Anat (2011), *Creaturely Poetics: Animality and Vulnerability in Literature and Film*, New York: Columbia University Press.

Pieterse, Annel (2014), '"The Danger Inside": Witchcraft and Community in South African Literature', *English in Africa* 41 (3): 27–55.

Pilane, Pontsho (2016), 'Feminism Has Always Been African', *Mail & Guardian*, 6 May, 13 pars. Available online: https://mg.co.za/article/2016-05-06-00-feminism-has-always-been-african (accessed 18 August 2021).

Plath, Sylvia ([1963] 1971), *The Bell Jar*, New York: Harper & Row.

Plumwood, Val (1996), 'Androcentrism and Anthrocentrism: Parallels and Politics', *Ethics and the Environment* 1 (2): 119–52.

Primorac, Ranka (2002), 'Iron Butterflies: Notes on Yvonne Vera's *Butterfly Burning*', in Robert Muponde and Mandi Taruvinga (eds), *Sign and Taboo: Perspectives on the Poetic Fiction of Yvonne Vera*, 101–8, Harare: Weaver.

Primorac, Ranka (2004), '"The Place of the Woman is the Place of the Imagination": Yvonne Vera interviewed by Ranka Primorac', *The Journal of Commonwealth Literature* 39: 156–71.

Prince, Mary ([1831] 2004), *The History of Mary Prince, a West Indian Slave*, ed. Sara Salih, London: Penguin.

Qureshi, Sadiah (2004), 'Displaying Sara Baartman, the "Hottentot Venus"', *History of Science* 42: 233–57.

Rhys, Jean ([1934] 2000), *Voyage in the Dark*, London: Penguin Classics.

Roberts, Dorothy (1997), *Killing the Black Body: Race, Reproduction, and the Meaning of Liberty*, New York: Vintage.

Romanis, Elizabeth Chloe, Dunja Begović, Margot R. Brazier and Alexandra Katherine Mullock (2020), 'Reviewing the Womb', *Journal of Medical Ethics*. Available online: https://jme.bmj.com/content/medethics/early/2020/07/28/medethics-2020-106160. full.pdf (accessed 17 September 2021).

Rooks, Elinor (2017), 'Picking up the Pieces: Embodied Theory in Bessie Head's *A Question of* Power', *Pivot: A Journal of Interdisciplinary Studies & Thought* 6 (1): 57 pars. Available online: https://pivot.journals.yorku.ca/index.php/pivot/article/view/40276/35276 (accessed 18 August 2021).

Rooney, Caroline (1991), '"Dangerous Knowledge" and the Poetics of Survival: A Reading of *Our Sister Killjoy* and *A Question of Power*', in Susheila Nasta (ed.), *Motherlands: Black Women's Writing from Africa, the Caribbean and South Asia*, 99–126, London: Women's Press.

Ross, Loretta J. (2005), 'African-American Women and Abortion: 1800–1970', in Abena P. A. Busia and Stanlie M. James (eds), *Theorising Black Feminisms: The Visionary Pragmatism of Black Women*, 141–61, London: Routledge.

Ryan, Derek (2013), *Virginia Woolf and the Materiality of Theory: Sex, Animal, Life*, Edinburgh: Edinburgh University Press.

Saha, Jonathan (2020), 'E Is for Elephant', in Antoinette Burton and Renisa Mawani (eds), *Animalia: An Anti-Imperial Bestiary for Our Times*, 55–61, Durham: Duke University Press.

Said, Edward ([1975] 1985), *Beginnings: Intention and Method*, New York: Columbia University Press.

Said, Edward ([1978] 2003), *Orientalism*, London: Penguin.

Said, Edward (1983), *The World, the Text, and the Critic*, Cambridge: Harvard University Press.

Saint, Lily (2017), 'Traces of Glory: On Wilma Stockenström's *The Expedition to the Baobab* Tree', *Los Angeles Review of Books*, 18 July, 29 pars. Available online: https://lareviewofbooks.org/article/traces-of-glory-on-wilma-stockenstroms-the-expedition-to-the-baobab-tree/ (accessed 18 August 2021).

Sam, Agnes (1986), 'Bessie Head: A Tribute', *Kunapipi* 8 (1): 53–6.

Samuelson, Meg (2010), 'Oceanic Histories and Protean Poetics: The Surge of the Sea in Zoë Wicomb's Fiction', *Journal of Southern African Studies* 36 (3): 543–57.

Sanders, Mark (2007), *Ambiguities of Witnessing: Law and Literature in the Time of a Truth Commission*, Stanford: Stanford University Press.

Sandilands, Catriona (2015), 'Queer Ecology', in Joni Adamson, William A. Gleason and David N. Pellow (eds), *Keywords for Environmental Studies*, 6 pars,

New York: New York University Press, 2015. Available online: https://keywords.
  nyupress.org/environmental-studies/essay/queer-ecology/ (accessed 18 August
  2021).

Sankofa (1993), [Film] Dir. Haile Gerima, USA: Mypheduh Films.

Schiebinger, Londa L. (2004), *Plants and Empire: Colonial Bioprospecting in the Atlantic
  World*, Cambridge: Harvard University Press.

Schreiner, Olive ([1883] 2008), *The Story of an African Farm*, Cape Town: Penguin.

Scott, David (2014), 'The Tragic Vision in Postcolonial Time', *PMLA* 129 (4): 799–808.

Serres, Michel ([1980] 2007), *The Parasite*, trans. Lawrence R. Schehr, Minneapolis:
  University of Minnesota Press.

Sethna, Christabelle and Gayle Davis, eds (2019), *Abortion across Borders:
  Transnational Travel and Access to Abortion Services*, Baltimore: Johns Hopkins
  University Press.

Sewell, Anna ([1877] 2012), *Black Beauty*, Oxford: Oxford University Press.

Seymour, Nicole (2013), *Strange Natures: Futurity, Empathy, and Queer Ecological
  Imagination*, Urbana: University of Illinois Press.

Shakespeare, William ([1606] 2004), *King Lear*, Ware: Wordsworth.

Shakespeare, William ([1606] 2005), *Macbeth*, Ware: Wordsworth.

Shapiro, H. (1974), 'Summing up', in G. C. Oosthuizen, G. Abbott and M. Notelovitz
  (eds), *The Great Debate: Abortion in the South African Context*, 232–4, Cape Town:
  Howard Timmins.

Shaw, Carolyn Martin (2002), 'A Woman Speaks of Rivers: Generation and Sexuality
  in Yvonne Vera's Novels', in Robert Muponde and Mandi Taruvinga (eds), *Sign and
  Taboo: Perspectives on the Poetic Fiction of Yvonne Vera*, 83–92, Harare: Weaver.

Sheehan, Paul (2002), *Modernism, Narrative and Humanism*, Cambridge: Cambridge
  University Press.

Sibisi, H. (1974), 'Abortion and Zulu Culture', in G. C. Oosthuizen, G. Abbott and
  M. Notelovitz (eds), *The Great Debate: Abortion in the South African Context*, 53–9,
  Cape Town: Howard Timmins.

Skloot, Rebecca (2010), *The Immortal Life of Henrietta Lacks*, London: Macmillan.

Slaughter, Joseph R. (2007), *Human Rights, Inc.: The World Novel, Narrative Form, and
  International Law*, New York: Fordham University Press.

Smith, Stephanie S. (2013a), 'The Challenges Procuring of Safe Abortion Care in
  Botswana', *African Journal of Reproductive Health* 17 (4): 43–55.

Smith, Stephanie S. (2013b), 'Reproductive Health and the Question of Abortion in
  Botswana: A Review', *African Journal of Reproductive Health* 17 (4): 26–34.

Soros, Eugene (2002), 'Yvonne Vera: Breaking the Silence', *Worldpress.org*, 23 September,
  14 pars. Available online: https://www.worldpress.org/Africa/736.cfm (accessed
  18 August 2021).

South African History Archive (1991), *Images of Defiance: South African Resistance
  Posters in the 1980s*, Randburg: Ravan.

Spiegel, Marjorie (1988), *The Dreaded Comparison: Human and Animal Slavery*, Philadelphia: New Society.

Stevenson, Angus ed. (2007), *Shorter Oxford English Dictionary*, Vol. 1, (6th edn), Oxford: Oxford University Press.

Stobie, Caitlin E. (2018), '"My Culture in a Tupperware": Situational Ethics in Zoë Wicomb's *October*', in Laura Wright (ed.), *Doing Vegan Studies: Textual Animals and Discursive Ethics*, 131–45, Reno: University of Nevada Press.

Stobie, Caitlin E. (2021), '"Creative Ferment": Abortion and Reproductive Agency in Bessie Head's *Personal Choices* Trilogy', *BMJ Medical Humanities*: 1–10. Available online: https://mh.bmj.com/content/early/2021/04/22/medhum-2020-012052.info (accessed 20 September 2021).

Stockenström, Wilma (1976), *Uitdraai*. Cape Town: Human & Rousseau.

Stockenström, Wilma ([1981] 2013), *Die Kremetartekspedisie* (Kindle edn), Cape Town: Human & Rousseau.

Stockenström, Wilma (1983), *The Expedition to the Baobab Tree*, trans. J. M. Coetzee, London: Faber & Faber.

Strathern, Marilyn, Jade S. Sasser, Adele Clarke, Ruha Benjamin, Kim Tallbear, Michelle Murphy, Donna Haraway, Yu-Ling Huang and Chia-Ling Wu (2019), 'Forum on *Making Kin Not Population: Reconceiving Generations*', *Feminist Studies* 45 (1): 159–72.

Stratton, Florence (1994), *Contemporary African Literature and the Politics of Gender*, New York: Routledge.

Swift, Jonathan ([1726] 1982), *Gulliver's Travels*, eds Peter Dixon and John Chalker, Harmondsworth: Penguin.

Torien, Barend (1988), 'Review of *You Can't Get Lost in Cape Town* by Zoë Wicomb', *Upstream* 6 (2): 42–3.

Triulzi, Sebastiano (2004–5), Interview Notes, York University Libraries, Clara Thomas Archives and Special Collections, Yvonne Vera Fonds (F0697), 2016-034, Box 007, File 03: par. 7–9.

Tucker, Margaret E. (1988), 'A "Nice-Time Girl" Strikes Back: An Essay on Bessie Head's *A Question of Power*', *Research in African Literatures* 19 (2): 170–81.

Van der Vlies, Andrew (2012), '"I'm Only Grateful That It's Not a Cape Town Book", or: Zoë Wicomb, Textuality, Propriety, and the Proprietary', *The Journal of Commonwealth Literature* 48 (1): 9–25.

Van Heerden, Etienne ([1986] 2011), *Ancestral Voices*, trans. Malcolm Hacksley, Johannesburg: Penguin.

Van Weyenberg, Astrid (2011), 'Wole Soyinka's Yoruba Tragedy: Performing Politics', in Daniel Orrells, Gurminder K. Bhambra and Tessa Roynon (eds), *African Athena: New Agendas*, 326–42, Oxford: Oxford University Press.

Varela, Francisco J., Humberto R. Maturana and Ricardo Uribe (1981), 'Autopoiesis: The Organization of Living Systems, Its Characterization and a Model', *Cybernetics Forum* 10 (2–3): 7–13.

Vera, Yvonne (n.d.), *Bird of Bright Plumage*, Toronto: York University Libraries, Clara Thomas Archives and Special Collections, Yvonne Vera Fonds (F0697), 2016-034, Box 004, File 02: 161.

Vera, Yvonne (1991), *Images of Women in Achebe*, Toronto: York University Libraries, Clara Thomas Archives and Special Collections, Yvonne Vera Fonds (F0697), 2016-034, Box 010, File 01: 2.

Vera, Yvonne (1993), *Nehanda*, Toronto: TSAR.

Vera, Yvonne (1995), *The Prison of Colonial Space: Narratives of Resistance*, Toronto: York University Libraries, Clara Thomas Archives and Special Collections, Yvonne Vera Fonds (F0697), 2016-034, Box 010, File 02: 279.

Vera, Yvonne (1998), *Butterfly Burning*, New York: Farrar, Straus and Giroux.

Vera, Yvonne, ed. (1999), *Opening Spaces: Contemporary African Women's Writing*, Oxford: Heinemann.

Viljoen, Louise (2012), 'Afrikaans Literature after 1976: Resistance and Repositionings', in David Attwell and Derek Attridge (eds), *The Cambridge History of South African Literature*, 452–71, Cambridge: Cambridge University Press.

Viola, André (1989), 'Zoë Wicomb's *You Can't Get Lost in Cape Town*: A Portrait of the Artist as a Young Coloured Girl', in Jacqueline Bardolph (ed.), *Short Fiction in the New Literatures in English*, 231–6, Nice: University of Nice Press.

Weingarten, Karen (2011), 'Bad Girls and Biopolitics: Abortion, Popular Fiction, and Population Control', *Literature and Medicine*, 29 (1): 81–103.

Wessels, Michael (2013), 'A Story of a /Xam Bushman Narrative', *Journal of Literary Studies* 29 (3): 1–22.

Westmore, Jean (1977), *Abortion in South Africa and Attitudes of Natal Medical Practitioners towards South African Abortion Legislation*, Durban: University of Natal.

Wicomb, Zoë (1987), *You Can't Get Lost in Cape Town*, London: Virago.

Wicomb, Zoë (1990), 'To Hear the Variety of Discourses', *Current Writing* 2: 35–43.

Wicomb, Zoë (1998), 'Five Afrikaner Texts and the Rehabilitation of Whiteness', *Social Identities* 4 (3): 363–83.

Wicomb, Zoë (2001), *David's Story*, New York: Feminist Press.

Wicomb, Zoë (2005), 'Setting, Intertextuality and the Resurrection of the Postcolonial Author', *Journal of Postcolonial Writing* 41 (2): 144–55.

Wicomb, Zoë (2014), *October* (Kindle edn), London: New Press.

Wilt, Judith (1990), *Abortion, Choice and Contemporary Fiction: The Armageddon of the Maternal Instinct*, Chicago: University of Chicago Press.

Wolfe, Cary (2007), 'Bring the Noise: *The Parasite* and the Multiple Genealogies of Posthumanism', in Michel Serres, (ed.), *The Parasite*, trans. Lawrence R. Schehr, xi–xxviii, Minneapolis: University of Minnesota Press.

Woolf, Virginia ([1929] 2008), *A Room of One's Own and Three Guineas*, Oxford: Oxford University Press.

Woolf, Virginia ([1941] 1992), *Between the Acts*, London: Penguin Classics.

Worden, Nigel ([1985] 2010), *Slavery in Dutch South Africa*, Cambridge: Cambridge University Press.

Young, Robert J. C. ([1994] 1995), *Colonial Desire: Hybridity in Theory, Culture, and Race*, London: Routledge.

Zeiss, Cecelia Scallan (1991), 'Myth and Metamorphosis: Landscape as Archetype in Quest Narratives by Samuel Beckett and Wilma Stockenström', *Irish University Review* 21 (2): 56–81.

Index

Printed in the USA
CPSIA information can be obtained
at www.ICGtesting.com
LVHW021043120624
782908LV00022B/27